STEEL RAILS TO THE SUNRISE

Port Jefferson, 1952.

Alfred R. Jaeger

STEEL RAILS TO THE SUNRISE

K-4s with mid-day train near Carle Place, 1951.   Harvey Weber

by Ron Ziel and George H. Foster

HAWTHORN BOOKS, INC.
Publishers / New York

To those whose interest and devotion to this work aided immeasurably toward its completion:
ROBERT M. EMERY,
a trainman whose patience and diligence in mapping the Long Island Rail Road, preserving its history and donating hundreds of hours to assisting the authors was invaluable;
HELEN CRONHEIM FOSTER,
part researcher, part troubleshooter, part editor, part secretary, and lovely wife.

ACKNOWLEDGMENTS

The authors are deeply indebted to the following institutions and individuals whose concern, assistance and historical collections contributed to the very essence of *Steel Rails to the Sunrise:* the Queens Borough Public Library and Marjorie Leek and Florence Block of the Long Island Division; the Brooklyn Public Library and Miss Louise Turpin of the Historical Division; the Suffolk County Historical Society, Riverhead; the New York Historical Society; the Southold Library; the Steamship Historical Society of America and Mr. and Mrs. James Wilson, Harry Cotterell, Jr., and Harry Jones; the Mariners' Museum, Newport News, and John Lockhead and Robert Burgess; the Smithsonian Institution and John H. White, Jr.; Dr. and Mrs. Kurt P. Cronheim; Mrs. Edith M. Ziel; Mrs. Dorothy H. Foster; Mrs. Aimee Reynolds; James V. Osborne; James McMahon; F. Nelson Blount; Elmer Lowell; Fred Martin; the *Long Island Forum* and Charles McDermott; Sylvester Doxsey; Clifford Prince; "Generator Jack" Schaffler; Joseph Burt and his Graflex plate camera; Frederick J. Weber; Mr. and Mrs. Walter Dolega; Mrs. Donald Ferguson, the daughter of Hal B. Fullerton; Thomas T. Taber; William H. Biesecker; E. L. Conklin; F. Rodney Dirkes; W. S. Boerckel, Jr.; Walter F. McNamara; William J. Rugen; F. G. Zahn; Arthur Huneke; Jefferson Skinner; Arthur L. Mirick; Edward Dersch; Alvin F. Staufer; Freeman Hubbard, editor of *Railroad Magazine;* Mr. and Mrs. Andrew Havrisko and their St. James General Store; W. S. Slade; Vincent F. Seyfried; Harry J. Trede; Felix E. Reifschneider; Alfred R. Jaeger; Norman Kohl; Robert B. Dunnet; Gene Collora; Jeffrey Winslow; Harold Fagerberg; R. Loren Graham; Miss Alma Kiehl; the Jermain Memorial Library, Sag Harbor, and Miss Russella Hazard; F. Schenck; Harrison S. Moore.

STEEL RAILS TO THE SUNRISE

Library of Congress Catalog Card Number: 75-214
ISBN: 0–8015–7147–2

3 4 5 6 7 8 9 10

Contents

Introduction	6
Laying the Rails Eastward	8
The LIRR Emerges from Chaos	30
The Halcyon Nineties	40
The White Boats	80
Crossing the River	97
Astride the Boiler	104
City and Suburbia	120
Way Out East	158
Steel Rails to Manhattan	184
Great Men of the LIRR	196
Juice-Jack Heaven	206
The Standard Era	214
Efficiency in Gray Paint	270
Deluxe Varnish Eastward	294
Appendix	310

Operator's view of an E-7s and her ballast train as seen from the Valley Tower at Valley Stream, 1936.
W. S. Boerckel, Jr.

Introduction

From the inception of *Steel Rails to the Sunrise*, I have watched the book slowly take shape, and have never ceased to be amazed at the quality and scope of the material. I have viewed this both as a rail enthusiast and as an author, having co-authored, with Frederick H. Richardson, *Along the Iron Trail* (Tuttle Publishing Company, 1938). My earliest recollections of steam railroading go back to the days when Richardson and I cut classes to watch the fast express trains on the Providence Division of the New York, New Haven & Hartford R.R.

I first met Ron Ziel while he was putting together his outstanding book, *The Twilight of Steam Locomotives,* and I was reminded of my own experiences with Mr. Richardson when we gambled on a book that would interest rail enthusiasts.

George and Ron have excelled in their new accomplishment. Striking pictures like this one of the LIRR have not been seen previously. Discovering and ferreting out historic unpublished photographs of this quality to tell the story of this interesting railroad, steeped in history and controversy since its inception, is truly a unique achievement. This book is not just a compilation of railroad motive power, but shows all the facets of railroading from stations to local color, and in addition presents seldom-published facts on the LIRR's fleet of ships. Since the paternal side of my family settled on Long Island and sailed their own packets up to Cape Cod, the two chapters devoted to the nautical aspect of the railroad's activities interested me greatly.

I recall the time in 1946 when Fred Richardson and I, flying an ancient Waco biplane, were forced down in central Long Island by a fast snow front. We hastened to head for New York City via the LIRR, and when a formidable Ten-Wheeler pulled into the small station in a swirl of snow, smoke, and steam my appreciation rose anew for "Old Reliable." A couple of days later we steamed back to this same station and took to the air again, and soon afterward, at 90 mph, we were chasing our departed train on its 50 mph dash to Greenport.

This book reminds me again of those fondly recalled days, and I am sure it will be frequently consulted, not only by the fully informed rail enthusiast, but by everyone who is interested in the history of Long Island.

F. Nelson Blount
Chairman and Founder, Steamtown, U.S.A.

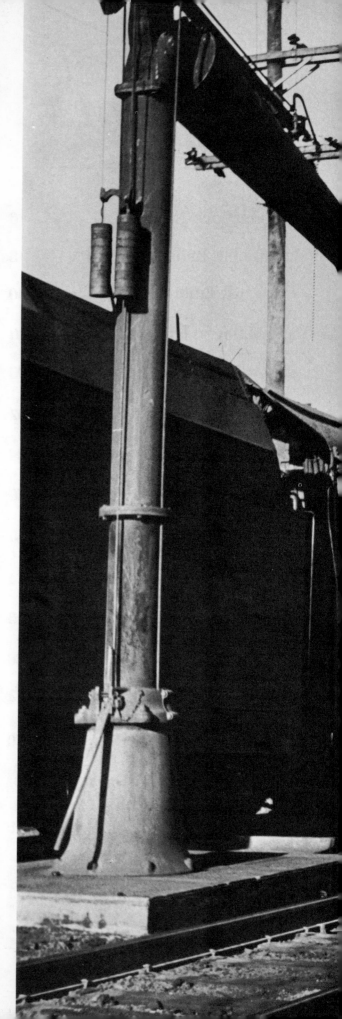

Meet at Smithtown, 1953. *Norman Kohl*

Laying the Rails Eastward

Down through the decades, railroads whose names have contained such far-sounding words as "Pacific" or "Western," or such romantic locations as "Santa Fe," "Cripple Creek," or "Deadwood," have stimulated the imaginations of the American people. Yet the seemingly prosaic Long Island Rail Road—small, unorthodox, sometimes ridiculed, and always barely tolerated by those who have come to depend on it the most, has a

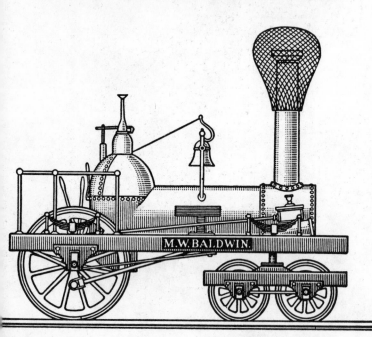

Collection of Harold Fagerberg

The Long Island Rail Road's First Locomotive
The *Ariel,* delivered in November, 1835, saw service on the LIRR for twenty years. A sister, the *Hicksville,* built a year later, was the first locomotive ever to use a steam whistle. It was remarked at the time that it made "a shrill, wild, unearthly sound; something like drawing a saw flat way across a bar of iron."

historic appeal as great and fascinating as the Western giants.

On April 25, 1832, the ten-mile Brooklyn & Jamaica Railroad Company was incorporated. Even as the iron rails were being laid through the rural community of Bedford and the farmlands toward East New York, Major D. B. Douglass, the principal engineer of the B & J, was making plans for a direct rail-boat connection to Boston, which, when concluded, would cut the steamer journey from New York from sixteen to eleven hours. This plan was given impetus by an engineering survey which found that the hills and rivers of southern Connecticut were impassable by rail. Wealthy and ambitious promoters from Boston and New York were attracted to the scheme, and the Long Island Rail Road Company received a charter from the New York State Legislature on April 24, 1834. The Norwich & Worcester, which ran from Boston to Providence and down to Stonington, Connecticut, was cooperative. All that remained was for the promoters to build a high-speed, thirty-miles-per-hour rail line from Brooklyn to the North Fork of Eastern Long Island and to establish a ferry service to Stonington.

The first big mistake in the development of the Long Island Rail Road occurred when the builders surveyed the main line. Indifferent to the needs of Long Island itself, they passed it through the endless pine barrens of central Suffolk County, midway between the villages scattered along the north and south shores of the Island. The LIRR was to rush express trains toward Boston, not to cater to the potato farmers of Suffolk, so the flat "middle route," relatively free of grade crossings and villages, seemed ideal for the purposes of the road.

When the Brooklyn & Jamaica was completed on April 18, 1836, the LIRR leased it and began laying rails eastward from Jamaica the same day. The lease, which charged the LIRR with a thirty-three-thousand-dollar annual obligation, included the B & J's two brand-new locomotives. The first one, named *Ariel,* was the nineteenth engine to be built by Matthias W. Baldwin, whose Baldwin Locomotive Works went on to construct over seventy thousand steam engines before all production ceased with steam's disappearance in the 1950's. The second engine, *Post Boy,* also outshopped by Baldwin, was nearly identical to *Ariel.* The B & J acquired and leased to the LIRR two additional locomotives, the *Hicksville* and the *John A. King,* in 1836 and 1838 respectively. The latter was the only engine ever constructed by the Poughkeepsie Locomotive Company.

By March of 1837, the railroad had forged eastward fifteen miles to what has become known as Hicksville. Using rails rolled in Liverpool, weighing over fifty-five pounds per yard, the Long Island track was of superior construction for that early date. The only village of any size between Jamaica and Hicksville was Brushville (now Queens Village). Beyond Brushville lay the vast, barren Hempstead Plain—probably the only genuine prairie on the Atlantic Seaboard, populated only by a few wandering herds of cattle. Passengers marveled at the complete desolation of the area from the two stops on the Plain, Clowesville (a mile west of the present Mineola station) and Carl Place (now Carle Place). Hicksville, the terminal for four years because the financial panic of 1837 had curtailed further construction, became the first of many large towns to be sired by the Long Island. Named for Valentine Hicks, the second president of the LIRR, this hamlet in a short time grew from a motley assortment of sheds and barns to a fair-sized town with several stores and a respectable hotel.

Meanwhile, the first two locomotives, *Ariel* and *Post Boy,* could not seem to keep out of each other's way. As *Ariel* was speeding an excursion train to the Union Course Race Track, she became involved in a right-of-way dispute with an unyielding cow. This misunderstanding resulted in

---

The Most Direct Route to Boston

As well as can be ascertained, the old map at *right* was printed when the main line to Greenport was completed in 1844. The property of N. R. MacLeod, this document is in excellent condition. It is reproduced here actual size—a tribute to the fine engraving techniques of the time. Except for the direct track to the North Fork of Long Island, only the branch to Hempstead deviated from the railroad's original purpose as a quick route to Boston. As the track which is now the New York, New Haven & Hartford Railroad in Connecticut extended only to New Haven at that time, the map must have been made no later than 1848.

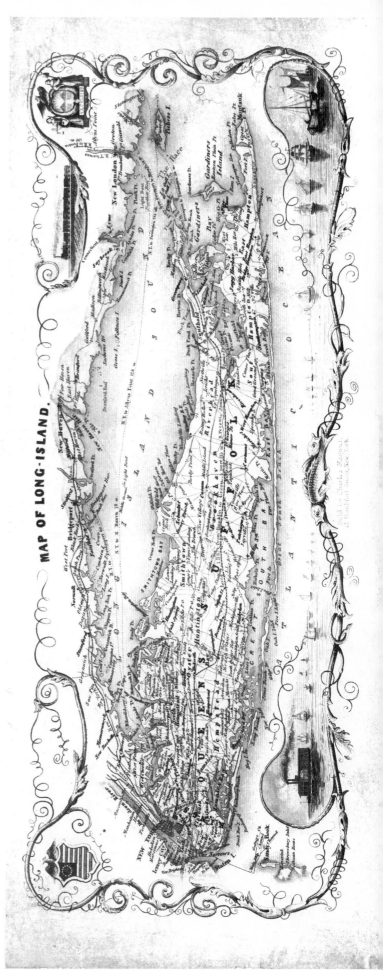

MAP OF LONG-ISLAND.

injury to both parties. Then *Post Boy,* pulling a second section of racing enthusiasts, smashed into the rear of *Ariel's* train. Accounts vary as to the ultimate fate of the cow, but no human injuries were suffered in the accident, generally believed to have been the first on the LIRR.

There was no cow, however, to blame for the unscheduled meeting between *Post Boy* and *Ariel* in 1852, which ended in *Post Boy* being sold "in pieces" to a firm near Boston, where she was rebuilt, shipped the same year to Savannah, Georgia, and put to work as a switcher by the Central Railroad & Banking Company. Now a confirmed rebel, *Post Boy* worked through the War Between the States hauling gravel trains on the Southwestern of Georgia. The venerable locomotive was put to work helping clean up the mess which General Sherman had made around Macon, and

---

L.I. Collection, Queens Borough Public Library

Early Commutation Ticket

The use of the Long Island Rail Road as a commuter system dates back to its earliest years. The ticket *above* is from August of 1859 and was good for passage between Brooklyn and Hempstead Branch (now Mineola).

---

pulled construction trains on the Macon & Brunswick R.R. Later, *Post Boy* worked a sawmill branch line. About 1876, she went into the passenger business on the Savannah, Skiddaway & Seaboard R.R., and was last seen in 1881 puttering around a sawmill near Waycross at the extremely rare age (for that time) of forty-five years.

As the construction crews progressed, the shrewd officials of the LIRR sought to eliminate as many grade crossings as possible before they became sources of trouble for the railroad. The railroad management frequently arranged meetings with the town fathers of on-line villages,

ostensibly for the purpose of solving any problems that might threaten to interfere with the orderly passage of the steamcars. In the course of these discussions the railroad officials would produce flasks of vintage whiskey. In due time, when the elected protectors of the people's interests were thoroughly inebriated, the railroad officers would persuade them to sign legal documents permitting the LIRR to cross existing roads, thus closing the roads to all traffic. Many of these roads are still in existence, with the railroad's embankment bisecting them right in the middle of the towns.

In 1841, the Long Island Rail Road reached Farmingdale and crossed into Suffolk County. By 1842 the tracks had extended to Deer Park, and on to Medford by early 1844. Meanwhile, rails were being laid westward from the North Fork, and the link was nearly completed by midsummer. The track gang at Punk's Hole (Manorville), composed chiefly of Irish immigrants, ran out of rail two miles short of the completion of their section. Delay in a shipment of rails from England threatened to postpone the opening of the line, but the enterprising Irishmen used heavy timbers crowned with strap iron as rails near Punk's Hole. For a few weeks, until the British rail was in place, trains had to cross this section at restricted speeds.

On July 27, 1844, three special excursion trains were run from Brooklyn to Greenport, and a celebration "to be referred to by generations unborn" (according to a contemporary resident of Southold) was held with a sumptuous dinner served out-of-doors, under large tents. The first train to Greenport amazed even the B & J's principal engineer, Major Douglass, by making the trip in three and a half hours instead of the scheduled five.

The early years of the LIRR were loaded with excitement, humor, passionate outbursts, and complete reversals of the original plans. In line with the early contempt of the railroad for the welfare of the Island's natives, many claims against it went ignored. Farmers became so incensed at the slaughter of their livestock and the fires caused by the wood-burning engines that orderly protest soon gave way to station-burning parties. Several trains were wrecked as a result of sabotage. Armed guards patrolling the tracks between Yaphank and Riverhead refused to report their friends, who merrily continued to tear up track and derail cars. Engineers and guards who rode the locomotives frequently exchanged shots with ambushers along the line. When the railroad sent a light engine or a handcar ahead of the trains, the farmers would let it pass and then quickly tear up a section of rail before the "Boston"—as the accommodation was commonly

LONG ISLAND RAILROAD!
NOTICE.

The Sunday MILK TRAIN will run as follows, on and after Sunday, May 26th:

GOING WEST.

Leave Syosset, at **7.14 A. M.**, for Hunter's Point.

GOING EAST.

Leave Hunter's Point at **12.30 P.M.** for Syosset.

Boat leaves James Slip, New-York side, at **12 M.**, to connect with above Train.

A. H. PALMER,

Office L. I. Railroad Co., } Hunter's Point, May 25th, 1861. } *Ass't Supt.*

GEO. F. NESBITT & CO., Printers and Stationers, corner of Pearl and Pine Streets.

Railroad Magazine

The Controversial Sabbath Train
The 1861 poster *above* advertised one of the Sunday milk trains which had so aroused the residents of Suffolk. These trains were a major scandal on Long Island just prior to the Civil War and resulted in several armed attacks against railroad property.

called—arrived. Finally, in one memorable episode, an escort engine fell through the Peconic River bridge after some Riverhead folk sawed through the timbers.

Many of the individualistic East Enders of the day were leery and quite superstitious of the iron horse which had trotted into their tranquil wilderness. Preston Raynor, relating stories of the early days,* tells the reactions of a boy known as "Long Charles" on seeing his first train at Manorville: "I tramped along at a pretty lively gait and reached the track fust one. There wasn't no train nur nothin' in sight, so I set down t' wait and musta fell asleep. Fust thing I knew, I heard thunderin'; so I jumped up and seen the sun was shinin' bright's could be. Then I got out on the track and thar she was comin'. I just stood there and looked and she kep' a'comin' and a'comin'; and fust thing I knew, she let out a squeal. That scairt me, so I turned and run and she kep' a'comin' right after me, a'squealin' at every jump. She kep' on chasin' me fur pretty nigh a half a

*Long Island Forum, November, 1943.

mile, an' she never gained on me much; but I was beginnin' to git het up and a mite winded, so I tho't mebbe I could jump down the bank a'fore she could ketch me, and so I did; but she never gained on me but just a mite."

One old woman, who lived along the track near Yaphank, lost her cow under the wheels of the "Boston." When the railroad refused to pay for the animal, the woman established a daily ritual of taking a large bucket of soap over to the grade, and, a few minutes before train time, coating both rails with the slippery liquid. After the train had stalled on nearly every passage, the railroad reconsidered and paid twenty dollars for the cow.

Over the years, the war grew more intense. In 1863, two thousand people, many armed, met with railroad officials at Manorville, to work out a truce whereby the road agreed to pay for half the damages which it caused. The disgruntled farmers, who were continuing to see huge conflagrations in their fields and in the pine barrens, and who were still losing livestock, remained unsatisfied; but the violence against the railroad subsided. Subsequently, the railroad struck upon the unique policy of charging engineers part of the damages for any livestock they hit. Though this must have slowed the schedules considerably, it no doubt reduced the accident rate as well.

By 1850, the "impassable" route through southern Connecticut had been opened, and the Long Island road's main reason for existence vanished. All-rail travel from New York to Boston was quicker and more convenient than the rail-boat route. The LIRR went into receivership and the major problems which plague it to this day—and will probably continue doing so as long as it exists—began to appear. The main line, running through nowhere, would have to be supplemented by branch lines or by competing railroads if the Island was to get the kind of rail service it needed. The LIRR took decades to adjust to this new role—a local railroad serving local interests —and in the process, it precipitated a war of competition and confusion. By this time it had become evident that the Long Island would gain more income from passenger service than it would from freight. This factor, unique among the nation's class-one carriers, has doomed the LIRR to a seemingly eternal cycle of bankruptcy and receivership.

Though a truce had ensued between the LIRR and those living along the right of way, due to the prosperity which the railroad brought to the farmers in the late 1850's, the Sunday "Milk Trains" brought on a new wave of station-burnings. The fundamentalist residents of the Island held a dim view of the "cool, calculated wickedness" by which the railroad violated the Sabbath.

Many people feared moral degradation would arise from this "desecration of the Lord's Day." The *Suffolk Times* of August 12, 1858, carried a letter which suggested: "better that all men in New York and Brooklyn should drink water for one day, than the morals of the people should be destroyed." The railroad finally withdrew all Sunday trains, but reinstated them as soon as the furor died down.

The Long Island Rail Road was having problems on the west end as well. In 1859, Brooklyn, blind to the fact that the railroad was the chief architect of its booming prosperity, banned the steam locomotives which plied the route along Atlantic Avenue to Jamaica. The replacement horsecars were even slower than the stagecoaches of past years, so the LIRR built a line from Jamaica to Long Island City, with a ferry to 34th Street in Manhattan. Within a few years, Brooklyn was begging the railroad to return its steam locomotives, earlier banned for smoke, noise, and nuisance. Too late, Brooklyn repented. The terminal moved to Long Island City and, decades later, plans to get the LIRR to Manhattan via a tunnel from Brooklyn were shelved in favor of the 34th Street tunnels to Pennsylvania Station. At length the railroad did return to Brooklyn, but only as a secondary terminal.

Before the collapse of the thriving Boston passenger business, the Long Island Rail Road had

The Earliest Photographs of the LIRR

The picture *above* was taken at Yaphank in the spring of 1865. It shows the brand-new locomotive *General Sherman*, with her crew. The young fellow at the far right was the news butcher. A regular employee on most nineteenth century passenger accommodations, he sold papers, cups of water, fruit, and candy en route. On August 26, 1865, six lives were lost when the *Sherman* collided head-on with the *General Grant*, a new Rogers locomotive, at Jamaica. At *right*, a train was posed at the famous Howard House in East New York. The month was April, 1865, for mourning bunting acknowledging the death of President Abraham Lincoln was displayed over the doors of the building. The huge cylindrical headlight on the engine was a very rare item during this period.

built only one minor branch—from Mineola to Hempstead. There followed a period of expansion which was marred by poor planning, a frequently surly and overbearing attitude on the part of the railroad's management, and no fewer than thirty separate railway companies, many of them subsidiaries of the LIRR and its chief competitors. This was coupled with a program to develop the desolate areas bordering on the main line. For ninety-five years the railroad tried, with limited success, to lure settlers to the scrub oak and pine barrens. It had some luck attracting farmers, but it was not until the post-World War I population explosion that the main line was finally settled as far as Lake Ronkonkoma.

Many of the popular movements and important events of the nineteenth century played a role in the development of the LIRR. In 1851, a group of Utopians, many of them from New Harmony and Brook Farm, attempted a collectivist venture near Thompson Depot similar to their previous efforts. The project, known as Modern Times, failed, but the present town of Brentwood rose on the site. In addition to Hicksville and Mineola, the railroad was directly responsible for the development of Deer Park, Farmingdale, Huntington Station, Suffolk Station (Central Islip), and other important towns in Nassau and Suffolk Counties.

Except for a collision between the locomotives *General Grant* and *General Sherman* in 1865, the Civil War did little damage to the LIRR.

In 1869, the first of the famous Methodist Camp Meetings was held at what is now North Merrick. These revivals were sponsored every summer from then until 1906, and the railroad contributed to their success by offering special excursion rates to the site.

In 1854, the Long Island Rail Road ventured a branch line from Hicksville to Syosset. The overly cautious expansion plans infuriated the towns which the main line had bypassed in the early forties. A forward-looking management could have rectified this situation, but in 1863 Oliver Charlick became president of the railroad. The twelve years in which he ruled were the worst in the Long Island's history and created situations which would have been hilarious had they not been so tragic. When Charlick refused to extend branches to the shore communities, those villages attempted to construct their own roads. He did all within his power to obstruct these plans and refused to cooperate in

any way. As a result, many newspapers clamored for the establishment of steamboat lines from the bypassed communities to New York. Trains were habitually late during those years, wrecks were common, and the railroad was called one of the greatest promoters of profanity on the Island by the *Suffolk Times*.

The only instances when the churlish Charlick could be made to act was when a rival road threatened to extend into a profitable new area. The Sag Harbor extension was a case in point. For years Charlick had ignored the pleas of that once prosperous village, whose chief industry— whaling—was rapidly dying out. When the Town of Southampton authorized a bond issue to aid the South Side Railroad in the construction of a branch from Patchogue in 1868, the LIRR jumped in, accepted a lesser grant, and dusted off the 1854 survey papers of a branch from the main line at Riverhead. The shrewd Charlick, realizing that the SSRR might still attempt to extend itself to the Hamptons, tapping the lucrative Moriches traffic on the way, built his branch from the desolate Manorville station in the heart of the pine barrens, effectively thwarting his competitors' chances. Charlick coerced the towns along the route into constructing the stations by the crude expedient of threatening to erect them miles away from the populated areas if the LIRR had to pay the costs.

An amusing dispute arose between the railroad authorities and the villagers of Quogue over the location of the depot. The former placed a platform and shed approximately where the present shelter stands, but the latter wished their depot to be built on Old Depot Road, despite the curve in the line, and since they were paying for it, as expected of a small village, they believed

Collection of Harold Fagerberg

they were justified in standing firm. The authorities threatened to move away the shed, as an admonition. Wrote a local historian: "The Quogue people kept a close watch on their 'station' (i.e. the shed) every weekday; and if the authorities attempted any dirty work at the crossroads on Sunday the villagers would have them arrested for Sabbath breaking. But the boss of the LIRR was a smart Irishman named Cunningham and the authorities felt that they could leave the matter in his hands. So one Saturday night he brought a train crew to Patchogue, laid over there all night, and early in the Sabbath dawn they came the rest of the way; and the 'station' was 'moved' ('dumped in the woods' several miles to the east) before the Quogue people had awakened from their slumbers, as a means of reducing the obdurate people to a proper state of penitence and submission."

After much wrangling, the Long Island Rail Road did build a branch from Mineola to Locust Valley between 1864 and 1869, which was ultimately extended to Oyster Bay in 1889. On the Syosset spur, Charlick and the residents of Cold Spring had a set-to over the placement of the depot, so he abandoned the entire grade which had been constructed from Syosset and curved the line south of the town, aiming to approach Huntington from the southwest. For years Charlick refused to allow his trains to stop even south of Cold Spring, as a punishment to the people who had the determination to stand up to him. At Huntington, Charlick had a violent argument with one of the promoters, so he curved his track once again and ran it two miles south of town. Huntington Station, the village which sprang up around the depot, has grown until it presently rivals the original town in size. The railroad continued on to Northport village, where in 1873 it was joined by the new Smithtown & Port Jefferson Railroad. Another of Charlick's protracted quarrels resulted in the junction being located over a mile south of Northport, giving that town two stations. Today, the original terminal is a lumberyard and passengers from Northport have to trek all the way to the East Northport station for rail service. As soon as Charlick saw the profitable nature of the South Side Railroad's branch to Far Rockaway, he ran a track nearly parallel to that rapidly expanding resort area. Oliver Charlick died in 1875. He left a legacy of misplaced branches and ill will which haunts the LIRR to this day. Conrad Poppenhusen, who took over after Charlick, found the mess irreparable, so the road went into receivership in 1877.

The receiver, Colonel Thomas R. Sharp, tried to rectify the mistakes of his predecessors and launched a vigorous public relations program to attract settlers to the Island. He encouraged the recreational and resort areas and was a promoter of the New York & Long Beach Railroad.

In 1881 Austin Corbin became the receiver of the Long Island Rail Road, and was made its president the following year. The railroad underwent a complete revitalization, realizing its greatest

Scenes on the Old Brooklyn & Jamaica R.R.

Although the B & J never ran its own trains, it earned money for its investors from the LIRR. Within a few years, the Long Island found the thirty-three-thousand-dollar annual leasing fee a prohibitive expense and received a modification of the terms. Unfortunately, the financial burden was not alleviated until years later, when the LIRR took complete control of the original ten-mile section of track. The wreck, *opposite page,* probably occurred during the early 1880's. Little is known of the mishap, except that the locomotive, a 4-4-0 American-type No. 21, was built by Baldwin in 1877. The scene is at East New York, near the Brooklyn-Queens border. The picture of Jamaica station *above* was made in 1878 by G. B. Brainard, one of Long Island's earliest photographers. Fortunately, his entire collection of thousands of wet-plate negatives is preserved at the Brooklyn Public Library. All the pictures credited to the Library which appear in this chapter and Chapter II and the photo on the bottom of page 43 were the work of G. B. Brainard. The picture *below* shows two trains ready to leave Jamaica for Long Island City and Brooklyn in the late eighties.

growth and experiencing its most exciting visions under the benevolent auspices of the great Austin Corbin. He was a man of great charm, possessing a rare ability to bring to fruition his brilliant ideas. It was during Corbin's administration that the link between Patchogue and Eastport was opened, the Wading River and Montauk branches were completed, more powerful locomotives and additional modern rolling stock ordered, and a new signal system installed. The gay prosperity of the late 1880's was evident as Long Island began to emerge in a form recognizable even in the twentieth century. Suburban towns were grow-ing up around the railroad; the wealthy aristoc-racy of New York was turning eastward to build huge estates and indulge in the noble sports of polo, riding to hounds, horse racing, and golf. The Long Island Rail Road under Austin Corbin was not only a vital part of those halcyon days, but was also largely responsible for them. The Vanderbilts, Heckschers, Cuttings, Pratts and many other prominent names of the era were closely associated with the dreams of the fabu-lous Austin Corbin as he faced the Gay Nineties with wonderful plans—doomed to failure through no fault of his own.

Piggyback in the 1880's

Originally a dummy engine named *Quincy,* built by Hinkley and Drury in 1862, the *Fred, upper left,* is shown at Hempstead in the early 1870's. The inboard-cylindered 2-4-0 was probably used for local runs at this time. Coach No. 10, one of the oldest in service, dates from around 1850. The *Fred* was sold to the Canarsie Railroad in 1876. Three-quarters of a century before most major railroads began to revitalize their freight service with the modern concept of piggyback, the LIRR provided this service, *lower left,* for Long Island farmers. The wagons were brought to the rail terminal at Long Island City and ferried over to markets in Manhattan. The photo *above* shows Mineola as it looked in 1879. The branch to Glen Cove (now the Oyster Bay line) cut off left of the little station. The original Hempstead spur, still in use for freight service nearly ninety years later, headed south parallel to the bridge, which is now the site of Mineola Boulevard. The picture was taken from a location in front of today's station. *Below,* engine No. 72, delivered in May, 1879, in the yard at Hempstead.

The Glen Cove and Northport Branches

Although the branch to the north shore of Nassau County extended to Locust Valley by 1869, it was referred to by the same name as the principal village which it served—Glen Cove. These two photos, both dating from 1878, show the Glen Cove depot and the terminal, including roundhouse, yard and station, at Locust Valley. At *right* is the Cold Spring station after Oliver Charlick finally consented to accept business from that town. Squat water towers were to be familiar on the Island scene for the next seventy years, since most towns had one for at least a brief period. The terminal at Northport, *lower right*, was a sleepy place indeed, especially after the junction to Port Jefferson was installed over a mile away.

The Smithtown & Port Jefferson Railroad

The western approach to Smithtown presented this appearance, *upper left,* only five years after the line was constructed in 1873. Although referred to as the depot at Setauket, the picture at *left* is probably only the freight shed, unless the doorway at the right of the building led to a small waiting room. A train was due, but unfortunately G. B. Brainard appeared to be preoccupied with the station buildings, as this October, 1878, scene reveals. One of the few locomotive shots in the Brainard Collection is this fine one of 4-4-0 No. 38 at Port Jefferson. The depot building is hidden by the train. Of great interest is the combination baggage-coach behind the engine. Lettered "Southern Rail Road," it illustrates the equipment exchanges which were commonplace at the time of the consolidation of the LIRR with former rivals. Port Jefferson remained the terminal until 1895, when the branch to Wading River was opened. The logo, *right,* was adopted by the LIRR at the time of the mergers of 1875.

LONG ISLAND RAIL ROAD.

HENRY HAVEMEYER, President.

Official Pocket Time Table.

SEPT. 15th, 1875.

Vignettes of the Seventies and Eighties

The lightweight construction of trains in the 1870's made possible the spindly wood bridges of that time. The bridge over Woodbury Road, *left*, was built in 1867, as the Port Jefferson branch was pushed eastward from Syosset. Three locomotives of the 4-4-0 American type were delivered to the LIRR by the Baldwin Locomotive Works in 1879. One of them, the *Arrow*, appears on page 17. Although the *Meteor*, *below*, is shown as No. 71, she was actually No. 74. The photo has been retouched to conform with the number on the tender. The remaining engine in this series, No. 73, was named *Comet*. Engine No. 87, *bottom*, was built by Rogers in 1883. She was part of a large class of engines which resembled turncoat camelbacks. The cab was set astride the firebox—not far enough forward to be a true camelback, but not far enough back to be considered orthodox. Eventually the strange hoods on these locomotives were removed, and their cabs were lengthened to tremendous proportions (see page 67). This photo was made at Long Island City on March 30, 1888, a few days after the snows of that year's great blizzard had melted. The people of Quogue eventually got a handsome two-story station, *right*, placed in their scrub-pine wilderness. Huntington and other large villages already had buildings of this standard LIRR design. Only the depot at St. James (page 279), which was identical to the Quogue structure, survives to this day. At that time the barren main line was sparsely populated, though boasting some fascinating station buildings such as the one at Lakeland, *below right*, now called Lake Ronkonkoma. The station, photographed in 1879, was an old converted farmhouse. The building behind it, apparently a church, may have been for sale, according to a sign on the porch.

The Winters Way Out East

On December 21, 1880, the locomotive *Springfield,* while clearing huge snow drifts off the main line near Waverly, ran into the rear of a snowbound passenger train. The incredible result, recorded by the camera of C. W. Conklin of Jamaica, is shown *above.* Referred to as the "Great Snow Blockade" in contemporary accounts, this was one of the most amazing train wrecks of all time. Waverly has long been renamed Holtsville, but its nearly forgotten claim to immortality should rekindle pride in the little community. The following winter saw engine No. 77 and a sister buried in snow past their running boards, *below,* west of Southampton station on the Sag Harbor branch. The photograph was made on February 5, 1882. On August 4, 1878, G. B. Brainard focused his primitive wet-plate camera on the station at Sag Harbor, *upper right.* On a drab winter day in 1882 an engineer misunderstood a signal and ran through the end of the platform at Sag Harbor *lower right,* causing engine No. 80 to bury her pilot in the debris. This story is authenticated by the engineer's son, James McMahon, Jr., the mayor of the charming old village.

Sylvester Doxsey

Early Depots on the North Fork

The Jamesport station *above,* shown in August of 1879, was only three years old at the time. It was extensively rebuilt in 1944, only to be demolished on July 18, 1963, and replaced by a sheet-metal shelter of dubious value. The Mattituck station *below* was a typical Long Island depot of its day. The station at Southampton was identical to it, and a number of other stations were quite similar. This portion of the main line has always been bordered with fertile farms, but its usefulness was nearly past when traffic dwindled to one train daily in the 1960's.

Two photos, Brooklyn Public Library

The Eastern Terminus

The Greenport Yard, *above*, as it looked about 1890. The yard lead is in the foreground and the freight yard is at the left rear. In the middle background is the station and the steamboat dock. The boat in the photo in all probability is one of the Montauk Steamboat Company's vessels which made connections with the South Fork, Shelter Island, the North Shore towns, and Long Island City. The four-stall brick roundhouse was torn down in 1921. One of the unique features of the roundhouse was that it was alongside the turntable, instead of leading from it. The turntable, always in the open, was still in use after virtually all the other facilities had been removed following the disappearance of steam power in the 1950's. The station is ninety-four and a half miles from the terminal at Long Island City. Had the Boston route remained in service, Greenport would no doubt have become quite a sizable town. Today, however, there is infinitely less activity in the yard than there was at the time of this picture. If the projected bridge is built to New England, Greenport may well become a boomtown, but that would probably have little effect on the railroad and the tenuous position of the main line east of Riverhead. One of the few engines from the 1890's of which a good photograph but no information survives is the little 2-4-0 tank engine No. 43, *right*. It probably came from one of the small roads in Brooklyn which was merged with the LIRR in the '90's.

The Blizzard of 1888

After the great blizzard of March, 1888, all the railroads of the northeast were in snowbound confusion, and the LIRR was no exception. *Above,* several trains are lined up in heavy drifts in eastern Queens. The College Point Station on the Whitestone branch *below* was hopelessly buried. *Opposite* are several coaches of distinctly different styles which were used during this era. The upper one, dating from 1877, and the middle coach, from the 1880's, were built by Jackson & Sharp of Wilmington, Delaware. The lower car, used for summer excursions, probably ran to the resort areas at Far Rockaway and South Brooklyn.

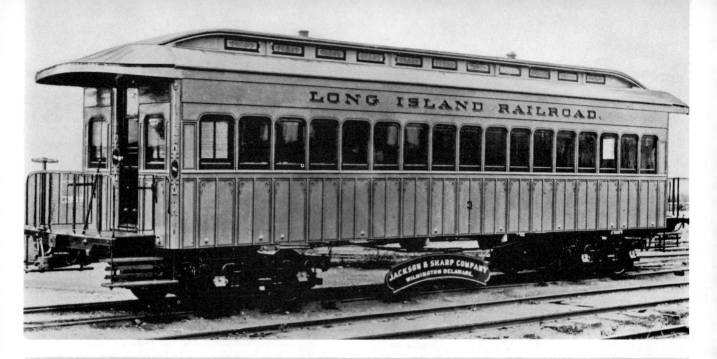

The LIRR Emerges from Chaos

The Long Island Rail Road, not heeding the pleas of the bypassed shore communities, realized its first threat from local competition in 1860. That year, the South Side Railroad of Long Island was projected from Jamaica to Patchogue. The Civil War delayed plans, but in 1865 the directors started raising money and letting contracts for construction as far as Islip. The two most prominent men behind the South Side were Charles Fox of Baldwin and Willet Charlick, brother of the then LIRR president Oliver Charlick, who was busily engaged in attempting to destroy the new line at every turn.

The main section of the South Side was completed from Jamaica to Babylon in November of 1867. By the end of 1868, the railroad had laid a line west from Jamaica to its East River terminus at Williamsburg. In April, 1869, the main line of the SSRR was opened to Patchogue, while the towns further east were subscribing $140,000 in bonds for an extension to Sag Harbor. Oliver Charlick's new LIRR branch to Sag Harbor, which was opened in June, 1870, captured the east-end business, and the SSRR rails were not laid east of Patchogue until eleven years later.

By October of 1865, the Brooklyn & Rockaway Beach Railroad was completed from East New York to Canarsie and enjoyed a booming business carrying vacationers to the surf-bathing areas of south Brooklyn. This accelerated the plans of the South Side's directors to open a branch to the Rockaways, which were becoming a fashionable resort area. In the rush to complete the branch by the summer of 1869, the SSRR laid track across seven hundred feet of farmland near Lawrence which had not been relinquished by the

owner, William B. McManus. A hot-tempered Irishman, McManus was not easily awed by the powerful South Side, and the following night he gathered a rowdy band of fellow Irishmen who so thoroughly tore up the track that every rail was bent beyond salvage. After a long legal hassle, the railroad paid McManus and the issue was settled. The branch became an instant success and in 1870 the railroad erected the South Side Pavilion, a two-hundred-foot long restaurant on the beach. By 1872, the South Side had ex-

---

The SSRR and the LIRR

The tenth engine purchased by the South Side Railroad, in 1869, was a second-hand 2-2-4T named the *Pewit*, shown *below*. It was originally built by Danforth, Cooke & Co. for the Central Railroad of New Jersey in 1860. The exact date and location of this picture is unknown and there are no clues to the ownership of the little locomotive at the time. The map, *right*, shows the Long Island Rail Road just after the great mergers of the mid-1870's. Dating from 1878, during the receivership of Colonel Sharp, the map shows the newly absorbed South Side Railroad and the Central Railroad as the Southern and Central divisions of the LIRR. Of particular interest are the many routes descending upon Flushing. The map has its inaccuracies, specifically the Whitestone Branch junction located to the west of Flushing and the Port Jefferson branch terminal at Mt. Sinai Harbor. In 1879 the Central branch was abandoned between Flushing and Hillside Avenue, near Creedmoor. Creedmoor is now the location of a state mental hospital, but at the time was a national rifle range. Trainloads of militia were brought there for practice. The most significant improvement came in 1881, when the Southern Division was extended from Patchogue to Eastport. It is interesting to compare this map with others in the volume to study the expansion of the LIRR and the many changes in station names.

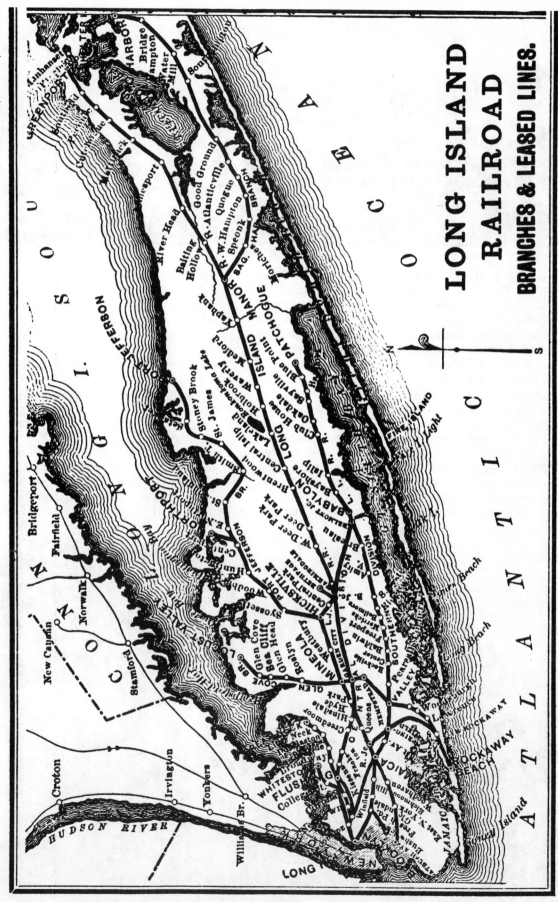

LONG ISLAND RAILROAD BRANCHES & LEASED LINES.

Collection of Harold Fagerberg

tended its tracks westward to the Seaside House (now Beach 103rd Street, Seaside Station). In 1875, the Neptune House (Beach 116th Street) became the final terminal. The SSRR, after acquiring a portion of the right of way of the New York & Flushing Railroad in 1870, built a terminal at Hunter's Point on the East River in Queens. This ended the construction years of the South Side, and it settled down to its brief existence as a successful independent railroad. The newspapers lavished great praise on the line for its smooth track, new equipment and conscientious manner of operation. In 1869, the road carried 246,660 passengers and 51,645 tons of freight. Only three years later, the figures totaled 617,899 passengers and 83,671 tons of freight.

Meanwhile, the people of Hempstead, dissatis-

fied with the service which the LIRR was providing over its branch to the main line at Mineola, contracted for the construction of the New York and Hempstead Plains Railroad. The road was to run westward through Valley Stream to 65th Street in Bay Ridge, Brooklyn. The new line was closely associated with the South Side system and frequently relied on it for assistance and equipment. In 1871, a railroad supplier named Pusey was elected president of the NY&HP, but was promptly discharged when he failed to honor his pledges to the directors. Pusey initiated a foreclosure suit and the bondholders illegally appointed a "receiver" without notifying the railroad. This resulted in Pusey, as agent for the receiver, seizing the railroad at Hempstead on January 8, 1872. That night Pusey and the re-

Authors' Collection

Collection of Joseph A. Moore

ceiver, Seaman Snediker, slept in one of the coaches, along with a constable and some hired men. The following morning the owners, finding these men asleep in the coach, silently moved the road's only locomotive down the track. When Pusey demanded its return, they defiantly chugged up and down the track, to the amazement of the early morning commuters who were awaiting the departure of the first train. As the engine neared the platform to receive passengers, the enraged Pusey began shooting at it. One bullet hit the dome directly in front of the engineer and the infuriated passengers threatened to lynch Pusey. After calming down, the passengers ran the train to Valley Stream by themselves. In June of 1873, the NY&HP was leased to the South Side for 999 years.

South Side Scenes

The SSRR's Richmond Hill depot, *above left*, as it appeared in the mid-1870's. The locomotive, a 4-4-0 named the *A. J. Bergen*, was built by Danforth Cooke & Co. in 1870. From here the line headed east to Jamaica, where the South Side depot was sandwiched between Beaver Pond and the LIRR, near the present 150th Street. At *lower left*, the LIRR engine No. 48 posed at the New York Boulevard crossing on the Southern Division in the early eighties. The conductor wore a uniform typical of the day. The rare photo *above* is the only known picture of the South Side's Rockaway branch and it shows the Rockaway Beach station with its ticket office in the early 1870's. The sign on top of the station reads: *Southern R.R. Ticket Office for Brooklyn and New York.* Opposite the station is the locomotive *Islip*, No. 17. This picture is the only one which the authors have found to be made from a tintype. The picture of Breslau (now Lindenhurst) *below* was taken in 1870. The new Grant locomotive, *J. B. Johnson*, was later No. 41 on the LIRR.

Collection of Harold Fagerberg

The South Side in Suffolk County

In 1878, the South Side station at Babylon, *above*, was a frame building. Fire Island, receiving prime billing on the depot wall, was just being discovered as a potential summer resort, although it could only be reached by a ferry ride across Great South Bay. The desolate Islip station, *below*, was a long carriage ride from town in those days. There are birdhouses on the track side of the roof, but smoke from the engines probably prevented any feathered occupants from remaining in those quarters very long.

Two photos, Brooklyn Public Library

Odyssey of a Flushing Engine

This picture of the Flushing & North Side train *above,* taken in the winter of 1872 by an unknown photographer, has become a classic Christmas card pose down through the decades. It shows the engine *New York,* just a few months after she rolled out of the Rhode Island Locomo-tive plant. This beautiful, tranquil scene is the sleepy farming village of Woodside, in Queens County. Somewhat altered, the *New York* is shown *below* in her LIRR livery as No. 11 at Long Island City sixteen years later, after the F&NS had been absorbed by the LIRR.

Collection of Harold Fagerberg

With the coming of Alexander T. Stewart's Central Railroad of Long Island from Flushing, the people of Hempstead found themselves besieged by three railroads fiercely competing for their trade. There just was not enough business in the village to warrant three depots, and soon all the railroads were in financial difficulties. The death knell for the South Side sounded in the financial panic of 1873. The road was taken over by the Poppenhusen interests, which by that time were in control of the Flushing, North Side & Central Railroad in partnership with A. T. Stewart. However, after several wrecks on the once-splendid South Side, the administration canceled plans to extend it past Patchogue and used the materials to repair the deteriorating Far Rockaway branch.

When Oliver Charlick was finally removed from his disastrous reign over the uncertain destinies of the Long Island Rail Road in 1875, control of the mismanaged line fell upon Conrad Poppenhusen. A wealthy immigrant from Germany and credited with building College Point, he was a benefactor to all who worked for him. In 1868, when College Point, like so many north-side communities, was clamoring for a railroad, Conrad Poppenhusen used his influence and his capital to help build what eventually became the Whitestone Branch of the LIRR. The New York & Flushing Railroad had been built between Hunter's point and Flushing in the 1850's and by 1866 the North Shore Railroad had been extended from Flushing to Great Neck.

By 1864, the New York & Flushing was in bad shape, due to a refusal on the part of the owners to maintain the line. This situation aroused the citizens in the area to subscribe to the construction of the Woodside & Flushing Railroad which

was built in direct competition with the original line. Oliver Charlick promptly took control of the ailing NY & FRR, dealing a serious blow to the new line. The Woodside & Flushing then reorganized as the Flushing & North Side Railroad Company with the backing of Poppenhusen and other prominent residents. It was built from Hunter's Point to College Point via Flushing, and on to Whitestone by the end of 1869.

In July, 1869, A. T. Stewart purchased over eighty-six hundred acres of the Hempstead Plains, where he planned to construct a fashionable town. By 1872, Stewart had made an arrangement whereby his Central Railroad of Long Island would be built from a connection with the Flushing & North Side through Floral Park to Farmingdale, and eventually to Babylon's Fire Island boat dock. Commonly called the Stewart Line, the Central Railroad was directly responsible for the development of Garden City. The portion between Floral Park and Babylon forms the present Central Branch of the LIRR. The only portion of the line from Flushing to Floral Park to survive the final consolidation of the LIRR is still in use—the dismal spur to the Creedmoor State Hospital.

Conrad Poppenhusen took control of the South Side and the Central Railroads, which, along with the Flushing & North Side, formed a system nearly as large as the Long Island. After the passing of Charlick in 1875, Poppenhusen took over the LIRR itself. He forged this railroad empire into a unified system, though he lost three million dollars in the process. The ensuing receivership set the scene for Austin Corbin, under whose leadership the new Long Island Rail Road system paid continuous dividends from 1880 to 1896.

Authors' Note: *Most of the material in this chapter courtesy of Vincent F. Seyfried.*

36

Two photos, Brooklyn Public Library

The Stewart Line

Unlike the grandiose schemes of so many nineteenth century promoters who developed Long Island, the plans of Alexander T. Stewart materialized rapidly and, eventually, successfully. To reach his sprawling enterprise of Garden City, he extended the Central Railroad of Long Island down from Flushing in the early 1870's. His first locomotive, the *Newtown,* suffered a boiler explosion at Whitestone station, *above left,* on September 25, 1872, but was rebuilt and later became the LIRR *Bayside*

(No. 6). The Central stations on Fulton Street in Hempstead, *above right,* and at Garden City, *below,* were handsome brick structures. Stewart took pride in the Garden City station especially, since this is where the prominent buyers of his properties arrived from New York. The LIRR crossing is marked by the water tower in the right background of the photo below. The nearby village of Stewart Manor perpetuates the memory of the enterprising developer.

The New York and Manhattan Beach Railroad

Originally built as a narrow gauge line, the NY & MB was constructed during the 1870's and the early eighties. It ran from Fresh Pond in a rough semicircle through central Kings County (Brooklyn) to a terminus at Bay Ridge. There was also a line parallel to Ocean Avenue, which did a brisk passenger business between Manhattan Beach Junction and Manhattan Beach in Coney Island from the day of its opening in 1876. This spur was abandoned in two sections between 1938 and 1941. The rest of the New York & Manhattan Beach Railroad is the present-day freight-only Bay Ridge branch of the LIRR. The LIRR had leased the NY & MB from 1882 until 1925, when it was formally merged into the Long Island. The 2-4-6T *above* is shown in 1883, just after it was converted to standard gauge operation when the LIRR leased the road. In 1888 tides had washed up to the foundations of the famous Brighton Beach Hotel, *below left*. Austin Corbin, president of the LIRR, had an interest in the hotel, so he arranged to have the six-thousand-ton, five-hundred-foot-long frame structure jacked up and loaded onto flat cars. In an engineering feat impressive even to

Two photos, Ron Ziel

this day, six locomotives eased the hotel two hundred yards further inland. The unusual monument *above* in Greenwood Cemetery was erected by the children of Oscar and Maggie Dietzel, who were among the sixteen fatalities of the wreck at Berlin, near Laurel Hill station, on August 26, 1893. Although weathered by seven decades, the sculptured accident still presents a macabre message. The photo *below* of LIRR rapid-transit engine No. 211 was made from a window of the Oriental Hotel. The train is posed at the distinctive station of that prominent resort place. Sheepshead Bay is in the background.

Collection of Harold Fagerberg

The Halcyon Nineties

The age of invention was at its peak. Westward expansion had given Americans a huge new land in which to mature. Civil War animosities were starting to fade. And the railroads, by reaching their steel tentacles into virtually every sizable town in the nation, provided an unequalled means of rapid economical transport and reliable communication, and had sealed the Union for all time.

The Long Island Rail Road was very much a part of this vigorous era. Under the enlightened administration of Austin Corbin in the eighties, the LIRR gained a large measure of respectability, and Corbin was largely responsible for the full life which the Island enjoyed under his leadership. In the 1890's the LIRR was completed to its greatest extent; and it actually paid dividends until 1896, when Corbin died.

There were problems, of course; and the Atlantic Avenue branch in Brooklyn proved one of the worst. The improved service on that line had precipitated such an exodus of new residents from the city that it was operated as a rapid transit system. Timetables as early as 1880 showed trains running at a fifteen-minute headway—ten minutes during rush hours—in each direction, nineteen hours a day. At night freight trains rumbled down Atlantic Avenue, adding to

the soot, noise, and danger of over two hundred steam train movements daily along the line. Property on Atlantic Avenue was depreciating and *The New York Times* editorialized on August 21, 1892: "Anyone who cares to see what a greedy railroad corporation can do in the way of destruction of a great thoroughfare should take one of the rapid-transit trains…at Flatbush Avenue… to East New York and back." There were complaints of the big avenue being unpaved because of the tracks and there were numerous accidents. But it was not until after the turn of the century that the grade was eliminated on Atlantic Avenue.

Early Rapid-Transit Engines

The two 4-4-0 tank engines *opposite* were typical of the larger ones in service during the early 1890's. The photo of No. 4, at East New York, is from the collection of Gene Collora and of No. 38, at Woodhaven Junction, is the property of Arthur Huneke. The timetable from 1880 also listed ferry connections to Manhattan. The map, issued in 1907, shows the LIRR at its greatest extent, and includes the routes of the Montauk Steamboat Company, a subsidiary of the LIRR.

Collection of Thomas Bayles

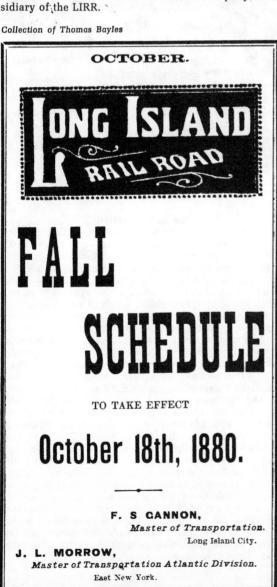

OCTOBER.

LONG ISLAND
RAIL ROAD

FALL

SCHEDULE

TO TAKE EFFECT

October 18th, 1880.

F. S. CANNON,
Master of Transportation.
Long Island City.

J. L. MORROW,
Master of Transportation Atlantic Division.
East New York.

No. 24.
Press of Rogers & Sherwood, 21 and 23 Barclay Street.

Collection of N. R. MacLeod

MAP OF
LONG ISLAND
SHOWING THE
Long Island Railroad System
AND
MONTAUK STEAMBOAT COMPANY'S LINES.
1907

SCALE OF MILES

Collection of William Biesecker

E. S. Thompson, Brooklyn Public Library

The El Connection

Since the elevated railroads were expanding through Brooklyn by the mid-nineties, a direct connection with the LIRR seemed expedient. The picture *above* was made at the foot of the Flatbush Avenue terminal in 1892. Taken on the corner of Atlantic Avenue and Ft. Greene Place, it shows a small Forney 0-4-4T of the type used on the runs to Rockaway Junction. In March of 1899, the El connection shown *above right* was under construction. Both pictures were made from about the same location. At *right* is a rare picture of the Brooklyn Bridge in the mid-eighties. The squat little locomotive was used for transferring the bridge cable cars from one track to the other. The platform was part of the Sands Street El station. The LIRR rapid-transit trains, after entering the El structure near the Flatbush terminal, rode down the line above Hudson Avenue, switched onto the Myrtle Avenue El and terminated at Sands Street. A portion of this line between Hudson Avenue and Bridge-Jay Station is still in use. From Sands Street, the passengers rode the New York & Brooklyn Bridge Railroad to the connection with the Second and Third Avenue El lines in Manhattan. A two-car local, *left*, sped through Woodhaven in 1893. Lower-quadrant semaphores mounted on wooden poles, such as the one in front of this locomotive, were the standard signaling devices of the era. These were installed during the administration of Austin Corbin and were a vast improvement over all previous methods of warning train crews of possible danger.

Fullerton, St. James General Store

Fullerton, St. James General Store

44

Fullerton, Suffolk County Historical Society

The Atlantic Division

The little Atlantic Avenue Forneys were extensively re-built during the mid-nineties and emerged looking like No. 203, *upper left*. The signal tower which appears in two of the pictures on the previous spread also shows in the left background of this photo taken by Fullerton at South Portland Street in 1898. Another rapid-transit engine, No. 218, is shown with her crew at *left*. Note the unique signal system atop the cab. The crew used it either to signal the engine's destination to the tower or to request movement. In the early 1900's the irate residents along Atlantic Avenue finally got their wish when the line was elevated or tunneled most of the way through Brooklyn. *Above*, two electric trains met at the East New York

tunnel at Stone Avenue (now Eastern Parkway). The final section of the elimination project between Brooklyn and Jamaica was completed in 1942. Shown *below* is the lower level of the Flatbush Avenue terminal in later years. The cars, designated MP-41 and built in 1904, were the oldest electrics on the LIRR. The present terminal was opened in 1906, and its appearance has changed little. To the right of the picture is the IRT Atlantic Avenue subway station. Although a connection was made so that LIRR cars could run right on to the subway tracks, the plan was dropped, but part of the connection is still visible. Now, passengers walk a few feet between the LIRR and the IRT platforms.

F. J. Weber, Authors' Collection

L.I. Collection, Queens Borough Public Library

The Long Island City Terminal

Before construction of the East River tunnels and Pennsylvania Station, the main terminal of the LIRR was at Hunter's Point in Long Island City. Here, railroad ferries carried as many as fifty thousand passengers daily between the depot and Manhattan. *Above,* the terminal as it appeared in 1895. *Below,* one of the Long Island's early camelbacks is shown switching at the terminal in 1901. When the troops returned from Cuba in

Fullerton, St. James General Store

QUEENS COUNTY BANK

LONG IS

Fullerton, Suffolk County Historical Society

August of 1898, they entrained for the yellow fever quarantine camps on Long Island at Hunter's Point. The 33rd Michigan Volunteers looked every bit the toughened veterans they were as they marched from the ferry dock, *above*, to their trains. The identity of the dapper civilian has not been established. In December, 1902, the terminal building burned to the ground, *below*, destroying the Company records.

Fullerton, St. James General Store

T.R. and the LIRR

The railroad was no stranger to Theodore Roosevelt when he came to depend on it for transport of his Rough Riders cavalry unit in 1898. When Col. Roosevelt established his training headquarters at Amagansett, all of the men and equipment for the outfit were carried by the LIRR. Having struck up a friendship with Special Agent Fullerton, the fiery Teddy and the management of the railroad worked in a spirit of cooperation. After the triumphant return of the Rough Riders from Cuba, they were whisked off as far as the LIRR could carry them—to Camp Wyckoff, on the barren Montauk Hills. There they remained in quarantine until rid of the yellow fever which many had contracted during the campaign against the Spanish. Roosevelt, who had become a national hero, made a rail tour of his beloved Long Island, where huge enthusiastic crowds welcomed him. Still wearing his uniform and broad-brimmed hat, T.R. spoke from the rear platform of Superintendent Potter's car, *left*. Hal Fullerton was the photographer on this occasion. The original plates are deposited with the Suffolk County Historical Society in Riverhead. Roosevelt is shown meeting the welcoming crowds at Babylon, *above,* and Greenport, *below.*

Fullerton, Suffolk County Historical Society

Fullerton, St. James General Store

The Port Washington Branch

The surviving railroad lines which descended en masse upon Flushing between the 1850's and the 1870's became the North Side branch of the LIRR after the consolidation period. Known as the Port Washington branch today, this twelve-mile line was electrified between 1910 and 1912. The branch from Flushing to Whitestone Landing, built under the auspices of Conrad Poppenhusen, was abandoned in 1932, although its electrification had been completed only four years earlier. One of the more fascinating incidents in the brief history of the Whitestone Branch was the furor which arose over the College Point station in 1893. This impressive building, which had been the pride of Poppenhusen two decades earlier, had deteriorated into a shambles. After repeated warnings about the "poor sanitary conditions," the local Board of Health seized the station and, according to *The New York Times,* "put out the ticket agent and telegraph operator and placed an officer in charge." When the superintendent rushed up from Long Island City, he was reported to have "fumed about in a highly indignant state." *Opposite.* a rear-end collision near Whitestone Junction in the early 1890's. At *left,* the station and engine house at Whitestone Landing in 1907. On this page, two views of the opening of Port Washington station on June 23, 1898.

L.I. Collection, Queens Borough Public Library

The Beach Branches

Built in 1880 as the New York, Woodhaven & Rockaway Railway from Glendale Junction to Rockaway Park, the Rockaway Beach branch was reorganized as the New York & Rockaway Beach Railway Co. in 1887 and leased to the Long Island Rail Road. In 1901 the line was merged into the Long Island as the Rockaway Beach Division. The branch was one of the first to be electrified in 1905 and became heavily traveled as the area developed into a year-round residential district. Special trains to Aqueduct Race Track provided additional revenue. The long wooden trestle over Jamaica Bay was a continual headache, plagued by frequent disastrous fires which destroyed large portions of the structure and in winter by ice floes which shoved it out of alignment. After a particularly severe conflagration, the LIRR abandoned its troublesome branch and sold the property to the New York City Transit Authority, which rebuilt it as part of the Independent subway system in the mid-1950's.

The Long Beach branch was built by the New York & Long Beach R.R. Co. in 1880. The following year the line was overextended five miles along the desolate and virtually uninhabited sand dunes to Point Lookout. After the LIRR purchased the line in 1886, it operated passenger trains to Point Lookout for a few years, then tore up the track east of Long Beach in 1895. In 1910 the Long Beach branch was electrified. The trestle over Jamaica Bay provided many occasions for good pictures, but few photographers took advantage of the opportunity. The four-car local, *left*, was chuffing over the structure around 1900, a few years before the line was electrified. The mixed train, *below*, had paused at the East Rockaway station on the Long Beach branch. In the summer of 1900, F. J. Weber photographed the Seaside Station, *lower left*, from the top of the Shoot-the-Chute at Rockaway Park.

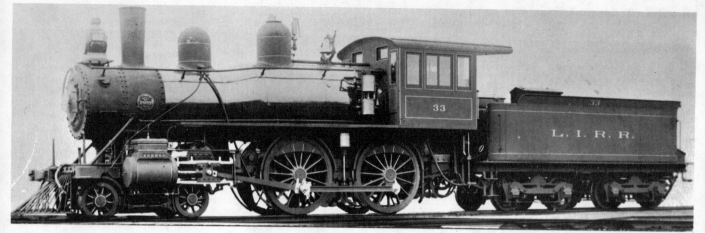

Collection of Gene Collora

Equipment in the Late Nineties

Typical of the graceful 4-4-0 type locomotives, LIRR No. 33 *above* was outshopped by Brooks in 1898. She only retained that number for a short time, however, since most classes of Long Island engines were renumbered late in 1898. The section car at *left* is a weird piece of equipment. Though driven by a piston connected to the rear wheel, its source of power, whether gasoline or steam, is a mystery. The driver could be a personification of "Ralph of the Railroad." The gas transport car, *below*, was used to replenish reservoirs of illuminating gas for the coaches at various stations. The Morris Park Shop buildings, *upper right*, were erected in the late eighties and most of them are still in use. This is the only known photo of the little inspection engine named "Pop," which is on the transfer table in the background. The table's vertical steam boiler has been replaced by electric power. The identity of the men is unknown. The little Prospect Park & Coney Island 0-4-0, *lower right*, was stored at Morris Park while awaiting the torch in 1897. The LIRR had purchased the small line in 1893 and operated it for a few years with its original equipment. Later the PP&CI was leased to the Brooklyn Rapid Transit Company, the line was electrified and its quaint locomotives, their usefulness past, were cut up for scrap.

Four photos, Fullerton, St. James General Store

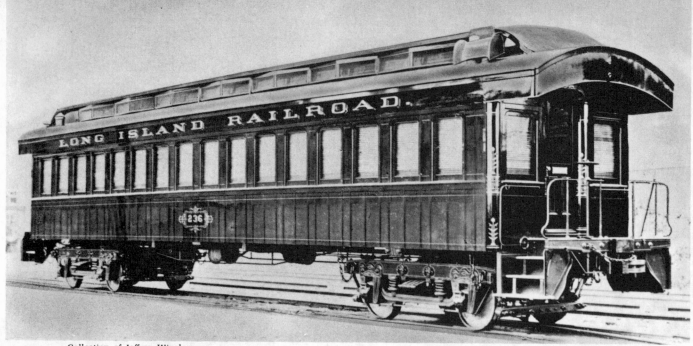

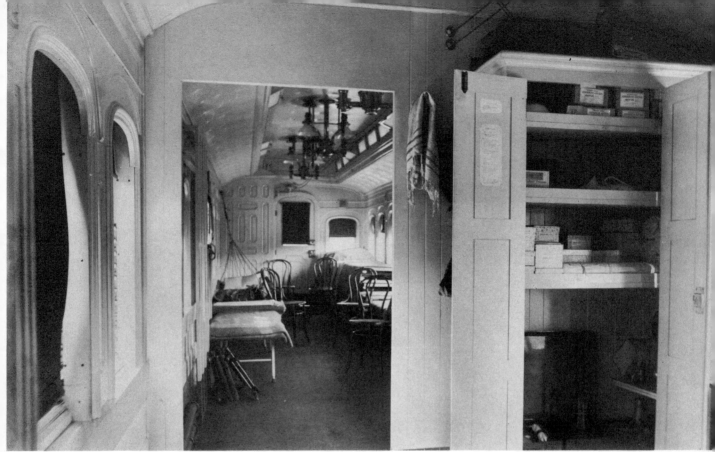

Victorian Coaches

It seems difficult at the present time to envision the rolling stock which was owned by the Long Island Rail Road around 1900. Examples of the ornate Victorian passenger equipment appear at *left*. Coach No. 236, typical of the handsome cars of the late eighties, featured plush seats, Pintsch gas lamps and wood slatted sunshades. Of particular interest is the fine gold-leaf ornamentation and the link-and-pin couplers. The epitome of the American car-builder's art was attained just prior to the advent of steel equipment, as evidenced by the picture of coach No. 258, built by the Wason Manufacturing Company in July, 1899. Among the last wood cars constructed for the LIRR were the magnificent closed-vestibule coaches of which No. 307 is an example. She was built by Jackson & Sharp, which had become a division of American Car & Foundry Co. All LIRR passenger equipment at the time was painted a dignified tuscan red with gold lettering and trim. It is doubtful that the classical beauty and tasteful refinement of this equipment will ever be duplicated. In 1898 the LIRR outfitted coach No. 117 as a mobile hospital. The car aroused much favorable comment in the press of the day, but no record is available as to how frequently and for what purposes the car was used. The

photo *above*, taken in 1901, shows the "transportation room." Hal Fullerton was standing in the fully equipped operating room when he made this plate. The car was under the jurisdiction of Dr. Valentine, the head surgeon of the LIRR. Although the railroad has always earned more revenue from passengers than from freight, in the 1890's the freight service was extremely vital to the development and growth of Long Island. In those days, the railroad dispatched or received over six hundred loaded freight cars daily through its various terminals. Frequently this total topped one thousand. When one reviews the scant population on Long Island then, these totals seem incredible. However, it must be recalled that the freight cars carried all the necessities of life to the residents at the time. It was the day of horse wagons and mud roads, so the LIRR was called upon to move everything from the lumber and bricks for the home-building boom to goods sold in the stores and used in the homes, churches, and schools. All the products of Long Island—potatoes, cauliflower, ducks, cordwood, oysters—were shipped on the LIRR. At the time the railroad had thousands of freight cars in interchange service. A stubby baggage car and a ventilated boxcar *below* stand amid stacks of fish crates on the Fort Pond Bay dock at Montauk.

The Severe Winters of the Nineties

One aspect of railroading which thoroughly captured the American imagination was the awesome struggle between men and machines and the blinding storms. The most celebrated storm was the great blizzard of March, 1888. The large Western roads, always on the alert for snow, were prepared. However, the entire East was caught without a single rotary snowplow, although they were manufactured in New Jersey. Rail transportation was snarled for days and many passengers were trapped in stalled trains.

The railroads learned the lesson of '88 well, and were prepared for the fierce snows of ensuing decades. The Long Island Rail Road had purchased a number of heavy wedge plows, but the pride of the Maintenance-of-Way Department was the huge steam-powered rotary shown here. This action photo, one of the finest ever made by Hal B. Fullerton, is among the plates which were salvaged by the proprietor of the General Store in St. James. The picture illustrates, as few have before or since, the drama and action which was associated with the steam rotary plow. It was taken during the blizzard of November 28, 1898. Drifts up to fifteen feet blocked many of the railroad cuts on the east end. The LIRR was so well prepared that most trains arrived on time and none were over a half hour late, despite the severity of the winds which drifted the snow back over the rails immediately after the passing of the snow trains.

The plows, each propelled by two or three locomotives, did their work so thoroughly that huge chunks of hurled snow smashed out windows in several stations. The agent at Huntington, fast asleep in his second-story bedroom, was half buried under a mound which an east-bound plow shot through the closed windows. At some stations the plows went through with such force that the snow was thrown over the buildings. As one story goes, a Manorville resident had just dug out his home and was starting to clear the cellarway when he heard a great roaring sound. Coming up to investigate, he was greeted by an avalanche of snow which propelled him back into the basement, as the rotary sped by.

Battling Snow on the West End

The two photos *above* show a snow train derailment during the Blizzard of 1898. A wedge plow and three locomotives had been clearing the main line in Queens Village when the accident occurred. The distinguished-looking gentleman supervising the rerailing of the 4-4-0's was probably the wrecking boss. The plow, set afire by its stove, provided warmth for the wrecking crew on that cold day. Jamaica station, *below*, was well cleared by noon on November 28, 1898. After a storm in January, 1899, a crew of Italian laborers, *upper right*, worked hard to clear the switches at Mineola for the first westbound train, behind engine No. 53. Two 4-4-0's, Nos. 106 and 107, *lower right*, became trapped in the snow and attracted quite a crowd.

Fullerton, Suffolk County Historical Society

Austin Corbin

Clearing the Rails in Suffolk

In a spectacle of smoke and snow, the rotary *above* forged eastward under the urging of two locomotives. *Upper right,* a wedge plow, speeding through Tuthill's Cut, east of Mattituck, spewed the drifting snow off the main line about 1900. Paused near wind-swept Amagansett in 1898 was a snow train, *right,* well equipped for duty way out east. The coach served as living quarters for the engine and plow crews. During "The Great Snow Blockade" of February, 1898, LIRR Superintendent Potter rode the plows and supervised the clearing of the line for three days and nights with no sleep, living on ham sandwiches. At Southold, a crowd had gathered over a hundred feet from the track to watch the plow go through. Even at that distance, they were completely buried by the thrown snow. The popular jibe that "a heavy frost would block the Long Island Rail Road," was laid to rest in the winter of 1898–99, not to be resurrected until the railroad was overwhelmed by the blizzard of December, 1947.

Long Island Forum

Fullerton, St. James General Store

Nassau County in the Late Nineties

In 1898, when Queens County elected to become part of New York City along with her neighbor, Kings County (Brooklyn), the three eastern townships seceded and organized Nassau County. The area was extremely photogenic, as photographer Fullerton proved in these pictures. The photo *above* was taken at Hyde Park on June 9, 1899. The engine, No. 79, is the same one which appears on page 54 before the 1898 renumbering. When the Post Office Department ruled that two towns in one state could not have the same name, Hyde Park, L.I., became New Hyde Park. The beautiful station in Massapequa, *below*, was erected in 1892 and demolished sixty-one years later to make way for the grade crossing elimination. This photo, made in 1897, shows a locomotive and coach No. 200, the ubiquitous superintendent's private car. At *right,* an inspection train paused a half mile east of Locust Valley in 1899.

Route of Proposed ONE RAIL or BICYCLE RAILROAD on Long Island.

Showing Amounts Paid at each Station for Railroad Service.

By far the most popular outdoor pastime during the 1890's was bicycle riding. There were several national and many local cycle clubs which boasted large memberships. One of the largest groups was the League of American Wheelmen. A forerunner of the highways of the twentieth century, especially on Long Island, was the extensive network of bicycle paths. One of the most traveled was the Cross Island Cycle Path, *upper right,* which ran north from Patchogue through Medford to Port Jefferson. This photo, taken by Fullerton in 1897, shows engine No. 92 posed at the path. The sign warns cyclists of the "Steam Railroad Crossing" as they pedal north across the pine barrens.

It seemed appropriate for the promoters of a fantastic monorail during the early nineties to seize on the appeal of the bicycle to publicize their venture. And so the Boynton Bicycle Railway, the vision of Frederick W. Dunton, a nephew of Austin Corbin, was conceived as a rapid-transit line. The map of the projected system shows how competitive the monorail would have been to the LIRR. In fact, the north shore route is a prime example of how the original LIRR main line should have been built. Except for the absence of a line paralleling the existing main line and the projected BBRy branch along Fire Island, the system was clearly intended to destroy the railroad. The 1894 stock prospectus which contained the map did not specify anything more about the dollar figures following the town names than what was stated in the headline. Being a major real estate promoter around Patchogue, Dunton built an experimental section of his proposed road about midway between that town and Bellport.

Dunton's claims were so extreme that one may well surmise his scheme was intended to be nothing more than a means of annoying Corbin. Calling the LIRR "outmoded," Dunton contended that the future growth of the Island would result in more money being spent to guard grade crossings than the total interest on the capital required to finance his ventures. He never mentioned the hundreds of grade crossings his line would require. Dunton promised to carry freight at half the rates of the LIRR, but he never gave any details as to how this would be achieved. Brazenly claiming that the double-track monorail "would have no ties to renew," Dunton went on to explain how the wooden supporting structure could be built for thirty-five thousand dollars per mile. He ignored the fantastically high maintenance costs for such a right of way.

Dunton, in promoting the Kings, Queens & Suffolk Company, as the system was officially called, also criticized the trolley lines. In reference to a passenger riding a car from Brooklyn to Jamaica, he wrote "if [the passenger] never ate his peck of dirt before, he will eat it all on that trip." Dunton claimed that, because of the unique type of rail service required on Long Island, "a standard gauge track is wholly unnecessary."

Dunton's line differed from its predecessor, the New

Map, Collection of Vincent F. Seyfried

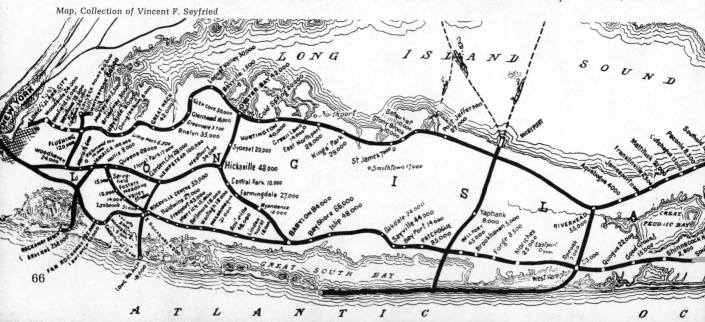

Two photos, Suffolk County Historical Society

York & Brighton Beach Railroad, which was the original Boynton Bicycle Railway, erected under the auspices of the inventor, Eben Boynton, at Coney Island in 1880. The Coney Island line, which was scrapped after only one season of operation due to a disastrous fire, utilized steam power in the form of a locomotive with one monstrous 96-inch driving wheel, *below.* Dunton, however, used electric power from the beginning of his venture. His famous car, *Rocket,* is shown *opposite,* at the terminal. In the background is the electric power generating station. Since Dunton was at odds with his uncle, Austin Corbin, and because of the publicity value, he transported the *Rocket* to his right-of-way on a truck pulled by fifteen yoke of oxen. The *Rocket* was a phenomenal machine, exceeding speeds of 60 mph on the two-mile monorail structure.

The prospectus, explaining the monorail principle, re-ferred to the upper rail as "being unnecessary, except at curves, when at rest and to transmit the electric current; but it inspires greater confidence." Austin Corbin reacted to all of this by suspending the special excursion trains to his nephew's enterprises. Although many people invested in the Boynton Bicycle Railway, it never materialized, and in 1902 the experimental section was dismantled. Some of the headline-seeking schemes to augment or even re-place the Long Island Rail Road, which were advocated by local politicians seventy years later, used many of Dunton's arguments. Like Dunton, they were wrong, and, in the manner of the visionary but misused Boynton Bicy-cle Railway, they created brief flurries, then died the ignominious death of all sensational plans in the face of public apathy.

Mile-a-Minute Murphy

When LIRR Special Agent Hal B. Fullerton met bicycle
champion Charles M. Murphy at a meeting of the League
of American Wheelmen in 1899, the two devised a scheme
which when executed became the most sensational
sporting event of the era. Murphy claimed that he could
pedal a bike at "a mile a minute," and Fullerton placed
the resources of the LIRR at his disposal to prove it. A
level section of track on the Central branch between
Farmingdale and Babylon was selected for the run and a
smooth plankway was installed between the rails. The
railroad modified a coach by placing a hood on the rear.
This prevented any wind force from striking Murphy directly as he pedaled behind the train with all his strength.
The great run was made near Maywood siding on June
30, 1899. As the run began LIRR Superintendent Potter
wailed: "The poor man will be killed." But as the end of
the planking neared, Fullerton and several other men
reached down, took hold of Murphy, and lifted him and
his bicycle into the train. The official time was one mile
in 57.8 seconds, though Murphy probably topped seventy
miles per hour at the height of the run. "Mile a Minute"
Murphy, who for a time was an international celebrity, in
later years became the first motorcycle policeman in
Nassau County. While workmen erected the planking,
left, Murphy tested his bicycle. Long Island engine No. 39
and the converted coach, *upper right,* were ready to go. A
plaque, *above,* marked the site of the run until recent
years. The most famous photo of the event, *right,* shows
Fullerton kneeling on the coach platform, giving instructions to Murphy. (This print was personally autographed
by the speed champion.)

Two photos, Fullerton, Suffolk County Historical Society

Collection of Arthur L. Mirick

The Oil Train

For many summers the Long Island Rail Road performed an odd ritual. During June and July the oil train roamed every branch, leaving behind a blackened, sticky right-of-way. The train, consisting of a locomotive, tank cars loaded with oil, flatcars outfitted with hoses and perforated side pipes, and a maintenance-of-way coach, was a strange sight as it slowly crawled along the track, dripping oil on the ballast. The purpose of spreading the oil was fourfold. It held down the dust which, in the era before sealed windows and air conditioning, was a great annoyance to passengers. The oil extended the life of the ties by soaking into the pores in the wood. The slick coating on the ballast also aided drainage and greatly retarded vegetation from growing along the right-of-way. It probably served to discourage trespassers as well. Although there is no record of when the oil train was discontinued, records do show that the LIRR spent ten thousand dollars to operate it as late as 1922. These three photographs (the work of Fullerton) were made as the train was putting down the goo near Central Islip on the main line on July 6, 1899.

Two photos, St. James General Store

The Forgotten Dreams of Austin Corbin

The greatest project envisioned by Austin Corbin was the plan to turn Fort Pond Bay at Montauk into a transoceanic port. Corbin was well aware that the prosperity which he brought to the Long Island Rail Road would not last unless he could improve freight as well as passenger revenues. A port at Montauk would have turned the LIRR into a major trunk line. Corbin's first step was to extend the Sag Harbor branch to a terminus at Fort Pond Bay. The Montauk Extension Railroad Co. was chartered in 1893 and the line from Bridgehampton to Montauk was opened in 1895. As Corbin ran trains from Hunter's Point to Montauk in record time (105 miles in 106 minutes), a great deal of support was aroused for his plan. Bills were introduced in Congress, surveys were made, and powerful business interests such as the Morgan empire were actively endorsing the project. Through Corbin's best friend, Charles M. Pratt, Sr., the vast fortunes of Standard Oil entered the picture as well. Pratt, who had founded Pratt Institute in Brooklyn in 1887, lived in Glen Cove at the time. Since the port of New York was becoming crowded and the Sandy Hook sandbar posed a threat to navigation, the advantages of the deep, sheltered harbor at Fort Pond Bay were tempting, indeed. The European terminus of the trans-Atlantic route was to have been Milford Haven in Wales. Not satisfied with merely attempting to attract the established shipping lines, Corbin and his associates organized their own line, the American Steamship Company. After visiting British representatives had approved the plans, the United States Army Engineers found that the costs of improving the harbor would be greater than was originally anticipated, not to mention the construction of docks and warehouses, as well as customs and immigration centers. Congress had voted down the project three times before 1896, but with the opening of the railroad to Montauk Corbin personally carried the fight to Washington. On the eve of final approval of the project, Corbin was killed in an accident. Pratt and the other associates tried to carry on, but without the great enthusiasm, dynamic personality, and personal convictions of Austin Corbin, the Fort Pond Bay project slowly died. The idea was revived from time to time over the next forty years, but nothing came of it.

After Austin Corbin

The Long Island Rail Road had reverted to its unfortunate destiny as a strictly local system when car No. 200 was caught by Fullerton's dry-plate camera in 1900. This was the superintendent's private car and was attached to a special inspection train when photographed in this idyllic setting at the Carmen's River bridge near Yaphank.

Collection of Thomas R. Bayles

73

The Main Line at the Turn of the Century

The dawning of the twentieth century found the Long Island Rail Road in a peculiar state of mixed destinies. After the wonderful vision of a port at Montauk collapsed along with the through route to Boston, the line was suddenly confronted with a new opportunity. In 1900 the LIRR president, William H. Baldwin, Jr., was negotiating with the Pennsylvania Railroad to have the Long Island enter the Pennsy's proposed new midtown terminal in Manhattan. Realization of this plan could mean a booming passenger business, but the attempts to attract more lucrative freight revenues were relegated to a secondary role, never again to become paramount in the planning of the policies of the LIRR. It was a strange coincidence that all the Long Island's most exciting dreams of the nineteenth century faded with the year 1899. By the end of 1900 the PRR was in charge of the Long Island, having promised to provide tunnels under the East River and terminal facilities at Pennsylvania Station in return for a controlling interest in the troubled road. The proudly individualistic LIRR showed few effects of the transition at first, and it took until 1928 for the Pennsy to relentlessly destroy the last of the traits which had prevented the Long Island from becoming just another branch of "The Standard Railroad of the World." The dramatic picture of No. 65, *opposite*, rounding the curve at Bethpage Junction, was taken in 1900. The five-car local *above*, leaving Westbury bound for Jamaica, dates from 1901. A new 4-6-0, No. 140, *right*, is shown pulling into Woodhaven in 1893. No. 85, a 4-4-0 flying extra flags, occupied the track at right. These Baldwin Ten-Wheelers lasted a long time on the LIRR. Sisters of No. 140, which was renumbered 116 in 1898, are pictured on page 130 as they appeared many years later.

Long Island Forum

Changing Town Names

One source of annoyance to Long Islanders was the habit of changing town names, which the railroad frequently indulged in. Sometimes this was justified, as in the case of West Deer Park. For years passengers got off there, thinking it was Deer Park. The residents of Deer Park petitioned the railroad to change the name of West Deer Park back to the original "Wyandance." The name was modified to the present Wyandanch. In most cases, however, it was the railroad, ever conscious of its "image," seemingly bent on substituting sterile or sophisticated names for the already existing quaint local ones. On March 20, 1892, *The New York Times* reported that the LIRR "has suddenly acquired such a mania for changing the names of stations along its line that many Long Islanders do not at present know where they live." At that date Good Ground became Bay Head; Breslau was renamed Lindenhurst; Ridgewood was changed to Wantagh, and South Oyster Bay received the Indian name, Massapequa. (One of the authors was incensed to discover, seventy-two years later, that the Queens community of Foster's Meadow was renamed Rosedale!) Fortunately, many of the affected communities raised such an outcry that they got their old names back. Baldwin (the sometime "Milburne"), Far Rockaway (briefly "Ocean City"), and Hewletts (the "Fenhurst" of 1892) were among these. The Waverly station of the late eighties, *upper left,* with its female agent and inquisitive bull, became Holtsville by 1899, *lower left.* Little is known of the mishap *above,* except that it occurred at Mattituck about 1899 and that there were no injuries. The bridge over the Shinnecock Canal, *right,* was not impressive compared to the beautiful truss span which is there now.

Collection of F. Schenck

Collection of Sylvester Doxsey

The New Montauk Division

A train leaving East Hampton, *left,* is shown in 1899, when the branch was four years old. The photo *above* shows Sag Harbor station in the early 1900's. The 0-4-6T which ran the shuttle train to Bridgehampton was an ex-New York & Manhattan Beach engine. Around 1890, the station building was moved from the end of the track to the location shown here. Miss Ethel Booth, a student telegrapher, remained inside the station while a locomotive was hauling the building a hundred feet to its new site. The wooden coach *below,* which was in work-train service, was demolished by an express in the Southampton station in 1904.

llerton, Suffolk County Historical Society

Collection of Richard B. Foster

The White Boats

Service to Greenport was opened amid many speeches on July 29, 1844, but not until Saturday, August 10, was the first complete trip made. At 12 o'clock a roaring cannon announced the arrival of the train from Brooklyn. The appearance of the steamer *Narragansett* in the harbor produced quite a stir among the staid inhabitants of the village that once had been known as Stirling. The locomotive carried flags bearing the names of New York and Boston, embellished with insignia representing clasped hands. The *Cleopatra* was the first steamship to be placed regularly on the new route. She was followed the next year, 1845, by the *Worcester* and *New Haven*. The passengers left Brooklyn daily at 8 A.M., reaching Greenport approximately four hours later. After a two-hour trip on the Sound, they arrived at Stonington or Allyn's Point on the Thames above New London, to connect with the Norwich & Worcester Railroad. The new route took all the travel and the railroad's stock steadily advanced. Letters and papers left Baltimore at 9 P.M. and reached Boston

Smithtown Public Library

NEW LINE
BETWEEN
NEW LONDON
AND
NEW YORK,
Via. LONG ISLAND RAIL ROAD !

COMMENCING
TUESDAY, JUNE 2d, 1857.
Leave Depot of the Long Island Railroad, South Ferry, Brooklyn, at 9 A. M, daily. (Sundays excepted) connecting at Greenport with the splendid Steamer
CATALINE,
Captain D. G. KEENEY, for New London, Norwich, Mystic and Stonington ; Landing at Pequot House Dock, each way.

Fare Between New York and New London				$2 25
" " " Mystic				2 50
" " " Norwich				2 50
" " " Stonington				2 50

Returning, the Steamer CATALINE will leave New London every Morning at quarter past 10, A. M, for Greenport, there connecting with Trains on the Long Island Railroad for New York.
☞ Freight taken at reasonable rates.
D. G. KEENEY, Capt.

E. B. SPOONER, Printer, " Star Office," 102 and 104 Orange Street, near Fulton, Brooklyn.

the following evening at 6. In the first year of operation the railroad carried 150,000 passengers.

In the golden days, hearts must have swelled with pride upon hearing the words, "the through route to Boston." The Long Island Rail Road invested some $400,000 in docking facilities and steamboats. It is interesting to note that Messrs. George Law and Cornelius Vanderbilt were directors of the LIRR at the time, and to reflect upon the $100,000 loan the railroad received from the state, the purchase of three steamers from Vanderbilt interests, and their rival interests on the Sound.

In July of 1846 the *Worcester* and *Cleopatra* were sold to the Norwich & Worcester RR. The LIRR was doing poorly. This was caused by heavy competition from the recently completed New Haven and Hartford Railroad and from boats of the Commodore's fleet, as well as Vanderbilt and Law's Norwich Line. With the completion of the Fall River Line early in 1847, the railroad sold the *New Haven* to Jacob Vanderbilt, who in turn sold her to the New York & Erie Railroad. By the 1850's the Long Island Rail Road had sunk into receivership for the first time.

The East Enders were proud of Capt. George C. Gibbs, who, after being besieged by fanatical financiers to develop a New York steamboat line, waited and, when the shouting died, placed in service the *W. W. Coit*, a boat large enough to cope with all but the heavy summer traffic. This vessel was put under supervision of the French Company's agents, remaining in control of the East End gentry, and not subject to manipulating city adventurers. The steamer already had quite a history, since, according to Dayton's *Steamboat Days*, the *W. W. Coit* had been taken into Civil War service in 1864 and recorded as a steamer. Later, as a dispatch boat, she carried General Gilmore to Charleston—the date is given as February 18, 1865 —and it is believed to have been *W. W. Coit's* ensign that flew from Fort Sumter, the first Union flag to go up after the Confederate surrender.

In 1870, under the management of Oliver Charlick, a new wharf was built in Greenport. Sag Harbor folks looked upon their new railroad branch as a blessing, but, after seeing Charlick's work, they preferred steamboats to being swindled by rail.

Another route to Boston was established September, 1872. The first steamer scheduled was the *Magenta*. Hoping to attract more traffic to the line, the Railroad added drawing-room cars and fast engines to speed the passengers and mail eastward. Meanwhile the *W. W. Coit* had stiff opposition from an old rival, the New York Steamboat Company's *Escort*. "Charlick the Churlish" put the newly built *Jane Moseley* into service on the Greenport to New London route in 1873. She was sold south in 1875.

Captain Gibbs, a shrewd businessman, started the 1875 season by making a trip over to New London. He encountered so much ice in the Sound that he

(Text continued, page 83)

Early Steamer Poster
The 1857 poster, *left*, shows how private enterprise adapted to the situation, opening a new line in order to provide for the Boston traffic.

Brainard Collection, Brooklyn Public Library

Long Wharf versus Maidstone Pier

The Sag Harbor Wharf Company was one of the oldest companies in the state. Its pier was built in 1770 and extended in 1804 and 1819, as the whaling industry expanded, until it was some 1,100 feet long. The company dissolved in 1886, but its assets remained in better condition than ever. Later however, with the extinction of the whaling industry, the pier fell into poor repair. Mr. Benjamin F. Huntting obtained a controlling interest in the pier and had it renovated. Soon he sold it to Austin Corbin for $20,000, double the amount of its original capitalization. The villagers were enraged at losing what they considered a home facility. Corbin never forgave Sag Harbor for what happened next. A new pier, commonly known as Maidstone, was built in 1888, and here the boats of the Montauk Steamboat Company docked. The LIRR put on opposition boats between Sag Harbor and New York, and a rate war ensued. Since the wharf property did not pay the railroad, it was sold to Fahys

and Cook at a very reduced price. The latter, who already owned the majority of the stock of the Montauk Steamboat Company, expended large sums to put the pier in top condition. When the Long Wharf Corporation dissolved in 1896, the properties were divided between the Fahys Watch Case Company, which received the wharf street and bulkhead, and the Montauk Steamboat Company, which took the pier. The railroad took control of the steamboat company, and acquired the lots at the shore-end of the pier by condemnation. The *W. W. Coit,* after serving in the Civil War, tried to run wildcat with the *Escort* on the Connecticut River between New York and Hartford, but could not compete with the established line. She was taken south, where she was used to carry peaches on the Delaware River. *Below,* she is shown in Washington Channel basking in the southern sun; *above,* several years later, in 1880, she was photographed at Long Wharf.

Mariner's Museum, Newport News, Va.

Collection of F. L. Scudder

Through Cars to Boston

Mr. Corbin decided in 1891 to use the LIRR's new extension to Oyster Bay as a base for a connecting link to acquire the lucrative Boston trade. The idea was to transport the train, minus its locomotive, via car ferry to Wilson's Point, Conn., where connection with the Housatonic Railroad could be made. The New York & New England Railroad, which was slowly losing its New England traffic to the more powerful New York, New Haven & Hartford Railroad, joined with the LIRR to form the Long Island & Eastern States Lines. This company acquired the steamer *Cape Charles, below,* which had been built by the Harlan & Hollingsworth Co. for the New York, Philadelphia and Norfolk Railroad Co. to transfer passengers and mail across Chesapeake Bay. The passage was not popular, as the water was too rough for comfort at the mouth of the Chesapeake, and the boat was sold to the New England Railroad, which had just built a branch through to South Norwalk. An engine of a work train, *above,* shuttled back and forth across the partially constructed float bridge at Oyster Bay, prior to inauguration of service. The bridge was about one thousand feet long and was served by a spur from the yard. By the spring of 1892 there were two daily trains running; it must have been quite a sight to see the white Pullmans, as they rushed through Queens on their midnight dash to the city. The accommodation was never a success on the New England side, although the NHRR's Pullman service did well. In order to obscure the fact that the NY & NERR was losing business to its competitor, cutouts resembling people were placed in the car windows. Shortly after this attempt to save face, the entire project was abandoned. The *Cape Charles* continued to sail for several years in the waters about New York, and for a season or two ran on the Sandy Hook route. In July, 1896, she was sold to Gulfport, Miss.; at that time she was valued at $100,000, and her speed was 20 mph. She was used alternately as a passenger boat and a towboat, once catching on fire; later she was acclaimed as one of the most powerful dredgers in the South—a far cry from the "plush and varnish" of the Northeast! An even earlier ship was the *Jane Moseley, top right,* built in 1873 by Lawrence & Foulks, Greenpoint, Brooklyn, for Oliver Charlick, president of the LIRR, and christened with his wife's maiden name. Capable of making 20 to 30 mph, she was put on the run from Greenport to Newport as a connecting link between New York and the eastern states. In July, 1873, while running between New York and Greenport, she broke her walking beam and was out of operation for a week. This line, too, was doomed to fail; Charlick sold the steamer to the railroad on March 3, 1875, for an unannounced price, and the latter sold her the same day to George H. Plant & Co. of Washington for a reported $85,000. In 1883 she was the first boat to be put on the Cape Charles–Norfolk route, but could not meet the demanding schedule and was used as an excursion steamer. Later she was named *Minerva,* and after fifty-nine years of service was abandoned at Shooters Island in 1932.

Peabody Museum, Salem, Mass.

damaged the paddle wheels on the *Coit* and had to lie over for repairs. The boat was run into by the Stonington Line steamer *Rhode Island* at Hell Gate on June 30, while on her way to New York in a dense fog, obliging her to miss one trip. This accident cut away the *Coit's* rail around the stern, part of the office, and part of the upper deck.

In June, 1876, the *W. W. Coit* became the first steamboat to land at Terry's Wharf in Southold. From then on, however, she was a regular visitor to that port. E. A. Terry recounts the following incident in *Steamboat Days in Southold:*

"Mr. Charles Ledyard, one of our early produce merchants, made frequent trips to New York and had trained his horse to meet the early morning boat. Mr. Baldwin Payne, a neighbor, would harness the horse and start him for the harbor. One morning someone, evidently thinking a driverless horse must be running away, stopped him and tied him to a post. The next time Mr. Payne started the horse to meet his master he put this sign on the wagon:

'Don't stop this horse but let him go it
To meet his boss who's on the *Coit.*' "

The railroad was losing the East End business to Captain Gibbs, so they put on an opposition steamboat, the *Frances*, with Captain Youngs commanding. A rate war followed, with competition between the rival boats, each trying to see which could reach the dock first to pick up cargo. The battle was wearing on the railroad, but Captain Gibbs thrived, becoming a thorn in the side of its management.

In October, 1886, Captain Gibbs incorporated the Montauk Steamboat Company, with a capitalization of $100,000. Two years later he ordered the *Shelter Island* built, and in 1890 sold the *Coit* to the New York and Stuyvesant Transportation Company. The *Shelter Island* proved such a good steamer that in 1891 her sister, the *Montauk*, was built. Gibb's brother, John, was placed in command.

Meanwhile, the LIRR, still after the Boston traffic, opened the ill-fated Oyster Bay–Wilson Point operation with the *Cape Charles.* On March 14, 1896, while making a landing at Greenport dock, the steamer *Montauk* collided with the smack *Lady Elgin.* The
(Text continued, page 96)

Old and Weary

The *Meteor,* the LIRR's only steamer used entirely for freight, made three trips a week between New York and Greenport, alternating with the *Shinnecock* to insure daily freight service to the East End. In 1902 she received a coat of paint and was sailed to Philadelphia under Captain Mitchell for a charter by a Chesapeake company. By 1905 she was held as a reserve boat. When the railroad had the *Meteor* she was already a well-worn boat, and is reported to have had a large piece of cement in her hold near the bow above the waterline as a remembrance of an early adventure. The Montauk Steamboat Company sold her in December, 1906, to the Roanoke and Baltimore Steamboat Company. Here she is shown by her later name, *Brazoria,* at the Newport News Shipbuilding and Dry Dock Company. Note the vestige of her previous owner—the Pennsy keystone still on her stack.

At Loggerhead Key

The new steamer *Shelter Island, above,* left Delaware in July, 1883, bound for the route between the East End and New York. The people who sailed up in her reported that she behaved splendidly, making 14 mph against high seas and wind. The President of Harlan & Hollingsworth said that his company had never built a better boat of her class, and the owners of the Montauk Steamboat Company and Captain Gibbs were very pleased with her. She plied the Sound until January, 1896, when she was chartered by William Flagler of Standard Oil Co., owner of the Ponce de Leon Hotel in Florida. A tug was sent from New London to break her free of the Sag Harbor ice. The steamer, commanded by Captain Mitchell, left the port with a good head of steam and made for southern waters. On February 22, when she was two hours out of Miami on the 140-mile run to Key West, she struck the rocks between Grecian and Mosquito shoals in six feet of water. The steamer anchored, and was kept afloat throughout the night by continuous pumping. The following morning she weighed anchor and headed for Miami, but the leaking increased and soon the fires in the boilers were extinguished. Three hours later, on a beautiful Florida morning, she sank in five fathoms of water off American Shoals Light. Tugs *Childs* and *Clyde* and several sailing vessels went to the scene of the disaster and brought what little furniture could be saved to Loggerhead Key. The LIRR acquired the *Nantasket, below,* in 1901, and she was put on the Glen Cove route; occasionally she made her 16 mph on the New London route as relief boat. Operations went smoothly for the little schooner until Monday, October 2, 1905, when she was running her early morning trip from Sea Cliff to New York. Off College Point she sighted tug *Emma J. Kennedy,* with schooners *Lawrence Haynes* and *Harry Prescott* in tow. The pilot of the *Nantasket* tried to swing the steamer away from the nearing schooners, but she did not answer to her rudder. She struck the schooners between the bows, tearing a great hole in the three-masted *Haynes.* As both vessels heeled dangerously the hawsers parted; the crew of the *Haynes* jumped to the *Prescott* just the *Haynes* sank. The passengers on the *Nantasket* were thrown to the deck by the collision and narrowly escaped death when the bowspirit of the schooner raked the steamer's deck. The bow of the steamer was crushed, but luckily she did not take water. Later she was sold and renamed the *City of Keansburg;* she was burned in 1928.

Two photos, Courtesy of Mariner's Museum, Newport News, Va.

Old Reliable

Built in 1879, the *Manhanset, above,* plied between New
London and Sag Harbor under the ownership of Capt.
James Smith. One of her most notable trips occurred in
February, 1899, when she broke the beef famine which
threatened Greenport by arriving with a load of meat
from New York the day after the local markets had ex-
hausted their supply. The little steamer was purchased
by the Pennsylvania Railroad in November, 1901, which
thus, in true Pennsy fashion, absorbed all opposition to
the New England Line. The price was not divulged, but
it was understood that Captain Smith placed a high figure
upon his holdings. Captain Mitchell of Shelter Island,
port captain of the Pennsy's Long Island Sound steamers,
was placed in temporary command. The *Manhanset* got a
complete overhaul early in 1903, *right,* soon after she
joined the Pennsy family. Shortly thereafter Captain
Youngs of Sag Harbor, who was sleeping in a small room
in back of the pilot house, woke to find the boat ablaze.
He rousted out the crew, all of whom jumped to safety,
but the ship was too far gone by the time the New London
Fire Department arrived. The firemen succeeded in flood-
ing the steamer and she slowly sank at her pier. The
steamer *Northport* was chartered to take over her duties
for the winter of 1904. In February, 1905, the Scott Wrecking Company raised the vessel and towed her to Staten
Island, where she was rebuilt. From all reports this work
was not too successful; the steamer failed her inspection
in March, 1907, and was condemned. The *Orient* took over
her New London route. The company weathered this
storm and managed to get the *Manhanset* running once
more, but she was leaky and no longer the dependable
boat she had been under Captain Smith. She was disabled again in May, 1910, while coming over from Connecticut; near Plum Gut she lost her propeller. The
plight of the *Manhanset* was reported by the U.S. cruiser
scout *Salem,* and she was towed into Greenport behind
an oyster boat.

J. Burt

Romance on the Sound

The *Wyandotte,* "Pride of Lake Erie," was purchased by the Montauk Steamboat Co. in 1905, after she had been used as an excursion and commuting boat between Detroit and small towns downriver. Captain McLaren was sent to Detroit to pilot the steamer to her new home. The one-thousand-passenger steamer was capable of making 17 mph. She traveled across lakes Erie and Ontario, steamed down the St. Lawrence River, through the Gulf of Halifax and out into the Atlantic Ocean on her trip to the Sound. The *Wyandotte* made the 2,500 mile trip under her own power in less than fifteen days. She was put on the Annex run, replacing the *Quaker City.* From there she went to the Glen Cove route and ended up on the New London route. The years passed peacefully for the steamer; here she is shown quietly slipping away from Long Wharf in Sag Harbor, *left,* on September 19, 1911. During that winter she was under charter to the New Haven Line, running between New York and New Haven. The company sold her in 1923 because she was not equipped to handle the increasing automobile traffic; she was limited to twenty cars, whereas the *Shinnecock, above left,* could carry sixty. Another of the line's ships that plied the same routes was the *Orient,* formerly the *Hingham.* Originally out of Boston, she served the line for many years, first working the Glen Cove route; in 1901, when the company was awarded the summer mail contract between Sag Harbor and New London, she was transferred to that route. The steamer developed high steaming powers and was considered one of the best boats owned by the line. In 1902 it awarded a contract to Tietsen & Lang's shipyards in Hoboken to cut the *Orient*

Off the Wharf

In 1903 the Montauk Steamboat Co. was in the market for another ship for the Block Island run. Manager VanCleaf and Captain Bunce went up to Bath, Maine, and looked over the steamers *Kennebec* and *Penobscot,* but decided on the *Sagadahoc* and sailed her back. She was built in New York in 1866 as the *Star of the East* and ran for thirty years on the route between Bath, Maine and Boston. It was only a few years since she had had a $100,000 modernization job, and the Montauk Line had to pay a handsome figure for her. In April, the Commission of Navigation approved the application to change her name to *Greenport,* the ship, *near left,* "being free of debt and seaworthy." In May, 1904, while docking at her slip, the steamer struck a barge with a glancing blow of her rudder. The full weight of the antiquated side-wheeler was brought to bear upon the steering wheel, which spun with frightening rapidity. The quartermaster was thrown to the top of the pilot house and came down across the drum of the revolving wheel; fortunately, he sustained only minor injuries. The company found the steamer very slow and expensive for the route, and sold her in the winter of 1906. On a Monday late in July, 1908, Engineer Joseph Smith sank with his locomotive off Long Wharf in Sag Harbor, *below.* He was backing the "shuttle train," engine No. 23, onto Long Wharf with two hoppers of coal destined for the boilers of the fleet of the Montauk Line. Smith did not know of any trouble until the tracks began to spread beneath the engine. The fireman, Edward Hubbard, hit the dirt, but Smith, still at the throttle, rode her down into eight feet of water, taking one hundred feet of pier, piling and cribwork with him. The big hook arrived at 8 P.M., brought by boss wrecker Carleton and his crew. They had to install a switch and lay three hundred feet of new track to get the sixty-ton crane into position. Engine 23 seemed to have an affinity for running into trouble on the wharf; a few years before she had jumped the track while working there, and more recently had backed a car of coal off the loading trestle.

in half and lengthen her out by thirty-five feet. With the added length and power she was as fast as any steamer of her size and tonnage on the Sound. One morning in September, 1905, a young woman left Sag Harbor on the boat, which was later boarded by a soldier at Fort Terry. The two young people were lovers on their way to New London to get married. But the steamer was late arriving at the port, and the couple had no time in which to have the ceremony performed. They dejectedly reboarded the steamer for the homeward trip, only to discover before the boat had been out very long that there were two ministers aboard, one from Albany and one from Shelter Island. At once the matrimonial skies brightened. When the Albany minister was approached, he agreed to tie the knot, but the Shelter Island man disapproved and created quite a scene to discourage the young people. The bridal couple was resolute, and as soon as the boat entered New York waters they were married on the hurricane deck in the presence of one hundred passengers and all the crew. While entering Plum Gut on April 19, 1907, the *Orient* broke her shaft and started to roll helplessly. The wireless operator at Fort Terry was the first to see her distress signals, and put in a call for a work tug from New London. In the meantime the government boat, *General Nathanael Greene,* was dispatched to remove the passengers from the steamer. On August 8, 1908, the *Orient* broke down on her trip from Sea Cliff to New York while coming through Hell Gate with three hundred passengers aboard, and was compelled to call for assistance. A N.Y., N.H.&H. transfer boat went to her aid and towed her to Astoria, L.I., where she disembarked her passengers and waited for repairs to be made to her steering gear.

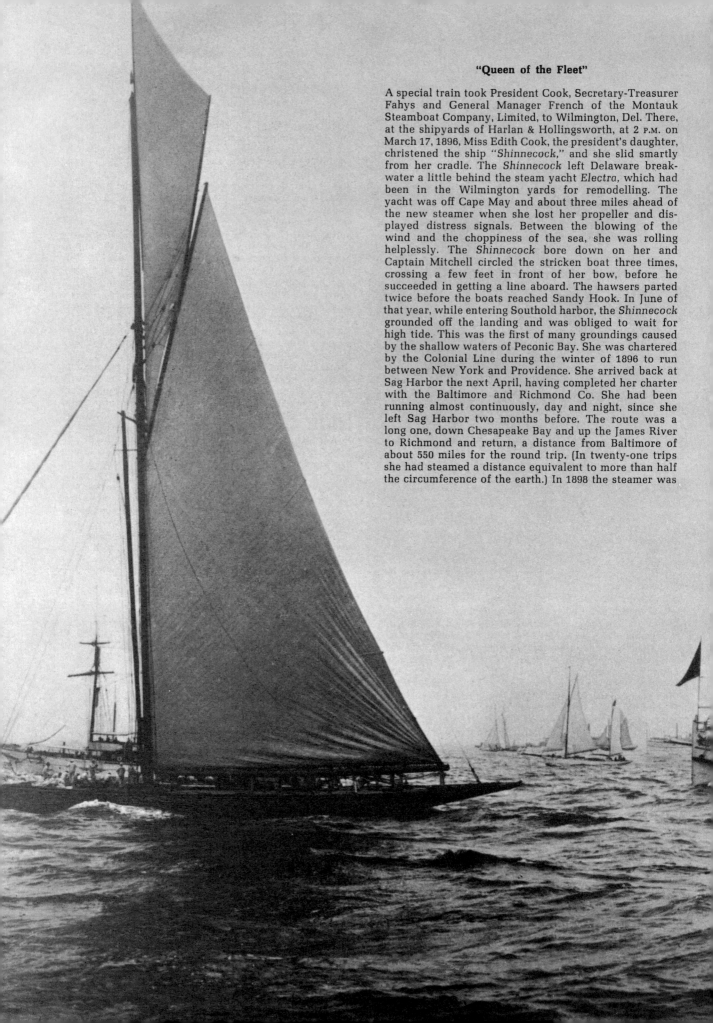

"Queen of the Fleet"

A special train took President Cook, Secretary-Treasurer Fahys and General Manager French of the Montauk Steamboat Company, Limited, to Wilmington, Del. There, at the shipyards of Harlan & Hollingsworth, at 2 P.M. on March 17, 1896, Miss Edith Cook, the president's daughter, christened the ship "*Shinnecock*," and she slid smartly from her cradle. The *Shinnecock* left Delaware breakwater a little behind the steam yacht *Electra*, which had been in the Wilmington yards for remodelling. The yacht was off Cape May and about three miles ahead of the new steamer when she lost her propeller and displayed distress signals. Between the blowing of the wind and the choppiness of the sea, she was rolling helplessly. The *Shinnecock* bore down on her and Captain Mitchell circled the stricken boat three times, crossing a few feet in front of her bow, before he succeeded in getting a line aboard. The hawsers parted twice before the boats reached Sandy Hook. In June of that year, while entering Southold harbor, the *Shinnecock* grounded off the landing and was obliged to wait for high tide. This was the first of many groundings caused by the shallow waters of Peconic Bay. She was chartered by the Colonial Line during the winter of 1896 to run between New York and Providence. She arrived back at Sag Harbor the next April, having completed her charter with the Baltimore and Richmond Co. She had been running almost continuously, day and night, since she left Sag Harbor two months before. The route was a long one, down Chesapeake Bay and up the James River to Richmond and return, a distance from Baltimore of about 550 miles for the round trip. (In twenty-one trips she had steamed a distance equivalent to more than half the circumference of the earth.) In 1898 the steamer was pressed into service by the U.S. Government to carry 2,450 sick Spanish-American War veterans to the city from their quarantine at Montauk Point. On her first trip she carried 271 sick soldiers; she was used for twenty-two days and the charter price was said to have been $1,000 per day. The job completed, the *Shinnecock* went to Staten Island and was thoroughly fumigated. In December the company was in the market for charter to carry her through till she could spend another summer traveling up and down the Sound on the Sag Harbor route, doing her usual three round trips a week. The exacting schedule she had to meet caused her to acquire the nickname of "Perpetual Motion." In this photograph from the Murdock Collection of the New York Historical Society, the *Shinnecock* was listing over with crowded decks after being chartered by the New York Pilots' Association for the 1899 Columbia-Shamrock race. She spent that winter under charter to the Narragansett Bay Line. The highlight of the season of 1900 was the carrying of a monster leather-backed turtle, caught off Block Island, to New York; it weighed over one thousand pounds. In September she was chartered for two months by the New York and Providence Line; from there she was leased to the Joy Line for the winter and spring of 1901, where she ran competition to the New Haven Line. It is understood that it was at the request of the New Haven Railroad that the LIRR failed to renew the lease. Labor problems arose on September 1 when nine members of the crew of the *Shinnecock* refused to work because they were dissatisfied with their supper. They were brought before Justice Tooker of Sag Harbor on a charge of mutiny which could not be sustained, and the Justice claimed "no jurisdiction." Justice Greene was appealed to, but he took the same view of the case. President Riemann of the Sag Harbor Board of

Trustees protested against having the men left in the village, and after some deliberation they were promised a good supper and taken back to New York on the boat. Legal action was taken by the MSB Co. against the Joy Steamship Co. to recover $2,982.03 with interest for breach of contract. The latter had chartered the *Shinnecock* in September of 1900 for sixty days at $112 per day, and not only had failed to pay in full but had refused to pay for stores and damages. On October 8, 1902, a bloody fight took place at Orient between a score of villagers and the crew of the *Shinnecock*. It was reported that the trouble arose from attentions previously shown to the young women of the village by the steamer's crew. When the ship arrived at Orient Wharf, it was confronted by a crowd of village men who insulted the crew with vile epithets and pelted them with decayed vegetables, flour, and anything else at hand. Finally they called the crew cowards and dared them to fight. The latter waited for the passengers to disembark, then accepted the invitation. All the officers took part, while the deckhands were held in reserve. In five minutes the malcontents were driven off the pier and the Montauk Liners claimed victory, although both sides nursed bruises, black eyes, and bloody noses. The *Shinnecock* was chartered for the winters of 1903–05 by the Flagler interests of Florida, and spent her time basking in the southern sun. In a thick early morning fog on July 15, 1907, she quietly slid fifteen feet up onto a sunken reef on the easterly shore of Hart's Island at the end of Long Island Sound. There was little excitement among the two hundred passengers, most of whom were asleep. Captain Mitchell sent First Officer White ashore in a small boat for assistance. When the tide turned, the *Shinnecock* swung about so that most of her port side rested on the reef. The *Sagamore* was pulled off her

Fullerton, Suffolk County Historical Society

Annex run and rushed to transfer the passengers to Pier 8 in the East River, amid a good deal of complaints at the delay. After this mishap, operations proceeded quietly for the boat until the afternoon of August 1, 1911, when an argument started below in the galley. Two cooks squared off with butcher knives and fought a duel to the death. The body of the dead man and the surviving combatant were taken ashore in Manhattan just as the steamer was about to set sail at 5 P.M. for Block Island. She steamed quietly during the night through the steadily increasing fog. By high water, at 4 A.M., the fog had become almost impenetrable. The *Shinnecock* snagged herself upon the soft bottom off Long Beach Bar, just east of the lighthouse south of Orient, so close to land that the men could jump ashore. On board the steamer it was claimed that the lighthouse bell had not been sounding its warning. The freight steamer *Manhanset* transferred the passengers to Greenport, while President Addison hurried to New London via the *Wyandotte* to secure help for the stranded boat. Scores of summer people from Shelter Island, Greenport and Orient flocked to the scene in sail and power boats. One woman passenger on the *Shinnecock* complained of having had too much excitement for one day: she had watched an operation on her mother just before sailing, had witnessed the duel between the cooks, and then had been shipwrecked. It took three tugs and a lighter of the T. A. Scott Co. all day to float the steamer, at an estimated cost to the company of $5,000. The job was completed at 5 P.M., when the steamer was hauled off the bar and finished her trip to Block Island, none the worse

for wear. Only one week later, on August 9, while peacefully steaming across Gardiner's Bay, the still morning air was ripped by the force of an explosion. The *Shinnecock* had blown her cylinder head at lam. Although no one was hurt, the ship was immediately anchored on the calm bay, while the little steamer *Manhanset* again came to the aid of the "Queen of the Fleet," taking off fifty of the passengers for Greenport and returning to take the remaining passengers to Sag Harbor. It was not learned until the next day that the damage was more serious than it had seemed; she had cracked her cylinder. The disabled steamer left Greenport at 6 o'clock for repairs at Whitestone, towed by the tugs *Wooley* and *Syosset*. The *Montauk* was assigned to her run until another vessel could be obtained. During World War I the *Shinnecock* served as a barracks ship at Quarantine Station, Staten Island. She was laid up at Whitestone Landing for a time and then reconditioned. It was probably during this period that her top deck was removed. In 1924 she was placed on the New London route; at this time the one-day round-trip ticket cost $1.80 for adults, $.90 for children. Normally the crew slept aboard, that is, if they did not have to spend the night at some such work as replacing a paddle broken by a piece of driftwood during the day. Here the *Shinnecock* is shown, *top left,* proudly steaming in Gardiner's Bay. The boys in Sag Harbor liked to ride the rollers from the wake of her propeller. In the twenties many famous people, among them Arthur Treacher and Mary Pickford, walked up her beautifully curved stairway. During the winter of 1925 she was chartered as a tender and excursion ship by the

Two photos, Taylor Collection, Mariner's Museum, Newport News, Va.

Admiral Line of New York, which planned to use her with the S.S. *H. F. Alexander* on their New York–Florida run. She was reconditioned and equipped with accommodations for two thousand passengers and a dance floor sixty by forty feet on the afterdeck, and an orchestra was carried on the boat. The railroad ended its "White Boats" in 1927, and the "Queen of the Fleet" was sold on March 16, 1928, to the Montauk Beach Development Co., which had formed the Montauk and New London Steamboat Line to run out of Fort Pond Bay. In the latter part of 1928 she was renamed *Empire State*. Her new owners, the Todd Shipbuilding Corporation of New York, had her overhauled and converted to an oil burner, then sold her to the Nantasket–Boston Steamboat Company. They gave the "Queen" her last name, *Town of Hull*. Now a full-fledged excursion boat, licensed to carry 1,877 pas-

sengers, she was used on the beach runs, moonlight sails and cruises through the Cape Cod Canal at the end of the summer seasons. In the 1944 hurricane she broke away from her moorings at Pemberton, cleared most of the harbor, and ended up being pounded again and again on the rocks off Peddocks Island. She was floated a month later, but her bottom was so badly damaged that she never saw passenger service again. Here she is shown, on October 17, 1946, in the process of being scrapped at Pemberton, *top right,* at what was once the repair pier. By September 28, 1947, *below,* this is all that was left of the "Queen of the Fleet." The *Shinnecock,* long recognized as one of the finest American steamboats, will be preserved in the form of a large scale model to be built for the new transportation section of the Smithsonian Institution in Washington, D.C.

On the Annex Run

The *Montauk*, *above*, as she backed off from the MSB Co. Dock at Orient Harbor. The *Old Glory*, later the *Nassau*, and LIRR ferries *Flushing* and *Rockaway*, *top right*, were tied up during the year of 1898. While on the Annex run, *right*, the trim little *Nassau* sat in the shadow of the *Lusitania*, pride of the Cunard Steamship Co. The ill-fated ship met her end on May 7, 1915, sunk by a German torpedo. The *Nassau* and the *Quaker City*, *left*, as they were moored to a float in the East River in 1904. Purchased that year, the *Quaker City* proved to be unprofitable on the Annex run, even though she could carry 1,200 passengers, because of the high operating cost of her two locomotive-type boilers. These were fired forward, thus placing the smokestack farther aft than was common on most steamers. The LIRR sold her in June, 1905, to the Maine Central Railroad Co., where she worked out of Rockland, Maine, under the name of *Sieur de Monts*. Then came a stint with the U.S. Quartermaster Department as the *Major L'Enfant*. From there she was promoted to the *General Mathews* until 1930, when she burned to the waterline. She was rebuilt into a tank barge the next year and saw service until 1941.

Fullerton, St. James General Store

The Second Montauk

The handsomely fitted *Montauk, left,* made her first run for the MSB Co. on June 27, 1905, leaving the pier adjacent to Montauk station at 12 o'clock and arriving at the new harbor on the east side of Block Island at 2 P.M. The forty-three-mile return trip to Greenport was made during a grayish southwest gale blowing at forty miles per hour. The twenty-four miles of rough sea between Block Island and Gardiner's Bay gave the boat a fine chance to test her seagoing qualities, which were pronounced admirable by all who were not forced to retire to their staterooms. On her way the boat passed the monitor *Terror* and three torpedo destroyers at their practice grounds east of Gardiner's Island. When the *Montauk* put into Sag Harbor late at night, the town fathers requested that she kindly not blow her whistle, as it had been mistaken for the fire alarm. The company had acquired the steamer at a cost of $175,000 from the Queen Ann Railroad, which had her built in 1902 as the *Queen Caroline* and ran her between Cape May, N.J., and Lewis, Del. She could make seventeen knots per hour. During the latter part of the 1907 season the *Montauk* ran unprofitable opposition on the Norfolk–Washington Day Line as an independent boat. She spent the winters of 1907–08 working out of Knight Key, Florida, where the crew boasted of having caught a 270-pound jewfish in April, 1908. She was out of Orient laded with 1,500 barrels of potatoes in September, 1909, when she grounded during a low tide. She had to spend the night there, and her cargo did not arrive at the New York markets until 10:30 A.M., causing much annoyance to the commission men who had sold the potatoes. The traffic manager was on board, and experienced the same difficulties the steamboat officers had to put up with. All went well as she steamed under charter for the Wilmington Shipbuilding Corporation in the spring of 1918, carrying day laborers between Philadelphia and Hog Island. After she was sold by the LIRR her name was changed to *Transford,* and she worked out of Providence. She was laid up during World War II and burned on September 30, 1945, at Claremont, Va. Former Annex boat *Sagamore, below,* is shown as she left Glenwood Landing on July 27, 1913, on the Glen Cove run to New York. The annex boat *Orient, lower left,* is about to pass under the Brooklyn Bridge en route from pier 17, at the foot of Pine Street, which was the LIRR slip adjoining the Wall Street ferry.

J. Burt

bowsprit of the little *Lady* went through the hull of the steamer above the waterline, but did not delay the *Montauk* from finishing her run. The *Shelter Island* was not so fortunate, as she was lost at sea while on winter charter in Florida. By July, the *Shinnecock* had arrived on the Sound and Gibbs found himself in keen competition for the disputed title "Greyhound of the Sound." In the eyes of Long Islanders she was a veritable palace, fitted out in Queen Anne style with a gold and white interior set off with red plush chairs and bright red carpeting.

In March, 1897, the Montauk Line moved to Pier 40, East River, at the foot of Pike Street. The *Montauk* encountered bad weather on the Sound in May, and ran into Sea Cliff where she laid over. Getting under way in the early hours, the Sound was so rough that she beat her way over to Bridgeport, many of the passengers wishing that they were anywhere else! In July the *Shinnecock*, while entering Orient harbor about 1 A.M., collided with the 86-ton schooner *Doretta Kahn* of Greenport, which foolishly had been anchored without riding lights directly in the path of the New York steamers.

The LIRR, always mindful of the excursion business, operated the Norwich Line's *City of Worcester* as well as its "Flyer of the Sound," the *City of Lowell*. While steaming through Plum Gut early one September morning, the *Montauk's* Captain Burns saw a fire on Orient Point Wharf. He headed for the dock, got out her hose, extinguished the spreading flames, and went on about his trip. The passengers knew nothing of the incident until morning.

On July 1, 1898, to promote the Montauk Line, Fahys & Cook carried the New York Press Association to inaugurate the daily trips to Block Island. The Long Island Rail Road opened a new route to Glen Island that July 14. The Glen Island boats touched at Whitestone's pier, and the railroad did a thriving excursion business from Winfield, Elmhurst, Corona, and Flushing. It was probably the *Harlem*, formerly of the Morrisania Steamboat Company, that covered what was later to become the Glen Head route. Meanwhile, the *Montauk* made special trips every Wednesday to Camp Wyckoff at Montauk Point, carrying visitors to the fort.

The exasperated LIRR finally decided to buy out the competition and on May 13, 1899, purchased controlling interest of the Montauk Steamboat Company, removing thirty-five years of opposition. In November the company leased the *Montauk* to the New Haven line to run between New Haven and New York.

The railroad then established three routes: the Sag Harbor Route—New York, Orient Point, Orient, Greenport, Shelter Island Heights and Sag Harbor, with connections to Block Island; the North Shore Route—New York, Great Neck, Glen Cove, Sea Cliff, Glenwood Landing, South Glenwood; and the New London Route—Sag Harbor, Shelter Island Heights, Greenport, Manhansett, Plum Island, New London. The 1907 map (page 41) also shows routes from Greenport, Sag Harbor and Montauk to Block Island.

One day late in November, 1901, there was a bloody fight on the *Montauk*, resulting from a clash between the engineer's and mate's departments, over coaling the steamer. Monkey wrenches and freight hooks were used as weapons, and several broken heads resulted. Finally the row was quelled by the captain of the steamer offering to fight every member of the crew single-handed. The *Montauk* departed on time

for New York, but the two gangs had to be lodged in separate quarters; the mate slept behind barred doors armed with a pistol and a bludgeon while one of his men kept guard. The steamer soon received an entire new crew.

In January, 1902, amid a flurry of activity, David M. VanCleaf, the manager of the Montauk Steamboat Company, arrived at Sag Harbor aboard the *Nantasket*. Immediately, work started about the piers where the fleet of steamers were tied up in winter quarters. Crews were placed aboard the steamers *Orient* and *Meteor*, their winter's sheathings removed and decks cleared, they were refueled and their boilers were fired. From Maidstone Pier *Meteor* broke her way through the ice to clear water. *Manhanset* was to be used as an intermediate passenger and freight boat, and *Orient* as a Sunday excursion boat. *Meteor* immediately relieved *Manhanset*, which then was stripped of her superstructure, rebuilt and modernized. In the early part of 1902 the *Montauk* was sold to the Algoma Railroad Company of Ontario, Canada, an affiliate of the Pennsylvania Railroad. Leaving on March 8, the *Montauk* steamed up to Lake Huron where she sailed under a British flag as a passenger and freight boat. The sale was made with the understanding that the ship would not be used to compete against the New Haven Railroad on the Sound. The place of the *Montauk* was filled that summer by the comparatively old *City of Lawrence*, chartered from June 25 to September 6. The line also acquired the *Sagamore* (ex-*City of Trenton*) which plied out of Pier 13, East River, on the Annex run and Glen Cove route.

In July, 1904, the *Islander* was chartered to replace the *Meteor* while she had repairs made to her boilers.

In the winter of 1905, the *Orient* was chartered off-line to replace the *General*, operating out of Newport. That same year the Montauk Steamboat Company purchased the docks at Sea Cliff.

The Montauk Line had reduced service, but by 1908 it was getting stiff competition for the New York freight from the Merchant's Steamboat Company's *City of Haverhill*. Then the Montauk Steamboat Company put the *Meteor*, which had been laid up, at the disposal of shippers. The farmers stuck to the new line and declared that they would stay with the competition even if the Montauk Company carried the freight free. There was considerable feeling in the matter, and thus the war for patronage went merrily on.

By 1916 the line was feeling the impact of highway traffic. The freight business to Sea Cliff and Huntington was practically gone. The East End passenger business, which accounted for 30 per cent of the company's revenue, was also fast dwindling. In May of 1917 the company was hit by a ruling of the U.S. Navy Department, forbidding the passage of vessels through Plum Gut between sunset and sunrise. This effectively ended the Block Island service.

Steamboat service between Sag Harbor and New London ended after the summer of 1927. The last trip of the *Shinnecock* from Sag Harbor was made October 9, 1927; for with the opening of the 1928 season Montauk Point was the terminus, thus ending the glorious era of the "White Boats."

AUTHORS' NOTE: *Most of the above material was gleaned from the Sag Harbor newspapers, the* Express *and* Corrector.

Crossing the River

Along with the development of the LIRR came the problem of transporting passengers to and from the terminal at Long Island City. To meet the difficulty, in December, 1886, Austin Corbin purchased the majority of stock of the East River Ferry Company, which operated three ferries from Long Island City to James Slip, East 7th Street and East 34th Street. The railroad then operated these lines and the Annex run to Wall Street, which seems to have been handled by single-enders or steamboats for the "plush" traffic. The other runs were held down by double-ended ferrys. Later the railroad purchased the boats of the competing Metropolitan Ferry Company, operating from James Slip and East 34th Street to Long Island City. The passengers were handled in New York by a spur of the old 3rd Ave. Elevated Railroad and by six trolley lines. The first ferry boat, the *Queens County*, a single-decked wooden side-wheeler, was put on in 1895, and was followed by two sisters, the *Kings County* and *Suffolk County*. When a fourth boat was added another source had to be tapped for names, since there were only three counties on Long Island prior to 1898, so she was called *Ravenswood*. Two years later, on October 26, the *Kings County* burned at Hunter's Point.

Change at Long Island City

The Flushing & North Side Railroad opened a terminus at Hunter's Point in 1854 and acquired two small single-ended steamboats for ferry service. They were the *Enoch Dean* and the *Island City*. The *Enoch Dean* was owned outright and operated between Hunter's Point and Fulton Market Wharf, while the *Island City* was chartered at five dollars per day and ran between Flushing and New York when she was not used for a replacement. Because of the *Island City*'s lack of maintenance and unreliability she was dropped and the *Mattano*, a newer and larger boat, was chartered in her place. In 1868 the *Southampton*, the first iron-hulled ferryboat in the Port of New York, arrived. Her upper cabin was removed in 1890. She is shown *(following page)* as she crossed the East River, on November 19, 1897. The next to arrive, in

1869, was the *Long Island City*, which ran between Hunter's Point and James Slip to connect with the railroad. She was constructed on the latest principles at a cost of some $60,000. In March, 1871, the Hunter's Point ferryboat *Suffolk County* broke her shaft, only a few weeks after she had been run into and badly damaged. The next year the East River Ferry Company launched at Chester, Pa., at a cost of $125,000, the *Garden City*, which was similar to the commodious *Southampton*. The company seemed to be looking after the interests of its patrons better than any other on the river. Harlan & Hollingsworth built the *Flushing* in 1877; by this time the *George T. Oliphant* had been put on the Annex run. The *Queens County* was sold to the Annex Line in March, 1878, to run between Brooklyn and Jersey City. The *Rockaway* arrived in 1879, to be followed by the *Long Beach* the following year. In January the *George T. Oliphant*, better known as the Wall Street Annex boat, ran into the Grand Street ferryboat *Warren* off the foot of Broome Street. The *Oliphant* broke her own bow to pieces and sank only a few minutes after some seventy passengers had been removed. It may have been at this time that the *Harlem* was acquired for the run. There was no warning when fire broke out suddenly in the *Garden City*, either in the lower cabin close to the smokestack or in the boiler hatch (accounts vary), as she left her berth at the foot of James Slip for Long Island City at 11:35 on the morning of December 13, 1883. The pilot quickly lifted the forward rudder pin so that the boat might be steered from the opposite end and gave the signal "back fast." Before the ten-year-old ship made the bridge, the cabin was wrapped in flames. In a desperate jump for safety the pilot landed on a bulkhead, dislocating his shoulder in the process. The engineer ran through the flames and reached the deck with his clothes ablaze, while the fireman, after opening the seacocks, found his escape route to the deck cut off and squeezed through a porthole to drop into the water. The thirty passengers and ferry hands on board saved themselves by jumping to the bulkhead of the ferry slip or dashing through the flames to the bridge. Most of the horses on the boat were run off onto the end of the Roosevelt Street ferry *Arizona* or onto the *Idaho*, which may have been crashed into (again accounts vary), while tugs *Devoe* and *Stone*, lying near, turned and played their fire hoses on the burning ship. The fire was extinguished at 1:15 P.M.; a subsequent search through the wreckage of the fallen cabin revealed five charred trucks and the bodies of four horses in the driveway. The iron

Murdock Collection, New York Historical Society

hull of the boat escaped injury; damages were estimated at $30,000. She was towed to Hunter's Point to be rebuilt. Newburgh, New York, was the scene of the launching of the *Manhattan Beach* and her sister *Sag Harbor* in 1884. The *Ravenswood* was sold to Henry Flagler, the developer of Florida and owner of the St. Augustine & Halifax Railroad, in 1886. She was destroyed by fire nine years later. The *Long Island City* was sold to John Gregory of Perth Amboy, N.Y., in June, 1897, and was converted into a barge, keeping the same name. The *Suffolk County* was sold to the West Jersey Ferry Company in June, 1893; she sank in August, 1900. In August, 1897, the Glen Island steamer *Sam Sloan* collided with the *Garden City* north of Brooklyn Bridge and both boats were badly damaged; considerable damage resulted also when the steamboat *Harlem* backed into the *Southampton* as she was leaving her ferry slip at Long Island City that same fall. The Montauk Steamboat Line was kept busy carrying veterans returning from the war in Cuba in 1898: the *Flushing* landed the 71st New York Volunteers, while the *Princeton,* from the Pennsylvania Railroad's Jersey City Ferry Company, was pressed into service to carry the 3rd Detachment from Jersey City to Long Island City. In March, 1899, President Baldwin purchased the twin-screw steamer *Old Glory* for the Annex route. She could carry five hundred passengers at a speed of eighteen miles per hour, thus greatly reducing the running time to lower Manhattan. One morning in 1900 the ferryboat *Sag Harbor,* while on the 34th Street run, was rammed by a three-masted schooner; the bowsprit of the schooner ripped into the forward part of the women's cabin, tearing off the roof, and plowed into the pilot house. Surprisingly, no one was hurt in this $5,000 accident. At 2:30 P.M. on February 23, 1901, the *Long Beach* left James Slip on her way to Long Island City, and the *Union* left Catherine Street slip for Main Street, Brooklyn. The *Union* was ahead of the *Long Beach* as they worked their way up-river against the tide. Coming down the river was a tug towing a string of barges; it started across the river in front of the *Union,* which came to a stop. The *Long Beach* didn't, and her port bow crashed into the *Union's* starboard quarter. The damage to the *Union* and her passengers was slight, as most of them were in the forward cabins. The *Long Beach,* however, lost fifteen feet of rail, and the stanchions were swept from their places and thrown back into the men's cabin. There was panic among the one hundred passengers, only two of whom were injured. The *Hudson City* was transferred from the Jersey City Ferry Company to the LIRR in March, 1904, for the sum of $14,000, and was the longest

double-ended ferry to work regularly in the East River. She became disabled on the afternoon of August 24 of that year while crossing from 34th Street to Hunter's Point. She drifted with the tide until she was off East 43rd Street, where a New York Central tug caught her and held on until a Long Island tug arrived to tow her to Hunter's Point. The *Sag Harbor* collided with the ferry *Harry B. Hollins* of the Broadway & East 42nd Street line on Sunday night in the first week of March, 1905, and both boats received considerable damage to their joiner work. As the different lines crossed each other it is remarkable that accidents did not happen more frequently. Early in 1906 all the MSB Co.'s boats had their stacks painted yellow with a blue keystone bearing the name "Long Island Rail Road." The line had two new ferry boats built by Harlan & Hollingsworth in 1906; the first down the ways was the *Babylon,* on June 23, and the second was the *Hempstead,* on July 21. Some four years later the Pecks Slip operations were closed. In June, 1910, the *Rockaway* was sold to the Norfolk County Ferry Company, and was operated for them until she was scrapped. At 4 A.M. on July 3, 1912, the *Garden City,* loaded with a small wooden shack, a few lengths of fence, several workmen and one passenger, sailed unannounced to Staten Island from Bay Ridge, Brooklyn. Her "cargo" was hastily unloaded and set up and the *Garden City* departed. Before anyone else realized it, the LIRR had, in a most clandestine manner, established a new ferry route. Although New York City officials strongly objected to this route, the railroad's plea was upheld. That is how the 69th Street Ferry, which operated until the Verrazano-Narrows Bridge put it out of business in November, 1964, was founded. In 1912 the *Flushing* was sold to the North River Ferry Company, but it was not until 1924 that she was renamed *Tarrytown.* Ten years later she was scrapped also. The *Long Beach* was sold in February, 1913, to the Wilmington & Penns Grove Transportation Company; she was dismantled in 1941. The *Garden City* was sold and converted to a tank barge in 1916, but kept the same name. In February, 1920, the ferryboats *Hempstead* and *Babylon* returned to their routes after being used for war service. They had outstanding records, each carrying nearly a million soldiers; this included bringing raw recruits to Long Island camps for training, transporting the trained soldiers in the dark of night to waiting transports, and ferrying the returning veterans to discharge points and to ports where they could get transportation home. Unfortunately, the soldiers were not as careful on board the ships as ordinary passengers would have been, and the boats had to

be overhauled before returning to their regular runs between Long Island City and Manhattan. In the winter of 1921–22 the railroad chartered two ferries, the *America* and the *Henry L. Joyce*, from the Ferries Holding Corporation. Early in 1923 the Pennsylvania Railroad transferred the ferry *Pennsylvania* from the Camden & Philadelphia Steamboat Ferry Company to the LIRR. The *Hempstead* and her sister *Babylon* were sold to the Holland Company, a subsidiary of the former Public Service Corporation of New Jersey, for service on the Edgewater Ferry, the former becoming the *Hackensack* and the latter the *Tenafly*. The *Hackensack* was renamed *Islander* when she was sold to the Massachusetts Steamship Company. The *Tenafly*, without deck housing or machinery, was used as a construction float in the fabrication of the Brooklyn Battery Tunnel in 1947. "Death Day" for the Hunter's Point Ferry was March 3, 1925, when the shabby old *Southampton* churned from her slip at Hunter's Point for the last time at 6:35 P.M. Passengers comprised two policemen, a *Long Island Daily Star* reporter and three others. At 6:36 P.M. the *Pennsylvania* left East 34th Street on her last trip. As the two craft came abeam their masters simultaneously rendered each other for the last time the passing homage of a whistle salute, that of the *Pennsylvania* being distinguished by its shrillness. The *Pennsylvania* was sold to the Hampton Roads Transportation Company and renamed *Old Point Comfort*. Later, in 1937, she was used on the Tappan Zee Ferry Line, and was scrapped at Round Creek in 1943. The *Southampton* went south in March of 1925 to work for the Lake Transit Company; she was renamed *Southland* and used as a ferry on Lake Pontchartrain in Louisiana. The vessel never made it

north again, and burned on August 22, 1925. The two immigrant Italian boys, *below*, worked as bootblacks on the 34th Street ferries. The plates on their caps read "LIRR bootblack."

Launching of the Syosset

The little work boats of the Long Island's navy started to appear in 1888 with the tug *Gladiator,* followed the next year by *Wrestler* and in 1895 by the *Montauk.* Four years later the *Syosset* was built by Neafie & Levy, Ship and Engine Building Company of Philadelphia; here are three photos, taken by Hal B. Fullerton, that show her construction and launching. In 1907, as the older tugs began to wear, the *Patchogue* was acquired. Tom McLaren recalls that the *Patchogue* was a "nasty" boat and hard to steer, but she showed lots of power in emergencies. He also recalls a winter's day at Long Island City when one of the boatmen slipped between two car floats as the floats were coming together, and McLaren grabbed him just in time. In his near brush with death the boatman lost only the heel of his shoe.

Collection of William J. Rugen

Harbor Workers

Other tugs arrived in 1918, 1919, and 1920; they were the *Cutchogue, Quogue* and *Talisman*, respectively. The *Meitowax* came in 1926, to be followed four years later by the *Long Island*. The *Talisman* was sold during the late thirties. As war clouds loomed, the tug *Garden City* arrived in 1941 and the wooden tugs *Cutchogue* and *Quogue* were scrapped. Next to go for scrap were the *Patchogue*, in 1959, and the *Long Island, above*, in 1961.

The LIRR closed down its marine operations on October 31, 1963, when the *Meitowax* and *Garden City, below,* and eight 19-car-capacity floats were transferred to the parent Pennsylvania Railroad, which now handles all the former's float activities. One of the eight transferred car floats was No. 20, *right*. The *Meitowax* was sold in the latter part of 1963 and sank off Cape Hatteras, N.C., while being transferred south; the PRR also sold the *Garden City*.

Gene Collora

Astride
the Boiler

The widespread adoption of anthracite coal on eastern railroads during the late 1800's led to the popularity of the camelback locomotive. Probably the most distinctive and most maligned of engines, thousands of these center-cab machines were operating in the Northeast by 1910. Because of the extremely wide Wootten firebox, the cab was constructed astride the boiler, to give the engineer greater visibility. It was hot, cramped, and dirty, for an engineman had only two feet of room between the boiler jacket and the cab wall. At high speeds engineers sitting above the driving wheels were in constant danger of being cut in half if a side rod should snap. The camelbacks ("snappers," or "Mother Hubbards," as they were called on various roads) were also dangerous because the two crewmen were separated. Instances occurred where locomotives careened for miles with a dead engineer at the throttle, while the fireman on his exposed rear deck was oblivious to any danger ahead.

The era of the camelback reached the Long Island Rail Road during the mid-nineties when a batch of older 4-4-0's was rebuilt into a fleet of sleek Wootten firebox engines. The years between 1903 and 1911 saw the greatest extent of camelback activity on the LIRR, with fifty-three locomotives of four different wheel arrangements dominating the roster. In addition to the twenty-one 4-4-0's, five 4-6-0's and three 2-8-0's were added to the roster of camelbacks in the nineties. The speed queens of the LIRR for nearly three decades were four big 4-4-2's, built by Baldwin in 1901. Fifteen 4-6-0's and two more Consolidations were delivered between 1901 and 1903. The remaining three camelbacks arrived secondhand from the Pennsylvania Railroad in 1903.

Leaving Oyster Bay

Although the camelback locomotive was more commonly associated with such railroads as the Jersey Central, the New York, Ontario & Western, the Reading and others, the handsome specimens operated by the Long Island Rail Road were among the finest in the nation. 4-4-0 No. 47, *left,* is shown crossing the old stone bridge at Oyster Bay in 1902.

Collection of William Biesecker

105

Collection of Carleton Kelsey

Graceful Little 4-4-0's

Before the turn of the century the LIRR had rebuilt twenty-one Rogers and Cooke 4-4-0's of 1888–91 vintage into the D-53 class of camelbacks shown here. Although in general ugly and ungainly machines, occasionally a handsome class of camelbacks was developed. The Long Island's D-53's were undoubtedly among the most beauti- ful ever constructed. In the photo *above*, No. 51, originally an 1889 Rogers engine, had come to grief at the wye in Valley Stream. She was bringing a commuter train from Far Rockaway on this morning in 1896, when she split the switch and turned over. Apparently nobody was in- jured and the grinning crewmen seem proud of their handiwork. The 4-4-0's were used in short-haul com- muter service in Queens and Nassau, and the electrifica-

Collection of Harold K. Vollrath

Fullerton, St. James General Store

tion of most of these branches by World War I retired many of them by 1915. Years later, No. 54, *below,* posed at Long Island City with a D-16, No. 203. No. 58, *above right,* was a queen of the camelback aristocracy as she emerged from the Morris Park shops to stand before Fullerton's camera on April 24, 1899. Of particular interest is the high-riding boiler, supported by a section added to the cylinder saddle. 4-4-0 No. 124 *below,* origi-

nally erected by Rogers in 1889, was rebuilt into camelback No. 56 by Baldwin only three years later. Comparing the two photos on this page, it may be noted that while only the running gear, cylinders and portions of the boiler remain of the original locomotives, no major changes were made on the tenders. Camelbacks 43 to 63 were constructed consecutively from engines Nos. 111-131.

Collection of Gene Collora

ROGERS LOCOMOTIVE & MACHINE WORKS
PATERSON, NEW JERSEY · UNITED STATES OF AMERICA

Chaney, Smithsonian Institution

Camelback Consolidations

Satisfied with the performance of its little 4-4-0's, the Long Island Rail Road decided to expand the camelback fleet in 1898 with the delivery of three 2-8-0's from Brooks. These brutish H-51's, numbered 151–153, were used mostly to haul freight drags from Long Island City to Holban Yard in Jamaica. Little is known of these engines, except that two more, Nos. 154 and 155, were ordered from Baldwin in 1903 and designated H-51a. The dates of their retirement are unknown, but they were all gone by 1928, when the big Pennsylvania H-10's arrived. The picture *above* shows No. 151, with the head brakeman's lanterns hanging on her smokebox door, as she wheeled a freight train through Richmond Hill in the late afternoon of Sept. 22, 1917. The builder's photo of No. 153 *below* was made when the big-boilered Consolidation was rolled out of the Brooks plant in 1898.

Collection of Sylvester Doxsey

Twentieth-Century 2-8-0's

Consolidation No. 154, *above*, as she looked when she was delivered from Baldwin. The latest photo of the H-51 class (and the only one showing an electric headlight) is the shot of 154, *below*, taken in 1921 at Long Island City.

Goodyear Collection, DeGolyer Library

Charles B. Chaney, Smithsonian Institution

Brooks Ten-Wheelers

The photo at *left* was taken at Woodhaven Junction shortly after electrification was completed. One of the camelback 4-4-0's is shown passing a work train on the siding. In 1899, Brooks turned out five 4-6-0 camelbacks, designated class G-53. They had sixty-and-a-half-inch driving wheels and were used largely in freight service and on work trains. One of them, *above,* was backing three carloads of ballast through Forest Park on a bleak day in the spring of 1924. The builder's photo of No. 126, *below,* illustrates the clean lines of these well-proportioned locomotives. No. 126 was retired in 1929, after three decades of service.

llerton, Suffolk County Historical Society

Collection of William D. Slade

111

Camelbacks in Jamaica

During the Jamaica grade-crossing elimination, just prior to the first World War, the G-53 Ten-Wheelers saw much work-train service. No. 123, *left,* is backing up with a trainload of fill toward the Jamaica station. A Long Island Electric Railway trolley was crossing Washington Street (now 160th Street) bridge as the photographer made this exposure from the Union Hall Street (162nd Street) bridge. No. 123 is seen *above* moving a train of empties at about the same time. *Below,* No. 124 as she looked in 1913. One of the last active camelbacks, she

survived in regular service until 1930. One night in 1891 a westbound train towing a huge steam digger tackled the bridges east of Jamaica station. The digger struck the Washington Street bridge. The structure, constructed of wood, was torn from its moorings and crashed to the tracks. Before the crew realized what had happened, the Prospect Street and New York Avenue bridges shared the same fate. Nearly half the water supply of Jamaica was carried in mains mounted under the bridges. The resulting flood and bridge debris halted train movements for hours. The huge digger survived intact!

Three photos, Collection of Jeffrey Winslow

Collection of Harold K. Vollrath

The Pride of the Fleet

The four 4-4-2's and fifteen 4-6-0's delivered by Baldwin in 1901–03, were the most celebrated locomotives on the LIRR roster during the first quarter of the twentieth century. They were big, powerful, and reliable. Most of the legendary experiences of Long Island enginemen occurred on these engines, and they left an indelible mark on the operational thinking of the railroad. No. 19, *above*, is shown as she appeared later, at Long Island City in 1923. No. 17, *below*, was photographed in 1910. Most of these locomotives were rebuilt with piston valves and superheaters during the late teens. All of them had received modernized cab roofs for the firemen and electric headlights by 1920. G-54sb No. 13, *upper right*, passed a set of old-fashioned pole gates guarding the Carlton Avenue crossing as she rumbled into the Central Islip station on a winter morning in 1922. One of the four E-51sa's dating back to 1901 blasted through Mineola with the Patchogue Express twenty-seven years later.

Two photos, Chaney, Smithsonian Institution

G. G. Ayling

J. Burt

Authors' Collection

Rare Pennsylvania Camelbacks

In 1899 the Pennsylvania Railroad constructed three camelback 4-4-2 Atlantics for the fast run to Atlantic City. After four years the PRR decided that camelbacks were not for them, so the trio was sold to the LIRR. Apparently the new owner was displeased as well, for they were scrapped in 1911. Not only were these the sole camelbacks ever used by the PRR; they were also the first of a fleet of locomotives of the 4-4-2 type which would total over six hundred engines on the PRR by 1914. There are virtually no pictures in existence of the E-1's on the LIRR, and very few on the Pennsy. The builder's photo *below* shows one of them at the Juniata Shops in 1899. Another one, No. 700, is shown, *left,* in Atlantic City the same year. An unusual feature of these engines was the combination Belpaire-Wootten firebox, clearly visible in both pictures. The six-wheel tenders were soon discarded in favor of more conventional ones. The E-1's, numbered 698, 700, and 820 on the PRR, became Nos. 198–200 on the Long Island. 4-4-2 No. 2, *above,* was bringing a train into Mineola from Oyster Bay in 1916.

Smithsonian Institution

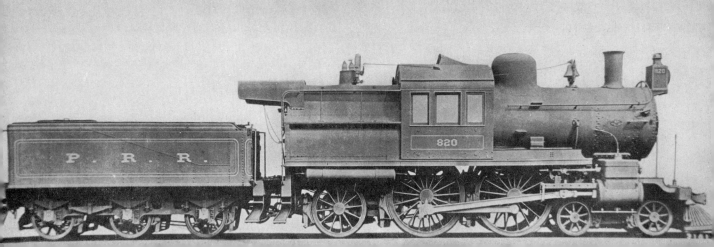

Fascinating Mishap

Derailments and wrecks were popular amusements in Suffolk County during the steam era, and engine No. 16 was an accommodating performer. She was the "hoodoo" locomotive of the fleet, often managing to put her wheels on the ground. On July 22, 1915, the big camelback broke the axle of her main driver near Blue Point on the Mon-tauk division. Local residents packed box lunches and pedaled out on their bicycles to view the bent rods, *below*, and the rerailing operations. A young lady, *above*, reminiscent of one of Charles Dana Gibson's popular drawings, appeared to be attracting more attention from the menfolk than the crippled camelback.

Two photos, Howard S. Conklin, Queens Borough Public Library

G. G. Ayling

Camelbacks in the Snow

During one of the severe winters of the early twenties, a camelback pushed the rotary *above* into Central Islip. There were few sights on the Long Island Rail Road more dramatic in the early 1900's than that of two locomotives shoving a wedge plow down the main line at better than thirty-miles per hour. A camelback and an old conventional 4-4-0, *upper right,* have teamed up to run a plow through New Hyde Park, and appear to be doing a marvelous job of covering the station platform which had been recently cleared. One sunny Easter morning, April 4, 1915, a heavy, wet snow had clogged the railroad so badly that several trains were derailed. 4-6-0 No. 123, *right,* was about to be rerailed by the big hook near Mineola.

118

Collection of Harry J. Trede

J. Burt

City and Suburbia

The year 1900 was a most significant one in the history of the Long Island. The Pennsylvania Railroad decided to build the East River tunnels and to pay $6,000,000 for the controlling interest of the Long Island's stock. W. H. Baldwin, president of the LIRR, stated that the sale was made in order to tide his road over a trying period and to insure its growth. A direct line now existed from the Island to the heart of New York City, and since it was able to deliver tens of thousands of commuters during the peak rush hours, a monumental exodus from the city was expected to follow. When in fact it did, a great social and economic upheaval resulted, as large numbers of middle and upper class citizens left the city to rear their families in the suburbs.

The much-heralded building boom, delayed by World War I, proved to be so great in the 1920's that even its most zealous prophets were dumbfounded. During these years it was not uncommon to see fifteen hundred to two thousand new

---

Transition at Jamaica

In the winter of 1902-03 Jamaica, *right,* still retained the relaxed nineteenth-century atmosphere of pre-Pennsy days. This picture, looking eastward along the double-track main line toward the Beaver Street bridge, was made from a platform shed roof. A few years later, Jamaica was electrified, *below,* and the main line was increased to six tracks.

Collection of W. S. Boerckel, Jr.

Fullerton, St. James *General Store*

houses a year erected in such towns as Jamaica, St. Albans, and Queens Village. Fortunately the LIRR, acting under the policies and with the financial resources of the Pennsy, met the vastly increased traffic with few service disruptions. Between 1901 and 1906 the railroad completely modernized its roster of steam passenger locomotives, and from 1904 to the first World War most of the trackage in Brooklyn and Queens was electrified. By the year 1927 the road had become the first class-one carrier to operate an all-steel passenger car fleet.

In 1911, the year after Penn Station was completed, the Long Island Rail Road carried 33,867,-228 passengers, over 30 per cent of whom were commuters. By 1929, the peak year in its history, the LIRR ran up a staggering total of 118,888,228 passengers, 61.7 per cent of them commuters. The vastly improved service to the city brought in millions of passengers, but the advent of the automobile and of competing rapid-transit and bus lines siphoned away much of the short-haul traffic. By 1940, a few years after the Independent Subway reached Jamaica, 80 per cent of the LIRR's commuters from Queens had deserted in favor of the "nickel-ride," and the Long Island's passenger total dropped to 67,501,730. In recent years the annual count of passengers has hovered around 71,000,000, most of them long-haul commuters from Nassau and Suffolk counties.

Two photos, Fullerton, St. James General Store

Collection of F. Schenck

The Rare 500's

The consolidation of the LIRR with such railroads as the New York & Manhattan Beach resulted in the former having various strange types of locomotives added to its roster. Since many of these were not destined to survive the electrification of Brooklyn and Queens local service a few years later, they were numbered in odd lots. This fact, coupled with the engine renumbering of 1898, provides much confusion for ferroequinologists (rail historians) who attempt to compile an accurate roster. Perhaps the most vexing class of such engines is the 500-series, the only known photographs of which appear on these pages. Since the NY&MB power had been designated in the 300-series by prefixing a three to the original number, i.e., No. 16 had become 316, it has been assumed that a similar arrangement was devised for the 500's—the highest numbers ever carried by LIRR-owned steam power. This shot of No. 524, *left*, was made from the base of the Union Hall Street bridge in 1904, and shows the new truss construction which carried Washington and Prospect streets over the widened main line. No. 512, *above*, was photographed the same year from a signal bridge near the present 147th Street. The new Baldwin camelback No. 15, *upper left*, is shown wheeling a train into the depot in early 1903.

123

Jamaica Elimination

One of the first and still one of the most impressive grade crossing eliminations was managed by raising the entire station and switching facilities at Jamaica. This operation was completed in 1913. To acquire fill for the massive un-dertaking, the railroad employed engines such as No. 8, *above*, to haul hundreds of carloads of sandy soil from Cold Spring. This load of empties returning from Jamaica was eastbound at Bellaire. The huge excavation which

Suffolk County Historical Society

remained after the completion of the project can still be seen north of the tracks west of milepost 31 on the Port Jefferson branch. Camelback No. 10, *above right,* was used in clearance tests for the mock-up of the Jamaica platforms. The signal boss toured his beat on horseback, *below left,* during the rebuilding of the main line through Rego Park in 1909. Dunton station, *below, near left,* was opened in 1914 and abandoned in 1942. The huge steel structure *below* carries the elevated tracks over Van Wyck Boulevard.

Collection of Harold Fagerberg

The Shops in the Peak Years

In the early 1900's, when the LIRR boasted a roster of over two hundred steam locomotives, the Morris Park Shops were alive with activity. A little 0-4-0T, *left,* leaving the elevated railroads of Chicago after only four years of service, arrived on the LIRR in 1898. Built by the Rhode Island works and numbered 321, she was assigned to the shop until her retirement in 1927. *Above,* an interior view of the backshop shows an array of 4-4-0's and camelbacks in various stages of heavy repair. The old steam crane *below,* which carried wheels around the shop area, was known as "Nancy" to the shop crews. During the early teens a LIRR employee named Fred Holman, who often brought his camera to work, made many of the photos on these pages.

Two photos, Holman, Collection of Jeffrey Winslow

The State Hospitals and the LIRR

The establishment of state mental institutions on Long Island resulted in considerable freight revenue for the railroad, since in addition to hauling virtually all the materials used in construction, the railroad kept these desolate complexes supplied with food and equipment. Trucks have now taken over much of this business, but the most lucrative part—the delivery of fuel to the huge power and heating plants—still belongs to the railroad. The delivery of soft coal is, in fact, one of the railroad's biggest sources of freight revenue at the present time. One of the most interesting locomotives to operate on the railroad was a little PRR A-3 class 0-4-0, Juniata-built in 1905. Although numbered 3 (later 03), and referred to as the "nut house engine," it never appeared on the roster of the Long Island. It was operated by the Central Islip State Hospital for switching on the grounds, and since its speed was restricted to 15 mph the monthly trips to Morris Park

for a boiler wash really tied up the main line and caused dispatchers many headaches. Both these photos of it were taken about 1915. "For years the railroad operated a special coach, No. 315, named *Central Islip*. The inside of each window was fitted with brass 'wicket-work' resembling that used at many ticket offices years ago. This car even had seat belts in certain seats."* The coach was used for transferring patients between institutions and was fondly called the "Creedmoor Creeper." The trackage leading to Creedmoor is still in service and is all that remains of Stewart's Central RR north of the main line. Earlier, the Creedmoor site had been a National Rifle Range where militia and Army troops trained. Few residents of Winchester and Springfield boulevards and Range, Musket, Pistol, and Sabre streets realize that these names were not arbitrarily designated by a developer, but reach into the rural past.

*From Harry Cotterell, Jr.

Collection of W. S. Boerckel, Jr.

Three photos, Collection of Harold Fagerberg

Suburban Tank Engines

In 1904 the LIRR bought five Baldwin 2-6-2T engines for use in short-haul commutation service. Nos. 20–24 were not satisfactory, however, and they were sold to the Jersey Central in 1911; the CNJ ran them until 1945. No. 21, *above,* is shown leaving Long Island City, and No. 22, *below,* is on the turntable there. No. 24, *right,* had been renumbered by the Jersey Central, by the addition of a prefix, "2." The four other 2-6-2 T's were similarly renumbered.

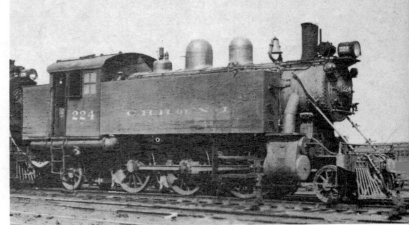

Collection of T. A. Gay

129

Two photos, Charles B. Chaney, Smithsonian Institution

The Twilight of Nineteenth-Century Steam

In 1892 the LIRR received ten G-52-class Ten-Wheelers from Baldwin. Two of them, Nos. 117 and 119 *upper left,* are shown at Long Island City in May, 1910. By 1924 No. 117, *lower left,* was one of the very few of these nineteenth-century 4-6-0's still in service. A comparison of this shot of the old Baldwin, relegated to the obscurity of occasional work-train service (in this instance, at St. Albans), with the photo taken fourteen years earlier, clearly illustrates the alterations of time. The slatted wood pilot of the varnish days had been replaced by more utilitarian footboards, the oil headlight had given way to electricity and the once-shiny boiler jacket became dulled with soot and grime. Both of these pictures, now at the Smithsonian Institution, were made by Charles B. Chaney (1875-1948), who spent most of his spare time taking thousands of photographs of the Pennsylvania Railroad. Fortunately, he traveled to Long Island often enough to make over five hundred pictures of LIRR motive power between 1910 and 1935. Morris Park, *above,* as it appeared in December, 1908. At left, the tracks of the Atlantic Division to Brooklyn. The Montauk Division, curving off to the right toward Long Island City, was elevated in 1913.

Two photos, Charles B. Chaney, Smithsonian Institution

West End Steam

Between 1889 and 1911 the LIRR acquired thirty 0-6-0 switch engines from Baldwin and Schenectady, two of which are shown, *left,* working the Carleton Avenue yard in Brooklyn around 1912. No. 183 (originally No. 23) was a Schenectady product of 1891 and No. 175 was outshopped by Baldwin in 1906. *Above,* as No. 78 was carrying a train past Sunnyside Yards in 1919, her fireman busied himself with wetting down the coal in the tender. *Below,* on a May afternoon in 1923 No. 90 pulled an eight-car train through Forest Park.

Chaney, Smithsonian Institution

The "Middle-Class" 4-6-0's

In addition to the Cooke and Baldwin Ten-Wheelers of the early 1890's, the LIRR had a series of Camelback 4-6-0's built by Brooks in 1898 and numbered 123–127. Between these engines of the nineties and the big modern class of G-5s Ten-Wheelers erected during the twenties, the railroad ordered nineteen 4-6-0's (1907–1917) as variations of the G-53 class. Numbered 128–140, G-53a, -b and -sc classes were gone by World War II. The G-53sd class (Nos. 141–146) were the last non-Pennsy steam locomotives to leave the LIRR. The entire group was retired in 1948–49. *Above left,* No. 132, a G-53a built by Brooks in 1907, was at Mineola during electrification in 1926. No. 133, *below,* one of the G-53b's delivered in 1911 is shown on the Morris Park turntable when she was new. Also new was No. 139, *right,* posed with her proud crew near Patchogue on May 16, 1913, shortly after arriving from Schenectady. Another G-53sc was No. 138, *below right,* rolling through Mineola in July, 1926, as a crew fitted protection boards over the newly installed third rail.

Holman, Collection of Jeffrey Winslow

Two photos, Fullerton, Suffolk County Historical Society

The Early 1900's

Upper left, a work train chuffed through the farmland at Albertson's on the Oyster Bay branch in October, 1902. Woodside station, *left,* was tranquil, indeed, around 1910. *Above,* raising clouds of dust a train briefly disturbed the peaceful hamlet of Hollis as it traversed the main line.

The station, still in use, was raised eight feet in 1915, and high platforms were installed. On May 17, 1910, the faculty and students of Pratt Institute were taken by special train to a picnic at Medford, *below.* For $330 the school arranged for the three coaches and a club car carrying "not more than 200 people."

Railroad Magazine

Rapid Electrification

Sensing the traffic crisis which lay just ahead, the railroad embarked on a massive electrification project immediately after the Penn Station agreement was closed. The first electric trains were dispatched from the new Flatbush Avenue terminal in Brooklyn, *above,* to Rockaway Beach on July 26, 1905. The first electric train to Hempstead, *below,* was photographed in Floral Park on May 26, 1908. With the opening of the East River tunnels in 1910 the Port Washington branch was electrified, followed by other lines. When the great building boom sired by the direct route to New York City arrived in the twenties, the LIRR met it without flinching. Expansion of the electrified lines to Mineloa and Babylon in the mid-twenties was undertaken as it became necessary. *Above right,* the first electric train to Babylon was greeted by a huge crowd on May 21, 1925. *Below right,* in July of 1928 a Multiple Unit (MU) electric train took an unintended plunge off the bridge at Hammel into Jamaica Bay.

Collection of W. S. Boerckel, Jr.

James V. Osborne

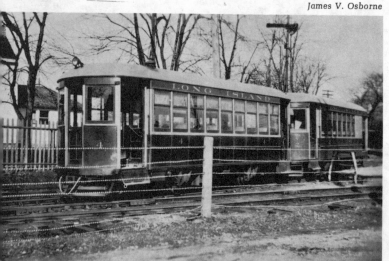

The Storage Battery Cars

The light traffic on the West Hempstead branch (or "Tigertown branch," so named because it went through a tough section) made steam trains a costly operation on that line. To help solve this the LIRR purchased from Edison-Beach in 1913 an electric car which operated on storage batteries. This car, No. 1, *above right,* provided such a rough ride that it was withdrawn the following year and "exiled" to the Bushwick branch in Brooklyn, where it agitated the stomachs of Bushwick-bound factory workers until the passenger service on that now-forgotten line finally died in 1924. In 1914 two larger Edison-Beach cars, Nos. 2 and 4, took over the West Hempstead run. Although these cars rode on four wheels like No. 1, they were much smoother and quieter. According to Felix E. Reifschneider, who supplied most of this information, the cars rarely experienced breakdowns and

Collection of Jeffrey Winslow

F. J. Weber, Authors' Collection

made the seven-mile trip from Mineola to Valley Stream (or "Rum Junction," so called because of the seven widely patronized saloons which could be seen from the station) in twenty-three minutes, including five or six intermediate stops. The cars were known to local residents as "dinkies," or, when they operated in Multiple Unit, as at *left,* "double dinky," or "double jigger." The railroad men disdainfully referred to the hapless cars as "moxie wagons." The biggest shortcoming of these cars was their vulnerability to snow; if more than a few inches covered the right of way, a steam engine and one coach were assigned to the run. Nos. 2 and 3 were combines,* while 1 and 4 were regular coaches; No. 3 also saw service on the Bushwick branch. Nos. 2 and 4 were equipped with third rail shoes, shortly before their retirement in 1926, to take advantage of the electrification between Mineola and the Franklin Avenue crossing. No. 4, *above left,* was photographed by J. Burt in 1926 at Mineola. The lower quadrant semaphores near the Howard Beach station, *right,* were typical of the block signals which once protected half of the LIRR trackage. The last of these had been dismantled by 1951.

*According to Vincent F. Seyfried, who closely collaborates with Reifschneider on such things, there may have been a car No. 3, but it was not a combine. There is only one known photo of the elusive No. 3, and it is a very poor one. Reifschneider concurs with Seyfried concerning car No. 3.

The Winter of 1910

One of the most proficient of Long Island's photographers, Joseph Burt, first took his big Graflex to the LIRR tracks on New Year's Day in 1910, where he made this picture of a train, *left,* coming down the Oyster Bay branch. The bridge carried the tracks of the New York & North Shore Traction Co. trolley line between Mineola and Hicksville. The impressive views of a 4-6-0 camelback, *upper left,* and a D-16 4-4-0, *above,* were made on January 16th. Mr. Burt, although now in retirement, fortunately has preserved all his fragile glass-plate negatives of the railroad. The D-16 class of locomotives was probably the most successful American type ever built. The Pennsylvania Railroad constructed 429 of these fine engines between 1895 and 1910. Ten were built for the LIRR in 1905, and twenty-one more the following year. There is no record of whether these thirty-one locomotives were included in the total, but they were identical to the ones operated throughout the PRR system. While most of them were short-lived and were retired in the late twenties, No. 212 was still in service as late as May, 1934. The D-16's and the thirty-one G-5s's that replaced them were the only steam power which the Pennsy built especially for the LIRR.

143

Ron Ziel

Trouble in Mineola

About 1920 a truck apparently skidded and stalled on the Jericho Turnpike crossing near Mineola. The "big hook," *above,* was called upon to clear the Oyster Bay branch of the obstruction. Crossing gates were installed here in 1924 and the grade crossing was finally eliminated in 1936. *Upper right,* a freight derailment in the heart of town on the night of December 20, 1922, wrecked the brick "MT" tower which had controlled the junction since 1890. After the Erie boxcar was hauled away the building collapsed, *lower right.* When the mishap occurred, the tower operator was sitting in the chair which is standing on the second floor. The big brick structure was a power sub-station. The present "Nassau" tower was later erected to replace the demolished tower. The old Mineola station, in the background, was replaced in 1923 by a much larger frame and stucco depot with raised platforms, located directly west of the Mineola Boulevard overpass. The most charming of the 1880-era stations to survive into the State administration of the LIRR, the East Williston structure, *left,* marked the end of electrification north of Mineola on the Oyster Bay Branch.

Three photos, J. Burt.

Tesla's Tower

Nikola Tesla was born on July 9, 1856, in Smiljan, Croatia (now part of Yugoslavia). By the age of 26 he had conceived the idea of a rotating magnetic field and was well on the way to constructing the first working a-c motor and generator. Tesla arrived in New York in 1884 with four cents and a book of poetry, for everything else had disappeared in a Paris railroad station. Soon after his arrival he approached Thomas Edison and was told: "Direct current, that's what people want. Forget alternating current. It's a waste of time." Edison must have recognized Tesla's genius for he gave him a job. Tesla however, didn't forget this early remark nor the later jokes which Edison made at his expense. So deep was this hurt in fact, that years later he refused to share the 1912 Nobel Prize in Physics with Edison, a "mere inventor." Not all of his inventions were as successful as the patent rights on alternating current which George Westinghouse purchased for $1,000,000. Shortly after the turn of the century Tesla built a 300-foot-high tower capped by a copper mesh dome, near Shoreham on the Wading River branch. From this facility he planned to broadcast cheap electricity and entertaining programs. J. P. Morgan and several other prominent businessmen were persuaded to put up $300,000. During the construction of this small "Radio City" Tesla had his supper specially prepared on a Long Island train every day, and each evening as the train waited in Shoreham station a porter would deliver the meal to him. The project was eventually abandoned for lack of funds and the huge tower was razed by the government during World War I. Tesla had invented "the arc light before Edison and the radio before Marconi, and he talked about cosmic rays a generation before other scientists learned such rays existed. In 1917 he even discussed plans for detecting distant objects by means of shortwave impulses reflected off the objects and picked up on a fluorescent screen" (radar). When Nikola Tesla died on January 7, 1943 at the age of 86, he had "become a forgotten man in the electrical age that owed him everything."*

*Quotations used by permission of Lyman M. Nash and Boys' Life, published by the Boy Scouts of America.

J. Burt

Glen Cove and Miller Place

Before 1910, Shoreham was known by the picturesque name of Wardenclyffe. The Glen Cove freight yard, *above,* was well stocked with loaded cars in 1903. An excursion train paused at the Miller Place station, *below,* about 1910, to let off these ladies dressed in their summer finery.

L.I.R.R FREIGHT DEPOT

The Idle Years in Huntington

The tranquil summer scene, *left,* typical of America long ago, shows a Wading River train leaving Huntington Station in 1904. New York Avenue, then a grade crossing, passed between the parked boxcars at right. The wooden station was replaced in 1909 by the modern structure farther east. The pickle factory behind the buckboard is the present site of F. M. Concannon's warehouse. *Below,* a freight paused near the location of the present station in March, 1903. In 1890 a horsecar line was built from the depot to Halesite—site of Nathan Hale's capture by the British. Called the Huntington Railroad Co., this subsidiary of the LIRR was electrified in 1898. In 1909, when the line was extended to Amityville along the present state highway, route 110, the grade crossing at New York Avenue was eliminated in order to permit the trolleys to run under the railroad. Subsequently this line was abandoned in sections between 1919 and 1927.

Oliver Charlick never forgot his battle with the people of Huntington in the 1860's (page 14). When he died in 1875, he left specific instructions that although mourning bunting might be hung in other stations and the ensigns on all of the LIRR boats should fly at half-mast, no observances were to be held at Huntington.

The LIRR freight depot was located on the trolley line north of Huntington in 1902, *lower left.* At the side of the building is seen the freight trolley which ran to the main station, and a discarded horsecar. Forty-five years after abandonment of the Huntington Railroad to the South Shore there was still no public transport to replace it, although the area's population had quadrupled! About 1905, a light engine was dispatched west from Huntington at the same time a circus train was sent east from Hicksville. The agent at Cold Spring, working on his records after hours, heard the dispatcher trying to raise the Huntington agent on the telegraph, to tell him to hold the engine. At that time there was a passing siding at Cold Spring, and the agent knew that the engines would meet head-on there. He ran to one switch and set it for the siding just as the circus special arrived. The light engine shot by on the main line and came so close to hitting the special that it knocked a marker light off the last coach! The big frame house which still stands north of the tracks at the west end of Cold Spring Harbor station was given to the heroic agent by the grateful railroad.

Fullerton, St. James General Store

Islip and Huntington After 1910

Right, peaceful Islip station with a D-16, No. 223, in 1911. The building was razed and replaced in 1963 by a pseudo-modern structure on the opposite side of the tracks. Agent G. G. Ayling of Central Islip station photographed his office about 1922, *lower right.* The telegraphic equipment, gooseneck telephones, and big Underwood typewriter were typical fixtures of the era. A D-16, No. 208, *below,* was photographed at Huntington Station in January, 1922. *Bottom,* another of the Juniata-built 4-4-0's pulled a solid train of wooden coaches into Huntington Station in 1916. The Huntington RR trolley conductor stood alongside a car assigned to the Ocean Electric Co., another LIRR subsidiary. These cars were frequently interchanged between the lines. The water tower in the background was removed in 1946; the signals in front of the depot, in 1958.

Collection of William J. Rugen

Collection of R. M. Emery

Along the South Shore

Until the tracks were elevated in 1964, the right of way through Babylon had retained much of the character it possessed when the view *above,* looking west toward the station from east of Deer-Park Avenue, was taken in 1907. *Lower left,* the handsome LIRR trolley, No. E-6, was typical of the open cars used during summer months. This one, constructed by the J. G. Brill Co., ran from Far Rockaway to Rockaway Park during the years 1898–1904, then was transferred to the Ocean Electric line. Another

Collection of R. M. Emery

scene drastically altered to make way for a projected grade crossing elimination was Amityville, *above*. Until 1964, the brick station dominated the area, and the only portion of the Huntington trolley line yet in existence was the span immediately over the tracks, which was used as a footbridge. *Lower right*, a photographer, apparently waiting for a train, stood on the platform of the old Bayport station in 1903.

Collection of F. Schenck

Collection of William Biesecker

Mid-Island Freights

Above, a freight train has taken the siding at Ronkonkoma station to make way for a mid-morning passenger train. *Below,* one of the few photos in existence of the old four-wheel cabooses belongs to a retired conductor, Raymond Robinson of Eastport. He was the dapper gentleman with the moustache seated on the rear platform when this photo of the Speonk freight was made in the

Patchogue yard in 1915. The engine, an H-3 Consolidation, No. 163, was built by Baldwin to PRR specifications in 1892. Eleven of these locomotives, renumbered 159–169 by the LIRR, were the first of more than four hundred steam engines which the Pennsy sold or leased to the Long Island over a period of fifty-three years. All but sixty-two of them were secondhand. The H-3's were nicknamed "Beetlehounds" by their crews.

A. Noble Chapman, Queens Borough Public Library

Patchogue's Past

The "traction mania" which swept the United States around the turn of the century had an effect on Long Island. One of the more ambitious outgrowths was a line which was projected from Patchogue north through Holtsville and Selden to Port Jefferson. During 1911 and 1912 the Suffolk Traction Co. built a line from the Patchogue Town Dock on Great South Bay to Holtsville, a distance of about seven miles. A later section was opened to Sayville. That was the extent of the Suffolk Traction Co., except for an additional section of track which was actually installed in Port Jefferson, but never saw service. The cars were storage-battery powered, very similar to the LIRR shown on page 141. *Above,* one of the cars is shown in Patchogue on the day of its arrival, via the LIRR, in 1911. The little cars struggled to eke out an existence, but the line was abandoned in 1919, leaving only a pair of rails which are still visible nearly a half century later on South Ocean Avenue in Patchogue. *Below,* two LIRR locomotives were snowbound on the ashpit track in Patchogue during the blizzard of December 13, 1904.

Howard S. Conklin, Queens Borough Public Library

Horse and Buggy Days

The photograph of Patchogue depot *above*, gives a clearer impression of life around a rural station in early 20th century America, than virtually any others which have survived to the present time. It was taken on March 25, 1905, when the chill of early spring required the horse-power for the hansom cabs to remain under wraps. The water tower and freight house have long been gone; the charming brick station was replaced by a modern stone and glass affair in 1963; acres of commuters' automobiles now cover the plaza, from which the hoofbeats have faded forever; but this picture immortalizes the flavor of a departed era. When Charles Evan Hughes ran his successful campaign for the governorship of New York, a special train, *left,* brought him to Patchogue on October 15, 1908. Unfortunately, time has damaged the plate on which this exposure was made. On that day, Mr. Hughes *right,* addressed a large crowd of Patchoguers, many of whom helped to elect him a few weeks later.

Way Out East

The east end of Long Island, until recently populated by individualistic tradesmen, conservative farmers and rugged seamen, has always been slower than the west-end towns to adopt the changing ways of the big city. From the time of its realization that the original reason for its existence had vanished with the building of the New Haven Railroad to Boston in 1850, the LIRR has played a major role in developing the areas way out east. The most concerted effort to open up the scrub-oak barrens east of Wading River on the north shore and Patchogue on the south was launched during the 1920's. Business and civic organizations all over the Island joined with prominent citizens, newspapers and the railroad to promote travel and settlements on Long Island. Using the slogan: "Hit the Sunrise Trail," they conducted a huge advertising campaign. Carl G. Fisher, the developer of Miami Beach, invested millions of dollars to turn desolate Montauk into a high-class resort area. The project briefly revived the plans of Austin Corbin to construct a deepwater port, but the Depression ruined the entire venture. The nearly vacant office building erected in Montauk village by the Fisher interests stands as an ominous reminder of past financial debacles to any latter-day developers.

In the early 1900's the east end was a place of prosperous potato farms in summer and deep snows in winter. Down through those pleasant

Two photos, Fullerton, Suffolk County Historical Society

decades the LIRR dispatched its luxury varnish and hot-shot freight trainloads of famous Long Island potatoes behind 4-4-0's and high-drivered camelbacks.

The management of the Long Island during the twenties was probably the most imaginative in the history of the road. It not only operated sumptuous trains to the eastern terminals but also sponsored a large band, singing groups, and huge athletic events, and generally aided in boosting Long Island. Because of the tremendous national death toll in grade-crossing accidents, the LIRR participated wholeheartedly in all the safety programs of the time.

In 1928 came the great purge. The Pennsylvania Railroad abandoned its policy of begrudgingly allowing a certain amount of autonomy to the LIRR and took over complete operational control. Native Long Islanders in management were replaced with surplus PRR officials and many of the little pleasantries which gave the railroad an individuality of its own were abruptly and senselessly destroyed. Locomotives which were still serviceable were scrapped to make way for standard PRR engines. The resulting demoralization of the once proud Long Island Rail Road men was compounded by the Depression and the great loss of passenger revenues in the thirties. The LIRR was never to recover completely from this triple blow.

Out on the Wading River Branch
An old boxcar, *left,* was unloaded at Wading River in 1905, to be used for living quarters for a crew of Italian laborers who were clearing land for the LIRR's first experimental farm. The enginehouse at the end of the branch is visible in the background. No. 11, one of the 4-6-0 camelbacks, as she pulled a freight toward Wading River in 1906, *below.*

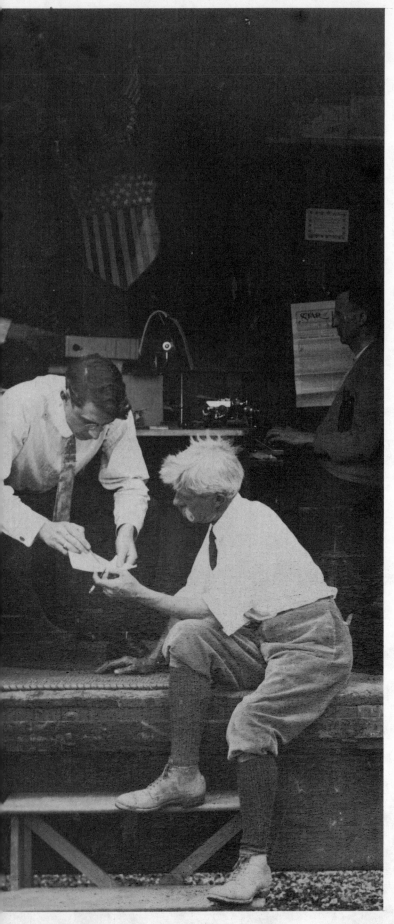

The Fabulous Fullerton

For three decades one man, Hal B. Fullerton, stood as the symbol of the dynamic surge which propelled the Long Island Rail Road into the twentieth century. In 1897 the railroad hired Fullerton as a special agent. Though primarily an agricultural expert, he spent most of his first seven years with the LIRR as its official photographer. His work, much of which is featured in this volume, is unexcelled. Hal Fullerton's first big venture on Long Island was to sponsor Charles Murphy's famous bicycle ride in 1899. After bitter experiences while pedaling his own bicycle, loaded with an 11- by 14-inch glass-plate camera, along the poor roads on the Island, Fullerton successfully advocated a road improvement program and became prime motivator of the fine system of bike paths which attracted cyclists from all over the nation. He ordered six bicycle-carrying cars to be built for the railroad and organized cycle excursion trains to various eastern stations. In one year, 1898, the LIRR carried more than 176,000 bicycles on these trains. Hal Fullerton had the dubious honor in 1901 of being the victim of what is believed to have been the first train-auto collision in the United States. Pinned under an 8- by 10-inch camera, he was unable to jump from the rear seat of a car as it was struck and thrown thirty feet at a crossing in Mineola. In 1905, acting on orders from the railroad superintendent, Fullerton purchased ten acres of the worst land he could find near Wading River. Here he built Peace and Plenty, an experimental farm to prove that Long Island soil could support good crops. In 1907 he purchased eighty acres near Medford, where he built Prosperity Farm. Over the next twenty years Fullerton became *the* expert on Long Island agriculture, growing nearly one thousand varieties of plants on the railroad's land. Agricultural experts from all over the world visited his demonstration farms. After World War I Fullerton was invited to France to aid in rebuilding the ravaged agricultural economy. As a direct result of the phenomenal success of these farms, the State Agricultural and Technical College was established near Farmingdale. In the late teens "Good Roads" Fullerton joined with Theodore Roosevelt to advocate a paved automobile highway network on Long Island. When Hal Fullerton finally retired as LIRR director of agriculture in 1927 his wife, Edith, took over. It was ironic that he left the railroad just before the Pennsy terminated the fabulous era which was so much the creation of his amazing talents. The Wading River farm had shut down years before and the Medford farm, having served its purpose well, was sold shortly after the PRR took over. Mrs. Fullerton died in 1931 and Hal B. Fullerton, agriculturist, photographer, author, world traveler, and railroad special agent *extraordinaire*, followed in 1935 at the age of seventy-eight. *Left*, on June 16, 1910, Fullerton is shown with Chief Clerk William Hartman in the boxcar which served as an office at one of the farms. The Medford farm, *upper right*, as it appeared in July, 1907, when the first crop was coming up. In 1910 the Fullerton family moved from Huntington to this farm. *Right*, Mrs. Fullerton with the LIRR exhibit at the Suffolk County Fair in Riverhead. This portable house, carried on two flatcars, won many prizes as it traveled around New York State during the twenties.

Chapman, Queens Borough Public Library

World War I and the LIRR

It would have been difficult to find a place which appeared less likely to be affected by the impending "war to end all wars" than central Suffolk in the early days of the century. The area consisted of a few villages connected by the single track main line of the railroad, and an expanse of wasteland with an occasional deteriorating house marking the futile efforts of earlier homesteaders. The pastoral quiet of Medford station, *above*, in 1907 and of two railroad men eating watermelon, *below*, at

Calverton in 1906 was typical of the tranquility then to be found along the main line. Shortly after the outbreak of war in Europe, however, a U.S. Army colonel and his staff, under the guidance of Hal Fullerton, selected a huge tract of land near Yaphank as the site for a military training camp. Prior to this, Yaphank's chief claim to fame was as the site of the killing by a freight train crew of the last native Long Island rattlesnake in 1900. The LIRR, in fact, was credited with the total extinction of rattlers on the Island, since the reptiles, loving to sun themselves on the shiny rails, would become groggy with the heat and fail to notice the oncoming trains.

With the entry of the United States into the European war, Camp Upton sprang to life. The railroad hauled all the supplies needed to build the facility; it laid the west leg of the wye at Eastport to allow a troop-train shuttle service out the main line, swinging over the Manorville branch and back to Long Island City over the Montauk branch; and it made ready for the one million men it was to carry into and out of Camp Upton within a few months. Except for one wreck east of Central Islip, which is still shrouded in military secrecy, the huge WWI troop movements went off smoothly, although old railroad men tell harrowing stories of those days. Often ships were held in New York, waiting for units to clear the camp. This resulted in many record runs by steel-nerved enginemen racing toward Long Island City with their precious loads of potential cannon fodder. One train of nine cars, drawn by a little 4-4-0, No. 98, covered the fifty-nine miles from Camp Upton to the East River in fifty minutes! When the slow orders all through Queens and Nassau are taken into consideration, the train must have hit almost 120 mph in places to achieve that time. Conductor Harrison Moore, riding the cab, can remember losing his lanterns "and everything else" on that run. Another 90-class engine, with Hiram Wykoff at the throttle, averaged 108 mph as it carried the post commanding officer, General Bell, and his staff from Ronkonkoma to Upton. The gen-

Collection of Mrs. F. A. Yeager

Charles B. Chaney, Smithsonian Institution

eral was so pleased with the time he brought cigars up to the engine crew. Irving Berlin immortalized Camp Upton with his musical comedy *Yip, Yip, Yaphank,* from which the popular song, "Oh, How I Hate to Get Up in the Morning," is still heard. So pressed was the LIRR for equipment in the bitter cold winter of 1917-18 that MU trailers were used on some troop trains. Since their lights and heaters were not operable in steam service, kerosene lamps were suspended from the light fixtures. The troops, freezing in temperatures which reached well below zero, cut up the wicker seats with their bayonets, piled them in the aisles and ignited them with the lamps. Officers and trainmen, not wanting to be lynched, tried to ignore these goings-on. When the camp was being evacuted in 1918, trains were dispatched through Patchogue at a ten-minute headway. *Above,* No. 9 was pulling ten cars of troops from the 691st New York Regiment through Sunnyside, en route to Long Island City. *Below,* one of the few pictures to escape the censors is this shot of Camp Upton station in 1917.

Collection of **Thomas R. Bayles**

Punk's Hole on the Main Line

When the Long Island Rail Road was extended through Suffolk County in the 1840's, Punk's Hole, midway between Yaphank and Calverton, was selected as a "wooding up" place for the Boston accommodation trains. Shortly thereafter, the odd name was changed to St. George's Manor. One day when the wife of the station agent was painting the porch of their little cottage across the tracks, he marched over, seized the paint and brush, and retouched the station sign to read simply "Manor." The agent's annoyance at the long, unorthodox station name prevailed, though in later years the railroad lengthened it to Manorville. The rule, "as the station is named so the town," was observed here and, although there is now only a shelter where the station once stood, *above,* Manorville retains the name bestowed on it by an irate railroad man long before this picture was made. *Left,* the tricycle handcar was photographed on the main line in 1906, about the same date as the picture above.

The Railroad in Riverhead

The pleasant brick and frame depot which serves River-head, *above*, was erected to replace a wooden structure. This photo, from a collection of official LIRR glass negatives now owned by F. Schenck, was taken on the opening day of the station, June 2, 1910. The picture, *below,* of the rerailing of PRR E-3sd Atlantic No. 917, after a derailment at Riverhead on September 6, 1934, came from W. W. Van Nostrand, a conductor whose five brothers were engineers on the Railroad.

Collection of F. Schenck

Bean Train Country

During harvest season on the North Fork, every express platform was loaded daily with crates and barrels of vegetables. Then the evening westbound local from Greenport stopped at each one, while the express car crews, usually aided by the trainmen, engine crews and some volunteer passengers, helped load the cabbages, beans and sprouts for their journey to the markets of Manhattan. One trio of husky Greenport youths made a daily habit of riding the bean train and loading the cars all the way to Manorville; they always got a free ride back on an eastbound train. The express platform at Peconic, *above,* and the Cutchogue and Southold stations, *below,* about 1910, in the days of the bean train. Train No. 211, *left,* at Manorville with G-5s No. 41 on the business end, posed for the camera of block-operator Boerckel, who was in charge of "MR" Cabin during this quiet summer of 1939.

E. L. Conklin

Washout at Aquebogue

Washouts after severe North Atlantic storms were frequent and played havoc with LIRR operations in Suffolk County. After a big nor'easter on November 17, 1935, the first westbound train from Greenport jumped the track near the Wilson Farm crossing, east of Aquebogue. Engine No. 44, a G-5s, *above,* rolled over on her side. The three crewmen riding the engine were the only ones injured. The impressive aerial view, *right,* was taken as an H-6s 2-8-0 arrived with a trainload of ballast and new ties to repair the damaged right of way. Another G-5s, No. 50, was sent to tow No. 44 into the shops. It was returning a favor; when No. 50 rolled over with the Cannon Ball express at Montauk three years earlier, No. 44 was dispatched to bring her in. A washout west of Quogue, after the '38 hurricane, resulted in the Railway Post Office car and four coaches turning over. The only part of the train left on the rails was the engine, a big PRR K-4s, and the last coach. Out east, about 1910, an argument developed between the postmaster and the agent of the new Laurel station as to who should tote the mail to the Post Office. It was decided that if the distance between the Post Office and the station was under a certain measurement, the responsibility would be the postmaster's; if over, it would be the agent's. The postmaster won when the distance from the south door of the station to the Post Office was measured and found to be just within the limit. Not one to lose a dispute, the railroad officials sealed the south door and took new measurements from the north door. This time it was found to be just over the limit!

New York Daily News Photo

Two photos, F. J. Weber, Authors' Collection

The North Fork

The afternoon local, known as the "Scoot," *above,* which ran from Greenport to Amagansett, is shown passing the site of the wreck pictured on the previous pages. This photo was made in 1930, shortly before the train was dropped from the timetables. The motive power is an E-7s 4-4-2 Atlantic type. Originally E-2s's, and built by the Pennsylvania Railroad shortly after 1900, the class was upgraded into the E-7s version in the twenties. Unable to handle the heavy steel passenger trains of the Pennsy, they were peddled off to the LIRR which, in consequence, was forced to scrap more powerful 4-6-0's and newer 4-4-0's. Many of these secondhand engines were in terrible condition and the Long Island, in addition to paying exorbitant rental fees (up to $100 daily per engine), was hit with heavy repair bills. Most of these light passenger locomotives were used for work train service and to pull occasional local trains; few lasted more than ten years. *Upper right,* Greenport station was photographed from the steamboat *Shinnecock* in 1925. *Right,* except for the removal of coal and watering facilities, the Greenport yard has changed little since this picture was made in 1938. The freight house at left, its end wall removed, now serves as a garage for busses operated by the Railroad.

Mrs. F. A. Yeager

Mrs. A. W. Robinson

Harold Fagerberg

Collection of Laura McGinness

J. Harvey Downs

The Elusive "Scoot"

Of all the memories cherished by East Enders, few are so fondly recalled as those of the little two-car local which for decades made a daily round trip between Amagansett and Greenport. It was powered by one of the Long Island's smaller 4-4-0's, and consisted of a combine and a lone coach. After a brief round of switching freight cars at Montauk, the little train would leave Amagansett at 10 A.M., shuffle over to Eastport, swing up to Manorville on the main line and run from there to Greenport, where it would lay over for the return trip, which began about 2 P.M. The local was known to most as the "Scoot," but because of her semicircular route she was also called the "Cape Horn Train." Some nicknamed her the "Bedbug" and others, correctly assuming that the railroad earned little from operating her, called her the "Peanut Train." Trafficking in mail, express, and a few local passengers, the "Scoot" finally died in February, 1931, amid eulogies from East-End newspapers, a victim of the combined onslaught of automobile and Depression. Her lonely run and humble status left precious few photographs. Most of those surviving are shown here, seeming to possess a mystical, almost ghostly quality, like the little old train herself. Rolling through the scrub-pine country, *upper left,* the "Scoot" is westbound between Riverhead and Manor, around 1910. On October 28, 1908, the conductor of a freight pulled by camelback No. 8, *left,* misunderstood his orders and smashed head-on into the "Scoot," in Jamesport station. The crew of the train posed with other railroad employees, *lower left,* at Amagansett in 1904. Engine No. 80, *above,* being turned at Greenport after bringing in the "Scoot," circa 1920. The train, in its last winter of operation, *right,* pulls into Aquebogue with a consist of steel cars behind a high-stepping Atlantic, E-7s No. 7497.

Changing Scenes at Moriches

About World War I, Hawkins' taxi posed beside the trim depot at Centre Moriches, *above*. In January, 1964, a few months before the weary building was demolished, the authors posed a new automobile, *below*, in front of it. They learned afterwards that the car belonged to the same Mr. Hawkins, who was at the station to check on his hack stand! On September 28, 1922, engine No. 91, *upper right*, split a switch at Centre Moriches. One obstinate old passenger steadfastly refused to leave the derailed coach until trainmen finally convinced him that the

Collection of Harold Fagerberg

car would not move for eight hours. Still protesting, the gentleman was spirited off to another train. The attractive little East Moriches station, *lower right,* built in 1898, burned down in 1936; 22 years later the station was discontinued as a stopping place for trains. The gentleman in the foreground was Joseph Weidmer. Every day for years he met the trains (in this instance the afternoon Montauk Mail, pulled by camelback 4-4-2 No. 2) to receive the mail. He became a familiar figure as he tugged a bright red wagon, loaded with mail, to the Post Office.

Collection of J. Burt

Collection of Elmer Lowell

E. L. Conklin

Collection of Robert M. Emery

Along the Montauk Line
Fortunately, nobody was occupying the rear coach of a passenger train halted at Eastport in 1915, *above,* when a camelback buried herself in it. On June 13, 1931, a new bridge, weighing over eight hundred tons, was installed *left,* to replace the old 215-ton span over the Shinnecock Canal. When the last evening train had passed, the old bridge was eased away while sand jacks lowered the new one into place. The heavier bridge was necessary to support the weight of the large K-4s Pacific-type locomotives which the Long Island began to lease from the PRR at that time. Twenty years later, when two of the heavy new Fairbanks-Morse diesels were to be double-headed over the bridge for the first time, the dispatcher phoned the roundhouse to check whether the structure would support their combined weights. When a clerk finally got the information and called back, the dispatcher answered: "Never mind, they just crossed it." In 1944, K-4s No. 5072, *right,* ran past the abandoned Shinnecock Hills station to pick up a mail sack. The building, which was erected in 1887, is now used as a Post Office during the summer; its ticket agency was shut down in 1932.

F. J. Weber, Authors' Collection

G. G. Ayling

"Doodlebugs" on the LIRR

With the rigorous economies enforced by the Depression, the Railroad found that it could no longer afford the luxury of operating one- and two-car steam trains which brought in little revenue. Trains that the Interstate Commerce Commission allowed it to drop, such as the "Scoot," quickly disappeared. Where the service had to be continued, the road turned to gas-mechanical ("doodlebug") rail cars which were adequate for the purpose. The "Patchogue Scoot," *above*, leaving Sayville, consisted of PRR gas car No. 4670, a Railway Post Office (RPO) car and a combine. PRR No. 4744, *left*, ran on the Wading River branch east of Port Jefferson after the discontinuance of steam service. The "Bridgehampton Jigger" steam train was replaced by the "Toonerville Trolley," *below*, which was photographed at Sag Harbor in April, 1939, shortly before the branch was abandoned.

Goodyear Collection, DeGolyer Library

Collection of Fred Payne

James V. Osborne

The Old "Jigger"

The "Bridgehampton Jigger" (as it was known in Sag Harbor), or the "Sag Harbor Scoot" (as Bridgehamptonites called it) is shown *above,* during an embarrassing moment in 1915. Since there were no turning facilities at the Bridgehampton end of the branch, the westward trip was made tender first, as it was when this derailment occurred. The conscientious crew, ever mindful of the welfare of their locomotive, covered the stack to keep moisture out. The National Golf Links in the Shinnecock Hills had its own station, *right,* for a brief period after 1908. The building stood just west of Tuckahoe Road, but by 1939 it had disappeared. In the summer of 1927 the engineer of the morning mail train noticed that he was being followed each day for the entire thirty-four miles of the route between Hampton Bays and Montauk by a pigeon. The bird would wait for the train at Hampton Bays, then fly along as close to the engine as possible; it often winged for miles right in the smoke. It would pause for rest at every station, then take off again with the train, arriving right on schedule at the terminal. There the pigeon would lie over with the train for more than two hours and follow it back to Hampton Bays, where it would disappear, only to be waiting for the same train the following day. Although the bird must have seen many other trains pass, it did not deviate for weeks on end from its daily practice of chasing the Montauk Mail.

Collection of Carleton Kelsey

The Nazi Invasion of Long Island

One dismal morning in 1942, a German U-boat surfaced briefly off eastern Long Island to dispatch a crew of saboteurs armed for the task of crippling the defense industries in the vicinity of New York City. The saboteurs, after stashing their equipment on Napeague Beach, walked up to the unlighted Amagansett station of the LIRR and purchased tickets for New York. In the dusky

J. Burt

predawn light, the Germans' first real glimpse of America must have been very similar to the view of the station, *above,* made eleven years later. At 6.30 A.M. the station was opened and the spies bought their tickets from agent Ira Baker. Catching the express for Jamaica at 6:57 they took their ride into history. Fortunately, the plotters were discovered by Federal authorities before they could carry out their mission. Several LIRR employees offered their services to turn the historic and elegant depot building into a museum of railroadiana, but the management decided against it and had the structure razed in 1964. There were sound economic reasons for dismantling other stations in Suffolk County, but the wanton destruction of the beautiful Amagansett station seems inexcusable. The trim hedges and fragrant rosebushes now surround an ugly metal shed. At *left,* the station in 1911, when it was one year old.

Rum Runners on the LIRR

In the late 1930's many a pleasant summer Sunday was spent by fans engine watching at Montauk. Such classes of Pennsylvania motive power as, *opposite, top to bottom,* K-2s and K-4s Pacifics and E-6s Atlantics were in abundance, as well as LIRR G-5s Ten-Wheelers. During Prohibition, rum runners would deliver contraband liquor to the desolate house tracks at Montauk. Enginemen who were part of the ring would bring the stuff from there to Morris Park, where it was smuggled out in the false bottom of a horse-drawn cinder wagon. Treasury agents, trying to trap the railroad men, boarded a camelback one night and ordered the engineer to dig through the coal in the tender. He refused, giving all manner of excuses. The agents shovelled through the coal themselves, until they reached a tarpaulin which covered a large watermelon. As they drew it off, the engineer began to yell that he was being persecuted for leaving a watermelon to cool in the coalpile. The red-faced agents never bothered him again, as night after night he delivered crates of Montauk hooch to the cinder wagon at Morris Park.

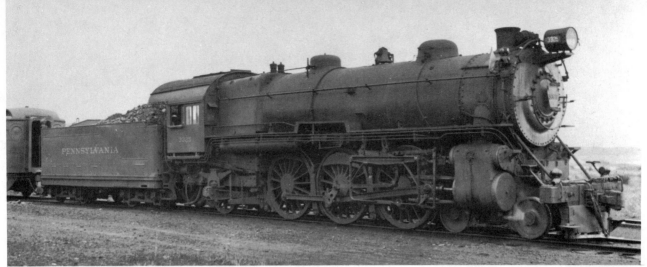

William J. Rugen

Edward Dersch

William J. Rugen

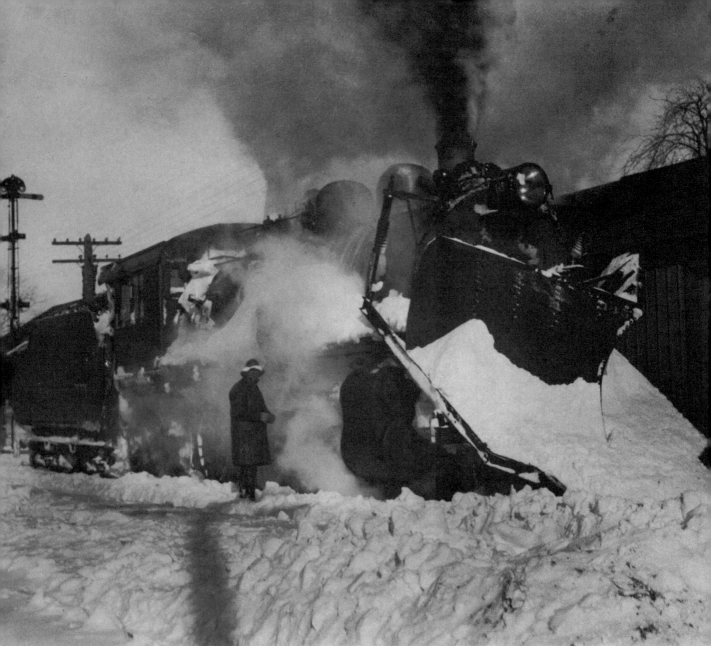

E. L. Conklin

The Blizzard of '34

In the 1920's and early thirties East End winters were often severe. Trains were stalled on the main line for days and even the most efficient snow-removal techniques could not handle every situation. One of the worst storms occurred in February, 1934. Conductor Harrison Moore, after clearing the track to Greenport, was ordered to return to Southold, where drifting snow reached to the coach roofs of a train stalled in a cut. Its wheels were frozen to the rails and would not budge. Trudging through snow up to his chest, Moore made his way to the Southold depot, where he called the dispatcher and informed him of the situation. The latter, snug in his warm tower in Jamaica, told Moore to close the couplers on his engine and on the rear car of the stalled train and then to "take a run on her." Protesting this would be foolish, Moore inquired if it was an order. "Yes, that's an order," the dispatcher replied, "do you want it in writing?" Moore, knowing that he had witnesses to the conversation at every station along the line, said that would be unnecessary. After sleighs had carried the passengers to safety, Moore told his engineer to back up fifty yards and make his run. The stalled train did not yield an inch, but the whole rear end of the last coach was smashed, the couplers broken and the front end of the locomotive damaged. The engine also blew her right cylinder. After conductor Moore had acidly informed the dispatcher of the results of his order, the crippled engine managed to limp back to Greenport. 4-6-0 No. 145, *above*, is shown clearing the tracks at Mattituck the day after the storm.

"Cross Crossings Cautiously"

From the earliest days of automobile travel, drivers have been incredibly careless at grade crossings. As far back as 1908 scenes such as this one, *right,* at Patchogue were commonplace on Long Island. The autoists would foolishly ignore warning signs, smash through gates (an average of one a day on Long Island by the mid-twenties), and ignore the fact that without some warning it was very difficult for a train on the move to avoid hitting a vehicle on the tracks. Many engineers ruefully observed that they had killed as many as a score of people during their years with the railroad. The toll was especially high on the long runs out east, where virtually every disaster seemed to involve the "Cannon Ball Express." The carnage was nationwide, and LIRR, like other railroads, cooperated in every way with local and national safety programs and with the Association of American Railroads. In 1925 Ralph dePalma, the famous auto racer, rode the cabs of Long Island locomotives to observe careless drivers. The slogan, "Cross Crossings Cautiously," was displayed, with appropriate illustrations, on billboards around the Island. Yet over five hundred persons were killed at Long Island grade crossings between 1935 and 1945, including seven men in the truck, *below,* which was struck by an E-6s at Mineola, in 1941. Grade crossing eliminations and improved crossing warnings have cut the death toll in recent years.

Conklin, Queens Borough Public Library

Ron Ziel

Steel Rails to Manhattan

By 1890 it had become evident that the future growth of Long Island would be limited by the ability of the railroad to handle effectively the heavy passenger traffic to and from New York City. The inconvenient transfer to ferries at Long Island City and the slow progress from the east side of Manhattan were both inhibiting factors in this development. During the late eighties Austin Corbin had considered two alternate plans for running the LIRR to New York: One called for a tunnel from Brooklyn to lower Manhattan and thence bringing the trains on up to Grand Central Terminal; the other was to cross the East River over the proposed Corbin Bridge from Long Island City to a point on Manhattan above Thirty-seventh Street, and again to terminate the trains at Grand Central. In conjunction with the port at Fort Pond Bay, either route would have called for making the Montauk division, as well as the main line to Manor and the Manor branch, four tracks wide. Corbin's sudden death ended all of his visionary projects, although the four-track survey was made during the building of the East River tunnels in 1905. By 1900, however, it was obvious that the Pennsylvania Railroad would receive a franchise to tunnel under the Hudson (North) River to Manhattan. It took control of the LIRR in exchange for providing the latter with tunnels to a proposed New York terminal. The Pennsylvania Tunnel & Terminal RR was chartered to leave the old main line to Jersey City at Harrison (Manhattan Transfer), cross the Jersey meadows, tunnel under Bergen Hill and the Hudson River, cross Manhattan under Thirty-second Street, pass under the East River through four tubes, and terminate at the proposed Sunnyside Yard on Long Island. The project, launched in 1902, became the most massive and expensive privately financed engineering feat ever accomplished. By the time of its completion in 1910, the combined tunnel and station project cost $125,000,000 (nearly three times that much if estimated in 1965 dollars). Originally planned for New Jersey, the Sunnyside Yard simplified movements through Pennsylvania Station, which was erected on one of the best locations in Manhattan, running between Seventh and Eighth Avenues and Thirty-first and Thirty-third streets. Most trains arriving at Penn Station discharge their passengers and continue to the sprawling servicing facilities at Sunnyside, the world's largest passenger-car yard. Unlike its rival, Grand Central, Penn Station is not a terminal and requires relatively few storage tracks which would occupy premium space.

Erecting Penn Station

While the major work of the New York project consisted in digging the immense tunnels from Weehawken, N.J., to Manhattan (6,644 feet), the most obvious structure, one whose development was more closely observed by the public, was the station building. It was the largest edifice ever erected for the convenience of rail travelers, and was as impressive as any product of modern civilization could be. The excavation required the demolition of over five hundred buildings and the removal of 3,000,-000 cubic yards of soil and bedrock. When the photo at *upper right* was made from Seventh Avenue in 1906, 7,800 feet of retaining walls were being poured while the contractor's donkey tank engines were removing trainloads of rock. Photographed from the tower of the Metropolitan Life Insurance Co., the beautiful building sparkled like a jewel set among the drab west-side tenements, as it neared completion in 1909. The famous sculptures of classical women and American eagles, *above,* graced all four main entrances to Penn Station. This set, on the Seventh Avenue side, faced down Thirty-second Street.

The Temple of Transportation

Overwhelmed newsmen coined many superlative phrases
to describe the magnificent station, but its resemblance
to Roman architecture (it was modeled on the Baths of
Caracalla and the Basilica of Constantine) inspired the
most appropriate title: Temple of Transportation. The
great edifice, *right,* was nearly competed on June 15,
1909, as many cranes hoisted the last slabs of Milford
pink granite into place on the main waiting-room cornice.
To surface the building 500,000 cubic feet of granite were
used. Other construction statistics were staggering—the
building covered almost eight acres, with twenty-eight
acres of yards below ground level. The "temple," designed by Stanford White of McKim, Mead and White,
was 784 feet long with 430 feet of frontage on Seventh
and Eighth avenues. It was supported on 650 steel col-
umns which, combined with the rest of the structural
steel, weighed 27,000 tons. The famous skylighted concourse roof required 220 tons of $^3/_8$-inch wire glass.
Nearly 1,000,000 cubic feet of concrete and over 15,000,000
bricks comprised the "flesh" between the steel skeleton
and the granite skin of Penn Station. Beneath the station
are twenty-one tracks which handle 750 trains daily,
nearly two thirds of them used for LIRR movements.

Wurts Brothers

The Great Event

The Pennsylvania Railroad, justifiably proud of its tremendous achievement, held a celebration when the PT&TRR was brought to a successful completion. Ironically, when the station was finally ready for inspection by the great men of the era, they did not arrive by luxurious Pullman cars from Washington, D.C., Philadelphia, and Pittsburgh, but by a humble train of LIRR commuter cars from Long Island City. The first revenue train, *left*, departed from Penn Station on September 8, 1910. It was more than two months later that the PRR began to use the station, to the delight of Long Island commuters, who must have felt as if the colossal structure existed exclusively for their benefit.

H. D. Bastow, Queens Borough Public Library

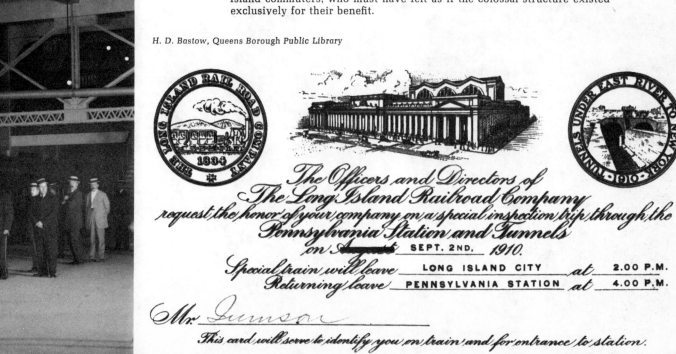

The Officers and Directors of
The Long Island Railroad Company
request the honor of your company on a special inspection trip through the
Pennsylvania Station and Tunnels
on ~~August~~ SEPT. 2ND, 1910.
Special train will leave ___LONG ISLAND CITY___ at ___2.00 P.M.___
Returning leave ___PENNSYLVANIA STATION___ at ___4.00 P.M.___

Mr. _Gunson_

This card will serve to identify you on train and for entrance to station.

Long Island Celebrates

The DD-1 electric locomotives, especially designed to handle trains to Manhattan, ran between Penn Station and Jamaica, in addition to their more celebrated runs from Manhattan Transfer in New Jersey. At Jamaica the trains which traveled beyond the electrified territory were held up briefly to change to steam power. The first train to leave Penn Station, however, proved the theory that has dominated most operational thinking at Jamaica ever since: it is easier for the railroad to change people than to change engines. So it was that except for the DD-1 era (1930-1950) LIRR trains from Penn Station have been Multiple Unit electrics. When the first MU train arrived at Jamaica from New York on the morning of September 8, 1910, the passengers changed for regularly scheduled steam trains to the eastern branches. Through a fortunate coincidence, photographs of all three of the Suffolk branches traversed by those trains on the opening day are available. All along the tracks crowds turned out to welcome the first "New York trains." *Below,* a profusion of 46-star flags greeted D-16 No. 201 as she sped along the main line near Medford. *Right,* few flags were in evidence at Patchogue as No. 99 brought in the Montauk train. H-3 No. 162, *lower right,* stood by at Northport depot as automobiles and the local trolley awaited the train to Wading River.

Fullerton, Suffolk County Historical Society

Chaney, Smithsonian Institution

Sweeping Changes

The completion of the tunnels and Penn Station accelerated the electrification on Long Island as the railroad braced itself to carry three times as many passengers and twice as much freight within the next twenty years. The writing was on the wall for the 4-4-0 camelbacks, such as No. 57, *left*, pulling a Port Washington train through the Sunnyside Yards from Long Island City on September 11, 1910. Within two years the branch was electrified and the sleek camelbacks were lined up at Holban Yard, awaiting their fate. The tunnels, *below*, were made of cast iron and of waterproof concrete two feet thick. In 1917 horses still pulled carriages out of the Thirty-first Street entrance to Penn Station, *right*, and streetcars rolled along Seventh Avenue. Within a decade the few automobiles shown here were multiplied into the city-wide traffic jam so familiar to a later generation. The "sweeping event," *lower right*, was a daily occurrence on the concourse floor. Arranging for one-way pedestrian traffic was an act of foresight by the builders of Penn Station. The stairs leading to street level were divided so that people leaving the station could use the center flight.

F. J. Weber, Authors' Collection

The Mariner's Museum, Newport News, Va.

Pennsylvania RR

Two photos, Pennsylvania RR

The Grand Concourse

Originally the platforms and tracks, *left,* were visible from the concourse floor, but this area was later covered over to increase the capacity of the station. During World War II the concourse was crowded with military people, as the photo *below,* taken from a similar angle, shows.

The concourse skylight glowed at night when viewed from the Hotel New Yorker on Thirty-fourth Street, *above.* The double-stacked building across Thirty-first Street is the power station that supplies utilities for Penn Station.

A Monumental Act of Vandalism

Pennsylvania Station was a glorious tribute to the finest builders of America. It was a thing of spaciousness, beauty, and good taste, and a monument to free enterprise. A. J. Cassatt, the PRR president who died in 1906, did not live to see the fulfillment of his work, and the lesser men who followed him were bent on the vulgarization of the building long before the ultimate calamity arrived. The designers would have been shocked had they lived to see the hideous, jazzy ticket awning which defaced the main waiting room in later years, or the ugly illuminated advertisements in the once-elegant concourse. The overheavy tax burden imposed on the structure drove the PRR ever deeper into the abyss of bad taste in attempts to recoup its losses. Finally, in 1964, when the building was only fifty-four years old, the wreckers came. Above the vociferous protests of architects, historians, railroad fans, *The New York Times,* and men of good taste everywhere, the 277-foot waiting room with its 150-foot ceiling, *left,* was closed; the long colonnades were torn down; and the Temple of Transportation was destroyed in the name of Progress. The great building, designed to last eight hundred years before major structural work would have been necessary, fought against her spoilers. So well built was the station that it took almost as long to demolish it as it had taken to erect it.

In April, 1965, an MU local, *below,* passed the remnants of Penn Station which were being dumped in the Jersey Meadows. Ironically, every PRR train to and from Penn Station rolled past this macabre scene. By January, 1966, the last of the concourse, *above,* was coming down.

Instead of hiding their shame, the people responsible for the desecration, which *The New York Times* called a "monumental act of vandalism," babbled proudly about the replacement, a modernistic arena and office building, which has no spiritual contribution to offer to the advance of society. The "new Penn Station" will be like dozens of other glass-and-steel tombstones that are turning New York City into an architectural graveyard. Norvel White, chairman of the Action Group for Better Architecture in New York, expressed the feeling of many of the three billion people who had passed through Penn Station in its half-century of existence: ". . . the old station, with its vast spaces, made a ceremony of arrival.

You knew when you got off the train and walked through the station that you had arrived somewhere important." The new station facilities, with ceilings at a maximum height of twenty-five feet, will leave travelers "in a subway station," according to White. The Pennsy official who referred to the spatial concepts of 1910 as being merely "waste space" expressed the prevalent mood of a nation adrift on a sea of mediocrity.

James Van Derpool, executive director of New York's Landmarks Preservation Commission, called the destruction of Penn Station "a tragic loss" over which "we will be consumed with regret." It was, in his words, the "supreme example of the architecture of the period." European countries preserve and rebuild their great landmarks (for example, St. Paul's Cathedral in London and the Brandenburg Gate in Berlin), but what is the United States government doing about ours? If the city and state of New York could not save so glorious a building as Pennsylvania Station, should it not have been the responsibility of the federal government to purchase it, take it off the tax rolls, and lease it to its occupants? The despoilers would have done well to heed the Biblical admonition of Proverbs 22:28, "Remove not the ancient landmark which thy fathers have set."

Great Men of the LIRR

Ron Ziel

Until the demise of the steam locomotive, which occurred at about the same time as the advent of the Space Age with its new order of heroes, railroad men, particularly engine crews, enjoyed the greatest respect in the romantic imagination of many Americans. It was fitting that they should, for a railroad man in the days of the steam engine had to possess a broad knowledge of all kinds of railroading, including such outstanding examples as snow fighting and highballing. If a flanger-snowplow operator should forget to raise its blades for an obscure crossing or switch, the ensuing derailment would probably cause his death. Engineers required nerves of cold steel when they wheeled their locomotives over 100 mph in pursuit of lost time.

A passenger trainman today, especially on the LIRR, requires the knowledge of an electrical and mechanical engineer, the patience of a Biblical prophet, the tact of a diplomat and, above all, a sense of humor. Most railroad men pass the test with flying colors. In the process of completing this volume, the authors traveled all over the railroad and observed many of the frustrating incidents that have become routine to trainmen. For instance, while a conductor was explaining operations at Jamaica to one of the authors, a woman, apparently in a panic because the conductor had not given her his immediate attention,

seized him by both lapels and shook him violently, while demanding to know on which track the Northport train was waiting. The conductor politely requested that she unhand him, then gave her directions. Trainmen are maligned, grabbed, yelled at, and blamed for everything that goes wrong in the routine of a commuter—even including his cold cup of coffee. When a wildcat shop-workers' strike delayed trains up to ninety minutes one day in November of 1964, the commuters furiously demanded explanations from the hapless trainmen. A trainman on the Port Jefferson run offers the secret of his success in handling the incessant flow of questions from some of the people with whom he has to baby-sit on the daily run to Jamaica. Whenever one of them asks a nonsensical question, such as "Why can't we go faster?" or "What happens if the engineer gets sick?" the trainman flashes his cheeriest smile and answers, "No problem." These soothing words seem to relieve many anxieties among the more timid passengers.

There is, of course, a more rewarding aspect to the life of a trainman. Many passengers are pleasant to have aboard and the trainmen enjoy their company. Often commuters seek out the cars worked by their favorite trainmen, and they sometimes develop lasting friendships. Some commuters form "clubs" on their trains. One such

Edward W. Hulse

Edward W. Hulse was born in Speonk on November 22, 1869. He operated trains 35 and 42, known as the Speonk Express, for many years and by the mid-1920's his fame had spread far beyond the Montauk division. When the railroad needed a bold hand to guide a VIP special or to make a dangerous run, it invariably called upon Ed Hulse. Hulse was the first man to be honored when the LIRR began naming its engines in 1924, *right*. A true railroad man and immensely proud of his calling, Hulse kept his sense of humor even when adversity struck. A pensioner recalls the day in the early twenties when Hulse's *Cannon Ball* hit a meat truck near Sayville at 90 mph. He had seen both occupants jump clear, so he hurtled onward. His friend, standing in the Center Moriches depot, never forgot the sight of Ed Hulse leaning way out of the cab and gesturing toward the stack, which had a long string of wieners stretched out behind it. It was recalled that "He went through Center Moriches like a bat out of hell, looking like a butcher shop, the engine all festooned with hams and strings of sausages." After having his name on No. 1 for six months, Hulse received a brand-new G-5s, No. 23, which was named for him in December, 1924. A year and a half later, when Hulse was wheeling his Speonk Express home to supper, his monogram adorned the cab of No. 27, *above*. This photo depicts a rare scene, indeed, a modern G-5s locomotive pulling a solid string of wooden coaches just a few months before the final demise of this ancient equipment.

Collection of Sylvester Doxsey

Sylvester P. Doxsey
Few pictures capture the resoluteness, confidence, and dependability of steam crewmen as this photo of Sylvester P. Doxsey and his fireman, Howard V. Owens. Posed in the cab of their big K-4s in 1933, these enginemen were waiting for the highball to clear their departure for Montauk. Doxsey rose to the head of the seniority list on the railroad, and was one of the last survivors of a generation that produced Eichhorn, Birchell, and Hulse. Living on into his eighties, he still recalled the days of the high-wheeled camelbacks in fascinating detail.

rare wit while handling a situation. Once an inebriated passenger was straddling a gangway between two coaches when a conductor requested his ticket. The passenger pulled out a monthly commutation ticket that he had just purchased but had failed to sign. The tippler, annoyed at the regulation requiring his signature, borrowed an expensive fountain pen from the conductor, signed the ticket, and dropped the pen overboard. Unruffled, the conductor took the ticket, punched it, and dropped it overboard. This is typical of the experiences related in the school in trainmanship—"charm school" to the men who took the course—which was attended by the LIRR trainmen before the opening of the 1964–65 World's Fair.

The Long Island, like most lines, has made its greatest legends in the cabs of its steam locomotives. In 1924, in one of the last—and perhaps the finest—expressions of its individuality, which made its first century of operations so fascinating, the LIRR chose to honor six of its engineers by naming their favorite steam locomotives after them, a practice that had been dropped by the railroads a half century earlier. Camelbacks Nos. 1 and 18 were named "Edward W. Hulse" and "James Eichhorn"; D-16 4-4-0's Nos. 212 and 223 were lettered "Seaman Birchell" and "Thomas H. Kelly"; and two of the older eight-wheelers, Nos. 84 and 92, honored "Walter Read" and "Charles McKeever." These six men were among its finest engineers during the railroad's prime years. All had mastered their trade well before 1900, and most were in engine service throughout their careers. Some of the men who fired for them grumbled that they were "company men," who continually demanded more steam on less coal and overworked their fireboys. That, however, was the highest accolade that could be bestowed upon a superior engineer. It was the man who ran his engine through floods

group, "The Tailgaters," rides the rear platform of one of the Port Jefferson trains every evening, year round. Another band of commuters has formed an exclusive club called "The Goodfellows" (named after Thomas M. Goodfellow, president of the LIRR), and has issued handsome printed identification cards to its members. Occasionally thirty or forty of the more affluent members of a club may band together to hire a parlor car for their train.

To cater to its boozing commuters, the LIRR has placed a number of bar cars in service. By removing the seats at one end of a coach, installing a bar and providing pink lights, the LIRR does a flowing business. The bar cars are always crowded and resounding with raucous laughter amid a constant flow of "Dashing Dan" cocktails. Because of the swaying of the cars it is hard to tell the tipsy passengers from the sober ones, although wives waiting for their mates at the station have little trouble finding out which car their men rode in.

At times a trainman, at the end of his patience with some of the topers and other undesirables with whom he is forced to contend, displays a and blizzards, pitting his acumen against them to make up for lost time, who was the hero of young boys and the envy of his fellow "hoggers." An engineer did not earn a reputation by coddling his fireman or shirking dangerous duty. The naming of these engines caused a great deal of favorable comment, including an editorial in *The New York Times* of June 12, 1924. It was a fine gesture, too good to last; the names were eradicated from the cab sides by the dour "underground coolies,"* as the LIRR men disdainfully referred to the Pennsy officals who took over in 1928.

One engineer who never had his locomotive monogrammed was Jack Schaffler, who began firing in 1919, was promoted to engineer six years later, and left when the PRR men came. He now owns a shop on the Flanders Road near Riverhead, where he repairs automobile generators. Although four decades have passed since "Generator Jack" left the railroad, he still spins his fantastic and fascinating yarns to all who listen, and the authors have seen paying customers quietly depart after patiently holding a sick generator in front of Jack for a half hour. When somebody comes to talk steam railroading Jack literally closes up the shop. A husky man, now in his sixties, Schaffler once hand-fired as much as sixteen tons of coal into a firebox on a four-hour run to Montauk in the twenties. For a few years Jack fired freights on the main line. One night, as his H-3 was working up Yaphank Hill, the engineer yelled: "Another train comin', join the birds!" The engineer slammed on the brakes just before he, Jack and the head brakeman jumped. The conductor dove into the coal pile. As the train ground to a halt, the dazed crewmen saw the "headlight of the other train" a few hundred yards ahead—a full moon centered right above the track at the crest of Yaphank Hill!

That same engineer had a habit of falling asleep at the throttle. One night, as they were backing along the barren main line, the conductor climbed in back of the tender and held a red lantern out on the end of a broomstick. Jack yelled: "Red light!" at the sleeping engineer, who immediately awoke, panicked, and hit the brakes. When the crew demanded to know the purpose of the unauthorized stop, the engineer began talking about a red light. The crew, laughing, said that he must have been dreaming. That engineer never slept on the job again.

*In reference to their arrival on Long Island through the East River tunnels.

One afternoon at Mattituck station three attractive young ladies were standing under the water tank as Jack was filling the tender. After gauging their location, he quickly shoved the spout upward and gave the girls a drenching under the run-off. The local newspaper headlined, "Fireman Gives Bride Shower," as one of the girls was to be married the following week. She and her groom personally delivered large pieces of wedding cake to Jack and his engineer at the station. In the days before widespread automobile travel, most newlyweds honeymooned by train. Jack recalls that when such a party was aboard, the engineer would blow the whistle and ring the bell all the way into Jamaica.

For a while Jack ran a switch engine down the Evergreen Branch in Brooklyn. Once, when he ran out of coal, he burned some new creosoted crossties, which made so much acrid smoke that women ran, gasping for breath, from nearby apartment houses. They threw so much junk out of the windows at Jack, as he recalls it, "I had so much stuff in the tender—pots, irons, breadboards—that I could have started a store." A great man with locomotives, Jack despised just one of them, a 1904 Baldwin 4-4-0, No. 100. He claimed that she steadfastly refused to steam for him. When he walked around her front, he swore that she gave him a "fresh look." One day, as his co-workers watched in amazement, Jack delivered a tirade against the defiant 100, yelling "You lousy no-good so-and-so, you're out to kill me!" Grumbling "I'll get even with you someday," he bid off the run and got another engine. Steam locomotives of the Long Island Rail Road possessed the same human characteristics that they did on other roads, as many old-timers will testify.

One of the greatest problems that plagued the railroad, almost until the last steam locomotive was dispatched from Jamaica in 1955, was the air pollution caused by engine smoke in Queens. No matter how hard the railroad tried to control smoke, thirty or forty locomotives under steam at Morris Park were bound to cast soot throughout a wide area. The prevailing winds carried the smoke over Richmond Hill, blackening houses, wash lines, and the good name of the Long Island Rail Road. When steam trains left Jamaica they frequently deposited soot all over eastern Queens. The railroad, ever sensitive to the vindictive assaults by civic groups and newspapers, posted "Watch Your Stack" signs along the right of way, appointed smoke watchers, and rewarded "clean

Chaney, Smithsonian Institution

Jack Schaffler was in engine service at the peak of the camelback era. During his firing days he preferred the center-cab engines to standard ones, especially since they separated him from crotchety engineers. His favorite engine, by far, was one of the big Baldwin Atlantics, No. 4. One night, as Jack was running No. 4 light from Ronkonkoma to Riverhead, he remarked to his crew: "Let's see what she can do." She did 114 mph coming into Manorville, after "rounding the curve at Yaphank on five of her ten wheels." This shot was taken a few years earlier, at Lynbrook.

---

burning" enginemen. Jack Schaffler's casual disdain for anything that interfered with his firing activities gave the smoke watchers some anxious moments. Once, as he was leaving Mineola, Jack was warned that the village of Hillside had posted a trio of smoke-seeking photographers on the station platform in that town. As Jack roared into the station at over 50 mph, he turned the smoke-lifters (jets of steam which were shot into the exhaust) wide open. The wind was perfect and the photographers and their cameras were doused by a heavy stream of brackish, black, hot water, which erupted from the smokestack of the engine.

Then there was the time when the road foreman of engines decided to show Jack how to fire without smoke. The engineer, hearing this, warned Jack to keep up steam or "I'll break all your bones." As the camelback pulled its train out of the station, the foreman insisted on firing, to show Jack how it was done. By the time they reached Queens Village, the boiler pressure had dropped way down. The engineer, intent on breaking a few bones, came back to the fire deck and started yelling at Jack. Upon learning that the foreman had been firing, the engineer threw him off the train and told Jack to get up steam. Jack gaily shoveled in a big load of coal and

raked the fire, sending a tremendous cloud of black smoke over the town. The resulting furor of complaints earned Jack a reprimand. Next morning, determined to avenge himself against the citizens of Queens Village, Jack stashed a bucket of wood shavings in his engine. As they sped through Queens Village station, Jack dumped the shavings into the firebox. This resulted in scores of commuters scurrying for cover as a shower of sparks rained down upon the platform.

Old-timers will remember that the Ku Klux Klan was a powerful force in Suffolk County during the 1920's. Jack Schaffler recalls that quite a few railroad men were Klan members. Some of them were engineers, "includin' at least one who had his name painted on an engine cab." Being a Catholic, and outspoken on virtually every subject, Jack soon was at odds with the local Klan "goons." Knowing they would give him trouble, Jack was, as usual, prepared. As he was stoking the firebox of a camelback on the team track at Ronkonkoma, a group of robed Klansmen began to berate him. Jack, a World War I veteran, removed a hand grenade from his pocket and pulled the pin. After giving the Klansmen ten seconds to clear out, he threw the grenade. The hole made by the explosion is still discernible, according to Jack. Having depleted his grenade arsenal, Jack then went to work wearing two black-painted pine cones on his suspenders. "That did the trick," said Jack. "Every time I showed up with those pine cones, they ran. They never got close enough to see that the 'grenades' were phonies."

Retired engineer Clifford Prince, now living on Shelter Island, recalled that his most unusual experience occurred when he was pulling the *Cannon Ball* with his favorite engine, K-4s No. 5406. Near East Hampton the engine gave a slight lurch and some gore hit his side of the cab, so Prince figured he had hit a cow that had wandered onto the track. When he reached Amagansett, he was shocked to find the entire locomotive covered with "assorted cow parts from the neck back." He had hit a herd of eight cows at 80 mph!

The Romance of Railroading

Even without the romance of steam, the life of a diesel engineer has its bright spots, as shown by this picture of engineer Frank McKeown sharing a cup of coffee with Sophia Loren at Long Beach station, *above,* in 1962. Miss Loren was starring in *That Kind of Woman,* a motion picture in which the Long Beach station was substituted for the Seaboard Air Line's Miami station. One LIRR engineer who carried the steam traditions into the drab diesel era was Cecil M. Craft. He is shown at the throttle of No. 29 at New Hyde Park in 1949, *above right.* In the 1960's, when most engineers wore the sport shirts of their downgraded profession, "Crafty" still donned the denim jacket, bandanna, and striped cap he wore in steam days.

Another engineer walloped a truckload of live ducks near Eastport. This was before air conditioning, and dozens of the ducks were sucked into the open car windows and vestibules. The train was full of running, flying, squawking, terrified ducks. At Westhampton many elated passengers detrained with their Sunday dinner, quacking noisily, firmly in hand.

Undoubtedly the most amazing adventure ever to occur to a Long Island Rail Road man—perhaps to any railroader—was the harrowing brush with death which a passenger brakeman, Henry F. Guertin, experienced in May, 1926. Rolling through Nassau at 50 mph, he was trying to close a jammed trap over the steps of the rear vestibule of his wooden coach. As Guertin braced himself on the grab irons and pushed the gate with both feet, he slipped and his legs shot out beyond the side of the car. At that precise moment the pole supporting the telltale, which was used to warn crewmen of the Ellison Avenue overpass, loomed alongside. Guertin's legs hit the pole, wrenching him out of the car. He spun completely around the pole and was thrown back onto the vestibule of the following car. Although dazed and bruised, Guertin suffered no injuries. The engineer and some of the passengers had seen the incident, which occurred in a span of less than two seconds. Guertin, now retired, has outlived all of the witnesses to his accident, but he has sworn statements from all of them to show to any latter-day doubters.

The spirit of Long Island Rail Road men is nostalgically recalled by old-timers in Richmond Hill. They remember that every New Year's Eve, when at least thirty locomotives were under steam in the yard, the shop men would tie down the whistles of all the engines at midnight. What more glorious way to welcome a new year than by the cacophony of thirty steam whistles sounding in unison?

The "No. 1" Trainman

In 1897 Frank Erthal hired out as a freight brakeman and began a rewarding fifty-three-year career with the railroad. An obviously dashing young conductor by 1910, *right,* he was assigned to the special trains that carried President Theodore Roosevelt to Sagamore Hill. Whenever Teddy received bouquets of flowers en route, he would toss one to Erthal, with the cheerful words, "For your mother, Frank." Erthal often recalled that "Mom got plenty of flowers from the President." Feeling that the train assigned to carry Admiral George Dewey deserved a special salute, Erthal fastened seventy-five signal torpedoes along the tracks. After the hero of Manila Bay had recovered from the explosions, Erthal explained that it was all in his honor. Dewey, obviously impressed, presented the crew with a box of expensive cigars. This was the era when many of America's celebrities rode the LIRR, and Erthal knew all of them: J. P. Morgan, "Diamond Jim" Brady, John Philip Sousa, Clarence Mackay, "Gentleman Jim" Corbett, John J. McGraw, August Belmont, Al Smith, and Bob Fitzsimmons. Frank's greatest moment occurred at Far Rockaway, when Lillian Russell stepped off the train to find herself surrounded by puddles of rain. Always a gallant gentleman, Frank took the darling of the nineties up in his arms and carried her the length of the platform. When Erthal worked the parlor cars to the old Gravesend Race Track, he often saw a wealthy gentleman who always tipped the crew generously. The following year, a towerman reported that a man was riding the steps on the rear of the last car. Raising the trapdoor, Erthal discovered the same generous horseplayer, now down on his luck, hunched on the steps and eating an apple.

When Erthal, a bachelor, retired in 1950 at the age of seventy, he was No. 1 on the LIRR seniority roster. Only two years later he was killed when he ran his automobile into the third car of an electric train in Babylon, apparently after he had suffered a heart attack. Frank Erthal died on the railroad that had been his long and fascinating life.

Collection of John Amman

Four photos, Collection of Jefferson Skinner

When Culture Rode the Rails

Life on Long Island during the 1920's was gay, and the railroad played its part. The Sunrise Trail Band, *lower left*, was one of the finest musical organizations on the Island, and it played in many concerts and parades. Often the band would ride special trains from Greenport and perform en route to New London. That they must have played well is shown from newspaper accounts, long lists of engagements, and honors bestowed upon them. The Trainmen's Trio comprised Matthew Balling, John Diehl, and Jefferson Skinner, *above*. Charles H. Burton replaced Diehl in later years, *below*. The Trio traveled as far west as Nebraska; they entertained at railroad events, at civic functions, and on the radio. It must have been wonderful, indeed, to ride a special while the Trio passed through the cars, strumming and singing to the accompaniment of the locomotive exhaust. In 1946, *right*, Jeff Skinner whooped it up with Balling and engineman James Kiebler on the pilot of a K-4s to celebrate the publication of the song, "Living on Long Island," written by Kiebler and Skinner. Kiebler was also responsible for the beautiful organ recitals at Penn Station during many Christmas seasons. The Ralph Peters Singing and Dramatic Society (named for a past LIRR president) was another one of the Railroad's successful ventures into the arts. All of these groups were dropped during the Depression. Jeff Skinner rose to No. 1 on the seniority roster and retired in December, 1965. His career was a prime example of the incredible waste of local talent on the LIRR. Jeff should have been in the Public Relations Department, instead of using his great talents to do little more than punch tickets.

THE TRAINMENS TRIO

Jefferson Skinner

The LIRR Athletic Program

The athletic program sponsored by the Pennsy in conjunction with the LIRR was so immense that it took over $2 million of the Pennsy's annual budget. Although the LIRR competed as merely one of a score of PRR divisions, the spunky "Sunrise Trails"—as all of the Long Island teams were known—frequently walked off with victories far out of proportion to their numbers. The entire program, which lasted from 1923 until 1931, was supervised by Harrison S. Moore, who held the full-time job of director of athletics. And a big job it was, with over seven hundred of the road's 13,000 employees participating. In 1920 the LIRR began sponsoring intramural sports between the departments of the road. When the PRR held its annual meets in Altoona each September, the LIRR sent teams to compete in every event: track and field, boxing, golf, tennis, baseball, basketball, bowling, wrestling, and rifle and pistol shooting. In 1923 Moore represented the Train Service Department on a four-man council set up to establish the LIRR Athletic Association. Two years later in Cincinnati, he helped to form the International Railroad Athletic League. He returned as the secretary-treasurer of that organization, a post which he held until the league was disbanded in 1931. When it came to giving employees time off to participate in sports or training, the director of athletics had the final say. Moore recalls that the supervisors of the other departments were not too happy with that arrangement. Like the Sunrise Trails Band and the Trainmen's Trio, the Sunrise Trails athletic teams traveled far to compete in events. Even when they ranged as far as Fort Wayne, St. Louis or Cleveland, a train consisting of as many as thirteen cars of employees, traveling on pass, was sent along to cheer them. The training grounds and site of the big events on Long Island was Ralph Peters Field, near Hollis. One of the more appropriate events held there was the annual competition between the track gangs. With an ample supply of ties, rails, and spikes, they would go to work laying short sections of track all over Peters Field.* In 1930 the PRR system championship baseball finals were held there. When the Sunrise Trails' star pitcher, George Manfredi (he later signed with the New York Yankees) was struck in the ankle by a line drive, Moore and a coach carried him off the field, followed by the team manager and a doctor, *above*. Moore was a trainman from 1906 until 1923, with only a brief break in 1914. After the Athletic Department was disbanded, he went back to train service ("What a letdown that was," he recalls). During the summers, until his retirement in 1954, he was a special conductor with the authority of assistant trainmaster.

*Latter-day LIRR men, noting that Holban yard now occupies the site of the old Peters Field, jokingly wonder if this is how the railroad's largest freight yard was originally layed out.

Roxey, the LIRR Mascot

Roxey's early life was that of a street waif. So unaccustomed to kindness was he that one day when a young lady, hurrying toward the Thirty-fourth Street ferry in New York, patted him on the head, he followed her onto the ferryboat and into the train. While he slept under the seat, she left the train, but Roxey didn't wake up until it reached Garden City. There he left the coach as a storm was beginning and sought shelter against the side of the station. When the weather grew worse, he dared to bark for admittance. The station agent, finding the dog huddled on the threshold, let him in and decided to adopt him in the name of the LIRR, naming him "Roxey" (or "Roxie", or "Roxy") after a dog he had once owned. The men of the railroad bought their mascot a nickel-plated collar with a silver plate inscribed: "I am Roxey, the LIRR dog, whose dog are you?" and renewed his license yearly. After Ralph Peters became president, he ordered that an unlimited pass be made of metal and fastened to Roxey's collar. With this went a general order giving the dog rights over all passengers and employees on any seat of any train, including the parlor cars. Even a U.S. President was not immune to this ruling. Roxey once invaded a private car that was to take Theodore Roosevelt to his summer home on Oyster Bay, and curled up on the bed. An indignant porter wanted to eject him, but the conductor, who happened to be present, pointed to Roxey's collar. Mr. Roosevelt himself walked in, heard the story, and allowed Roxey to stay.

The little dog's favorite place above all others was on the engine. He would perch on the fireman's seat—never going on the right side, where he might be in the way—and watch the countryside sweep by. His only enemy was the automobile; perhaps he foresaw the time when cars would rival his beloved trains. For twelve years Roxey roamed the line, stopping whenever the notion struck him to visit his numerous railroad friends. He died in 1914 and was buried at Merrick Station, *below,* near the right-of-way. At first his grave was well tended, but with the passing of the years and the people who loved him, the monument, like many other traditions, was left to deteriorate.

Other dogs have played significant roles in the history of the LIRR. From 1909 to 1916 the railroad had a pack of bloodhounds guarding its property. Their presence resulted in a sudden drop in the number of crimes committed against the railroad, especially the dynamiting of station safes and other thefts. One dog, named Sheba's Bob, caught over two hundred criminals in three years. The railroad also loaned the dogs to local police for work on nonrailroad cases. Sheba's Bob, for example, located more than twenty lost children. On October 24, 1914, Herman B. Duryea, a prominent businessman, hired a special train to pull his elegant private car from Westbury to Penn Station. Inside the car lay the body of a two-and-a-half-year-old Pomeranian, sealed in a satin-lined casket, en route to final interment near Shiloh National Military Park, Tennessee.

Another LIRR mascot, lesser known than Roxey, was Butch. A bronze plaque honoring this canine was cast from a Long Island engine bell and mounted in the Glen Cove station.

Collection of Arthur L. Mirick

"Roxie"
Long Island Railroad

Robert M. Emery

IN MEMORY OF
ROXEY
L.I.R.R. DOG

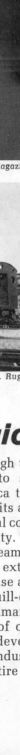

Juice-Jack Heaven

Although the Long Island Rail Road contributed more to steam-motive-power development in America than roads twenty times its size, it is rather its accomplishments in electrification and internal combustion that have been preserved for posterity. The LIRR has always been a leader in non-steam motive power. It was the first road to install extensive electrification and the first to purchase a road diesel. A DD-1 ancestor, a gearless quill-drive 4-4-0, No. 10003 on the Pennsy, ran primary tests on the Long Island under five miles of overhead a-c trolley. These and other major developments set the standards for the railroad industry in North America and, indeed, in the entire world.

Jeffrey Winslow

Diversity of Power

The scene at Jamaica, *above,* was a typical one during the dieselization period. It shows the three major forms of motive power at "Jay" Tower—a K-4s No. 5387, a DD-1 electric, and a diesel. The LIRR, which is forever trying to squeeze more passengers into each coach comfortably, operates a fleet of 132-passenger double-deck coaches like the one at *upper left,* Although these cars were initially successful, the more recent development of "3 and 2" seating for 128 riders in the newer conventional coaches has curtailed orders for additional "up and downs." *Left,* a Sperry Rail Service car on Buckram Trestle near Locust Valley in 1963 was conducting its annual search for defective rails. *Below,* a train comprising brand-new "World's Fair" electric cars crossed the Manhasset Viaduct in January, 1965.

Authors' Collection

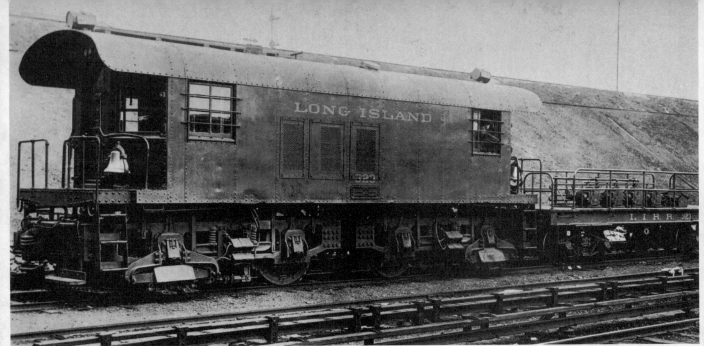

Collection of Arthur L. Mirick

"Phoebe" and Her Friends

The primitive electric locomotive, *above,* was one of the most important locomotives ever built. Constructed by the Juniata Shops in 1905, "Phoebe" was the Pennsylvania RR's first electric. The DD-1, GG-1 and other famous classes of Pennsy electric power, as well as great portions of electrified trackage and the tunnels to Manhattan, were the end-products of this homely box. She proved that "it could be done," and many of the engineering problems in the ensuing batch of DD-1's were worked out on this unit. By 1916, however, she was obsolete, so the PRR sent her to the LIRR where she hauled the Flatbush Avenue freight and puttered about Morris Park until 1937. Outstanding characteristics of this locomotive were the two large bells on her left side and her tender—a compressor car. "Phoebe" may well have been at the head end of a train which passed "PR" Tower in Brooklyn one quiet night many years ago. It was the job of the tower operator on the early morning "graveyard shift" to dispose of the garbage. Usually he stuffed it in a bag and tossed it into a passing gondola car, or into one of the old open garbage trucks which traversed Atlantic Avenue. On this particular occasion, however, he packed the garbage into a box, neatly wrapped it, tied it with string, and waited for the train to pass. When he threw the box, it bounced off the car and landed on the sidewalk. Before the operator could retrieve the parcel, a motorist stopped, jumped out of his auto, and, looking anxiously in every direction, grabbed the package and drove off. Every night thereafter the operator carefully wrapped the daily garbage and threw it onto Atlantic Avenue. He usually waited until a passenger train was passing, to give the illusion that the package had fallen off the train. Without fail, either an automobile would stop or a pedestrian would seize the bundle and run off with it. The delighted recipients of these "lost" parcels must have been embarrassed and annoyed, particularly at Christmas time, to find that their prize was only gift-wrapped garbage. *Below,* an MU train, leaving Jamaica for Penn Station, is led by one of the LIRR's famous "owl-eye" round-roofed cars, during a snowstorm in 1964.

Ron Ziel

Pennsylvania RR, from Alvin F. Staufer

Electric Switchers

The Long Island Rail Road, always a leader in bold concepts and improved operating techniques, was one of very few railroads (along with her parent, the Pennsy) to use electric switch engines. The Pennsy built forty-two little 0-6-0 B-class electrics, of which fourteen saw service on the LIRR for thirty years. Originally constructed as pairs of MU'd units, they often operated separately on both roads. In addition to these, twelve of the units belonging to the PRR were assigned to switch at Sunnyside Yards in the New York area. The Long Island B-3's, built in 1926, posed at Lewiston, Pa., *above*, as an H-8sb and an H-6sa pulled them eastward from the erecting floor at Altoona. Shortly before their retirement, two B-3's, *below*, worked under the catenary at the Bay Ridge float bridges in Brooklyn.

F. G. Zahn

Two photos, F. G. Zahn

Solution for a Big Problem

Assuming that they would be able to overcome the problems of developing a successful electric locomotive to operate to Manhattan, Pennsy engineers went ahead with construction of the tunnels and station years before the motive power was perfected. When Penn Station opened in 1910, the PRR was still in the process of constructing thirty-three two-unit box-cab DD-1 electrics, which eventually proved to be the perfect solution for the job. With the extension of overhead catenary under the Hudson River in 1933, over two thirds of these world-famous engines were transferred to the LIRR, where they henceforth shuttled between Penn Station and Jamaica. DD-1 No. 354, *above,* was whipping through Kew Gardens with the *Jamaica Mail,* consisting of a crew rider and Railway Post Office cars, bound for Port Jefferson, Montauk, and Greenport. Some of the DD-1's, *below,* had their cab-roof overhangs removed in a bland effort to "streamline" them for the 1939 World's Fair. Possessing huge electric motors which were connected to the drivers by siderods, these fascinating machines resembled dummy steam locomotives. One is reportedly being rescued for historical preservation by the Pennsy.

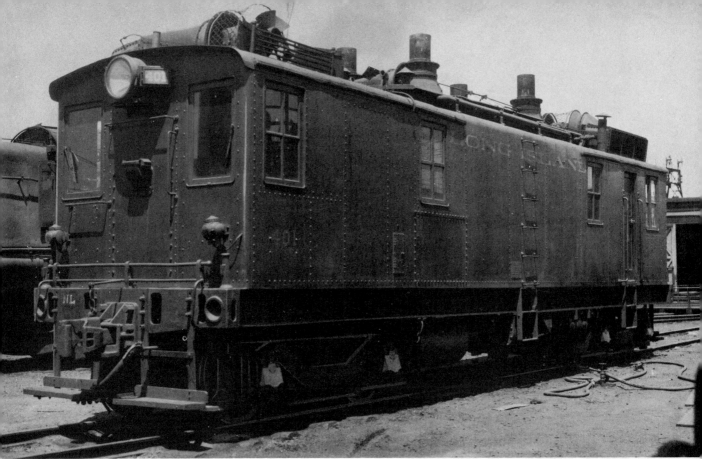

William J. Rugen

Setting the Pace

The unimpressive box on wheels, *above,* is probably the most significant of all the LIRR's accomplishments, for it sparked a revolution which altered the railroad industry in the United States for all time. No. 401, built jointly by Alco, General Electric, and Ingersoll-Rand, was the first diesel locomotive ever to see road service in America. Originally called an "oil-electric," No. 401 was put in service in 1926 and followed by a similar unit in 1928. A smaller oil-electric, No. 403, *right,* is shown at the North Fourth Street yard in Brooklyn. The yard was abandoned in the 1950's. The New Haven Railroad has trackage rights over the LIRR to Bay Ridge. In 1952, three box-cab NHRR electrics, *below,* brought a freight around the curve at New Lots.

Robert M. Emery

Jeffrey Winslow

W. S. Boerckel, Jr.

The Big Fling

One of the most popular attractions at the New York World's Fair of 1939–40 was a large and interesting exhibit put on by the railroads. Being the "host railroad" for this extravaganza, the LIRR hauled all of the locomotives and equipment. In addition to being on display, many engines were fired up for the impressive "Railroads on Parade," a pageant depicting the history of American railroading. Two LIRR cranes, *above,* laid the bedplate which supported the huge PRR S-1, No. 6100, as she operated under her own steam with the drivers turning while she remained stationary. The contemporary poster featuring the graceful trylon and the perisphere, displayed in a coach window, *left,* was one of many ways in which the LIRR promoted the Fair. A quarter of a century later, the railroad spent a great deal of money and energy on the second New York World's Fair which was built on the same Flushing Meadows site. A LIRR DD-1, *below,* led a PRR GG-1 and the Seaboard Railroad's crack Silver Meteor on a publicity run to the futuristic World's Fair station.

W. S. Boerckel, Jr.

World War II and the LIRR

The railroads were hit hard by the war. Just when operations had greatly increased, due to gasoline rationing and various restrictions on other forms of transport, tens of thousands of the most able-bodied railroad men were taken into the armed forces. Nearly 15 per cent of the work force of the LIRR left in 1942, but the Railroad was rescued by the women of the area. They went on the payroll in the offices, agencies, and on the trains; there were even a few "Rosie the Riveters" in the locomotive shops. Female trainmen, *above*, known as "Wheels," became a common sight. The gentleman standing at the rear is William J. Rugen, an important historian of the LIRR. On October 25, 1940, a trainload of Republic pursuit aircraft was loaded aboard flatcars, *below*, for a record three day cross-country dash to bolster General MacArthur's forces in the Pacific. This part of the train was waiting at Pinelawn siding for the rest of the crated planes to be brought out of Republic Aviation Corporation's plant at Farmingdale.

J. Burt

The Standard Era

To all appearances, the Long Island Rail Road spent its last twenty-five steam years as an extension of the New York Region of the Pennsylvania Railroad. When the PRR took over operational control in 1928, the LIRR steam roster was still 70 per cent "non-standard"—i.e., not of PRR manufacture or design. Three years later, however, only 30 per cent of the steam locomotives on the Long Island were not of Pennsy origin; and most of these were relatively new 1920-era 4-6-0's and 0-8-0's.

Regardless of class, the characteristics of the "standard" PRR engines were similar: square Belpaire firebox, massive boiler, horizontal strap-steel pilot, high headlight, keystone number plates on passenger power, and a simple design. The Pennsylvania locomotives which deposed the camelbacks and the turn of the century Ten-Wheelers and Americans were all leased to the Long Island, with the exception of H-10s's and G-5s's, which were actually purchased. After extensive electrification of the PRR lines east of Harrisburg in the early 1930's, there was plenty of surplus steam power to send to Long Island. The mother road saw to it that the older LIRR steamers due for backshopping were retired, even though many might still have had a decade of useful service ahead of them. In contrast to the well-maintained LIRR machines, a large number of the Pennsy engines arrived in scandalous mechanical condition. Most of the more than three hundred locomotives which the PRR leased to the Long Island were quite satisfactory, however, and performed well during their Long Island tenure.

Standard Symbols

Undoubtedly one of the finest classes of locomotives ever built, the PRR E-6s Atlantics upheld their legendary performance records on Long Island. No. 198, *right*, laid down a veritable smoke screen as she shot past mile post 17 on the main line, shortly after World War II. As a prelude to the standardization of the LIRR, its symbol was incorporated into the familiar Pennsy keystone herald, *above*, in the early 1920's.

214

Harry J. Trede

The Venerable H-6sb

In 1916, the LIRR purchased fifteen secondhand freight locomotives from the Pennsy. Since the PRR had just completed a program of putting 1,206 heavy 2-8-0 Consolidations into service, it was willing to part with fifteen of its 1,835 older H-6sb "Consols." These engines, built between 1905 and 1907, were the basis for much of the criticism that the Pennsylvania was foisting worn-out "hand-me-downs" onto its hapless stepchild. It appeared that the PRR Road Foreman of Engines could not have sent worse wrecks if he had scouted the entire system. All the H-6sb's were in need of heavy repairs. One had seven spot welds on one side of its frame. Another leaked so badly that it could hardly pull its own tender. The fifteen were completely rebuilt at Morris Park, and the effort was worth it. They saw over thirty years of service on the Long Island—longer than most new engines. H-6sb No. 306, *right*, switched at Long Island City in February, 1942. On Armistice Day in 1936, No. 312, *below*, moved a work train west of Valley Stream, which included several wood coaches, downgraded to crew car service.

W. S. Boerckel, Jr.

A Long-lived Locomotive

The LIRR seldom retained locomotives which were over thirty years old. One exception was the H-6sb class, thirteen of which were over forty when they were scrapped. Apparently No. 301, one of the last of this class when withdrawn from service in March, 1949, was the oldest engine ever owned by the railroad. Built by Baldwin in 1905, No. 301, with her sisters 308 and 314, survived in active service until her forty-fourth year. The ancient 2-8-0 *above* spent her last years switching. Here she is shown moving an overhauled B-3 electric from Morris Park to the Bay Ridge branch. Shortly thereafter, she awaited the end, in Holban Yard, *right*.

Rarely Photographed

Although at least seventy H-9s Consolidations and twenty-four 0-6-0 switch engines were leased to the railroad between 1928 and 1949, there are few good pictures of them. One H-9s, *upper left*, apparently carried away by the joyous celebrations marking the end of World War II, put her wheels on the ties at Glen Cove on the afternoon of V-J Day in 1945. Like most freight power, the H-9s's were often pressed into passenger service. A victim of the hideous postwar "face-lifting" which cluttered the fronts of so many Pennsy engines, reversing the positions of the headlight and generator and placing a huge platform on the smokebox front, H-9s No. 2826, *lower left,* pulled into the Merillon Avenue station in 1949. *Above,* the only B-6sb ever to run on the LIRR, shown at Dunton Tower in August, 1938; B-8 Nos. 919, *right,* and 1108, *below,* at Atkins Avenue on the Atlantic Branch.

Two photos, A. R. Ward

The Good Die Young

Between 1916 and 1924, three divisions of the American Locomotive Company turned out eighteen superb 0-8-0 switchers for the railroad. Nos. 251–269 were the last non-standard engines to be built for the LIRR. One of them, No. 257, survived as late as 1952. Since the big C-51's were the greatest creators of smoke within the New York City limits, they were the first steamers to be replaced by diesels. Six of the big brutes, extremely handsome as switchers go, are shown here. Nos. 254, *upper left,* and 259, *lower right,* were working the Long Island City car-float bridges in February, 1947. In the mid-forties Nos. 253, *left,* and 258, *right,* puttered about their business at Fresh Pond. The trim lines of the C-51's show clearly in the photo of No. 261, *below,* pulling a cut of cars near Dunton about 1937. In their earlier days, 0-8-0's such as No. 260, *upper right,* at Forest Park in 1926, often handled manifest freights eastward from Long Island City.

F. Rodney Dirkes

220

Three photos, F. G. Zahn

Standard Mikes and Unorthodox 4-6-0's

The heaviest freight locomotives ever to operate on the LIRR were ten L-1s 2-8-2 Mikados which the road leased for a few years to help out with the heavy freight traffic created by World War II. The L-1s, a large class on the PRR (574 were in service), was as popular among freight crews as her twin sister, the famous K-4s Pacific, was among crews in passenger service. The two classes were so similar, in fact, that they were designed to use the same boiler. One of the big Mikes, No. 3590, was photographed at Fresh Pond, *upper left,* in 1944. No. 3408, *left,* was leaving the east portal of the East New York tunnel. No. 1286, *lower left,* was snapped Bay Ridge-bound on that branch in October, 1945. Block operator W. S. Boerckel, Jr., who since the time of this photo has advanced in position on the Long Island Rail Road, was manning the "HC" (Hempstead Crossing) tower in Garden City on March 8, 1938, as the G-53sd, *right,* trundled by with the general manager's inspection train, consisting of a coach and business car No. 2000. The open observation car 2000, named *Jamaica,* became the pride of the luxurious Cannon Ball of the 1960's. The letters "NL" stenciled on the pilot beam were PRR code for New York Region, Long Island. No. 142, *below,* pulls a mid-day local near Merillon Avenue in 1940.

F. Rodney Dirkes

Vanished Scenes

This impressive aerial view of the Morris Park engine yard was made on October 28, 1949, during a national coal strike. Gatherings such as this, of forty steam locomotives, twelve DD-1 electrics, and but one diesel (upper left), were to disappear from Long Island forever with the mass arrival of new diesels a few months later. The view is looking east toward Jamaica. The two tracks in the right background are from the Atlantic branch. The wide road is Atlantic Avenue, which parallels most of the line to Brooklyn. *Above*, a shop crew forged a new part on a steam-powered press in the late thirties. *Below*, two men in the roundhouse worked to repair the crosshead on G-5s No. 38, while steam still poured from her cylinder.

New York Daily News Photo

F. J. Weber, Authors' Collection

Two photos, Collection of Gene Collora

F. J. Weber, Authors' Collection

The Great Depression

The stock market crash of 1929 hit the LIRR hard. As traffic continued to drop, rows of steam locomotives, *upper left*, were stored in Holban Yard. *Left*, a set of driving wheels from a 2-8-0 being guided onto the lathe. The smokebox front for No. 309, *right*, stood in the roundhouse as the H-6sb was overhauled in November, 1931. One ingenious device, more of a public relations ploy than anything else, was the big smoke washer, *above*, at Morris Park. When the funnels were lowered over the engine stacks on the team tracks, the smoke was "washed" by jets of steam. The end result was supposed to be clean white steam emerging from the top of the washer, while sludge poured out the bottom. The H-9s, H-6sb, K-4s, and the G-5s were all strategically placed so none were quite able to have their soot rinsed. While the *Long Island Press* was lambasting the railroad for allegedly blackening half of Queens, the *Brooklyn Daily Eagle* launched an unprovoked war against the railroad in the 1920's. At a time when all responsible business organizations were boosting Long Island with the Sunrise Trails project, the *Eagle* resorted to smear and smudge to "save" Brooklyn from the nasty LIRR and its ogre parent, the Pennsy. This campaign of vilification reached its lowest point when, on January 19, 1923, the *Eagle* published a malicious letter against the LIRR. Though the letter was later proved a forgery, the paper still continued to aim its editorial guns at the one organization which was more responsible than any other for the growth of Long Island.

Yard Scenes

H-10s Consolidation No. 109, *left,* stood by while a three-year-old G-5s rolled across the Morris Park turntable on January 25, 1932. Another 2-8-0, No. 119, *upper right,* switched a PRR coach in the Long Island City passenger yard in the spring of 1949; the United Nations Secretariat Building, under construction at the time, and the Chrysler Building are prominent beyond the East River. In 1932, the desolate Fifth Street freight yard, float bridges, and unused *Quogue* and sister tugs, *lower right,* testify to the drop in traffic spawned by the depression.

F. G. Zahn

Two photos, F. J. Weber, Authors' Collection

Collection of Gene Collora

F. Rodney Dirkes

William J. Rugen

West End Steam

Steam slowly leaking into the cylinders of G-5s No. 26, *left,* caused her to roll unattended out of the roundhouse and nose into the turntable pit at Morris Park. This embarrassing mishap occurred in mid-winter, but the wrecking crane on the turntable and the roundhouse crew soon extracted the wayward 4-6-0. With many passenger engines trapped in the roundhouse, commuters rode home behind freight power that evening. Ice in the flangeways of the Village Avenue crossing in Rockville Centre derailed a wooden wedge plow on February 20, 1934. The H-6sb which was pushing it, No. 314 *(lower left)* smashed right through it, killing the plow operator. Virtually unknown to even PRR historians is the fact that many of that road's most famous locomotives were leased to the LIRR. Among them was the prototype K-4s Pacific, No. 1737 *(above),* built in 1914. By 1928 she had been joined by 424 identical sisters to form the largest and most celebrated fleet of passenger locomotives in the United States. Though this photo was made in 1935, as late as 1947 this most renowned of Pacifics was still high-balling commuters eastward from Jamaica. *Below,* in the summer of 1949 a Consolidation moved a troop train along the Bay Ridge branch in Brooklyn.

F. G. Zahn

Jamaica, the Train-Watcher's Paradise

Because of heavy commuter traffic in and out of Jamaica during the rush hours, steam trains were often dispatched at a four-minute headway. In between periods the ready tracks at nearby Morris Park were crammed with Ten-Wheelers, Pacifics, Consolidations, and Atlantics. One of the few good pictures of the rare K-3s class of Pacific on the LIRR shows No. 8659, *left,* under the old wooden coal tipple in the late thirties. A new steel and concrete coaling facility was built on the spot during World War II. Although only thirty K-3s engines were constructed by the PRR (they were decidedly inferior to the E-6s and K-4s classes which were developed about the same time), five found their way to the LIRR, once again raising the issue of obsolescence being forced on the road. In 1948, the Federal Government placed many of the nation's greatest documents, including the Declaration of Independence, the Constitution, and the Bill of Rights, on a six-car train, painted red, white, and blue. The Freedom Train *(above),* under military honor guard, visited Jamaica where over one hundred thousand people filed through the beautiful cars. A K-4s, No. 3655, *below,* chugs out of Jamaica in 1949. The water scoop under her tender was an unnecessary accessory on the LIRR, which never had track pans.

Collection of Gene Collora

Two photos, Jeffrey Winslow

F. J. Weber, Authors' Collection

F. G. Zahn

F. Rodney Dirkes

Heavy Haulers Dispel Myths

Although outclassed by other locomotives, K-2sa Pacifics, such as No. 3228, *upper left*, and the K-3s engines were strong machines. The tough little G-5s 4-6-0's, *left*, although designed specifically for rapid-acceleration commuter service, were often called upon to haul freight drags. Here No. 25 rolled a string of boxcars and hoppers past the Bellaire station in 1949. *Above*, an H-10s Consolidation powered the Patchogue freight eastbound through Merrick on the Montauk division in 1940. *Below*, an H-6sb highballed through Freeport in 1931. All the Pennsy engines were powerful and fast; the G-5s's could haul fifteen coaches at fifty miles per hour, and the K-4s's

often moved twenty cars at similar speeds, while the hulking H-10s's moved 110 carloads of potatoes without assistance. Despite these known facts, in a booklet published by the LIRR in 1959 to commemorate its 125th anniversary a photo of a 2400 series diesel appeared with a caption which read in part: "Trains like this sometimes have as many as seventeen cars today. The old steamers seldom could handle more than seven or eight." This grossly exaggerated statement, typical of the platitudes on diesel performance issued by most railroads, was perhaps correct—if the author had the *Ariel* of 1835 in mind.

F. J. Weber, Authors' Collection

Norman Kohl

Hans Thorsen

Harry J. Trede

Apex of the Atlantics

The most famous and successful example of the 4-4-2 Atlantic-type locomotive was the Pennsylvania Railroad's classic E-6s. It was originally designed by Alfred W. Gibbs, the Chief Mechanical Engineer of the PRR in 1910. After the prototype was built, the road went on to erect two more of the class for test purposes, before building a fleet of eighty in 1914. These marvelous engines were still holding down tight passenger schedules forty years later, having survived two generations of replacements and seen fine locomotives, which had been built when the E-6s's were in their thirties, sent to the scrap yards. There was no thought of scrapping them until the diesel had nearly cleaned steam power off the Pennsy. If the diesel had not come, the "Big E" would probably still be wheeling passengers out of Philadelphia and Jamaica. The legend of the E-6s lies as heavy over Long Island as it does over the divisions of the PRR, for in the brief span of twenty years ending September, 1949, twenty-eight of them (one third of the total built), saw service on the LIRR. No. 779, *upper left,* shown on the Oyster Bay branch in 1944. At Oakdale in 1945 No. 1238, *left,* was assigned to train 50, the Patchogue-Babylon "Scoot." On a wintry day No. 198, *above,* smoked up Bellerose as she trailed a single coach.

237

Jeffrey Winslow

Joseph Fischer

The Big and Little E's

At least sixteen E-3s Atlantics built in the early 1900's were sent to the LIRR a quarter century later. They were too light to be of further use on the PRR, so that road got handsome profits from the decrepit machines by extending their service for at least ten years on the LIRR. *Above left,* one of these, probably No. 917, putters down the Oyster Bay Branch west of Mill Neck, with a near-capacity train of three steel coaches behind. Sister 3148, *above,* leaves Jamaica, while the most famous of all E-6s's, No. 460, with Sylvester Doxsey at the throttle, waits clearance down by Hall Tower. On June 11, 1927, the 460 was chosen to take the Lindbergh Special from Washington, D.C., to New York. This train, hired by a newsreel company to speed the films of Col. Charles A. Lindbergh's triumphal return to Washington, consisted of the E-6s, a baggage car-turned-darkroom, and a coach to provide additional braking power. Two competing newsreel firms hired airplanes to fly their films to New York, as the 460 ran 216 miles in 175 minutes at speeds

frequently nudging 115 miles per hour. A DD-1 electric carried the newly developed films the last nine miles to Penn station and fifteen minutes after their arrival they were flashed on Broadway screens—a full hour ahead of the competition! It was the E-6s's—perhaps the steam locomotives'—finest hour. After spending twenty-seven more years in the service of the PRR and the LIRR (see page 180), the 460 was chosen as the sole E-6s to be preserved by the Pennsy for historical purposes. Two other famous E-6s's, Nos. 737 and 779, both favorites of one of the most respected PRR engineers, Martin H. Lee, also spent much of their careers on the Long Island. The E-6s's added laurels to their performance records on Long Island by speeding trains to the East End. Engineman Clifford Prince recalls traveling the main line between Wyandanch and Calverton "taking milepost after milepost at 37, 38 seconds each" (104 miles per hour), with No. 420, at the head of the "Fish Trains" to Greenport. During World War II No. 1694, *left,* posed with two 4-6-0's at Oyster Bay.

239

Robert B. Dunnet

Edward Dersch

The Oyster Bay Branch

H-10s No. 107, *above*, had taken the siding, while her crew made faces at a passing passenger engineer at Roslyn Heights on May 14, 1951. *Below,* a few months earlier, Ten-Wheeler No. 32 was pulling into the majestic Mill Neck station. No. 30, *right*, left the main line at Mineola to bring a trainload of homebound commuters up the branch in 1944.

F. G. Zahn

MILL NECK

F. Rodney Dirkes

Arthur Huneke

Arthur Huneke

The Pennsy Makes Good

In a virtual repeat of the E-6s story a decade before, the PRR turned to an obsolete wheel arrangement in the early twenties and came up with a winner. The problem: how to speed suburban commuters into Pittsburgh and Philadelphia. The solution: take the basic E-6s boiler (also used on the heavy 2-8-0's) and roll a 4-6-0 chassis under it. The result: the heaviest (237,000 pounds), most modern, and most efficient 4-6-0 passenger locomotive ever manufactured in the United States. After successful tests with the initial engines of an order totaling ninety, the Pennsy's Juniata shops in Altoona, Pa., began erecting a fleet of thirty-one additional G-5s's for the LIRR. The Long Island, ever fond of Ten-Wheelers, found the G-5s ideal for the rapid acceleration and quick stop commutation runs, as well as for long hauls to Montauk and in freight service. They had sixty-eight-inch driving wheels, exerted 41,300 pounds of tractive effort, and operated under 205 pounds of steam pressure. The main complaint of enginemen was that the lack of a trailing truck created such fierce vibrations that the fireman could hardly keep his balance to sling coal. The G-5s's possessed voracious appetites and, lacking automatic stokers, were extremely rough on firemen. Four G-5s's rested at Oyster Bay, *above,* in 1935. As the end of steam approached in early 1954, No. 32, *right,* is shown passing Nassau Tower. While two G-5s's, *left,* waited the diminishing calls to duty, one of the few shopmen still assigned to steam work welded a smokebox part.

The Phases of Transition

The arrival of the G-5s class of locomotive, completed in 1929, signaled the end of the 4-4-0's and camelbacks. Norman Kohl, the unofficial photographer of the Oyster Bay branch, is responsible for these pictures showing the evolution of the G-5s over a generation. In the dusk of the older engines, *above,* a brand new G-5s posed with a 1904 American, No. 98, and what may well have been the last active camelback, Ten-Wheeler No. 12, in 1931. About this time all the newer classes of Pennsy power were in service on the LIRR, along with a few holdovers such as Nos. 98 and 12. It was by far the greatest time for engine watching in the history of the railroad, but precious little film was exposed during those early years of the Great Depression. *Below,* four G-5s's lined up for their portrait at the turntable in Oyster Bay in 1938. The turntable motor once jammed as No. 27 was riding it, and she made scores of revolutions before a gathering crowd of onlookers who were amused by the futile efforts of the hapless hostler to stop it. The main change in the outward appearance of the class occurred in 1942, when PRR keystone plates, *right,* replaced the round number plates on the smokeboxes.

Jeffrey Winslow

Harry J. Trede

Sooty Splendor

Scenes such as the one, *left,* with vast plumes of smoke and steam silhouetted against a leaden winter sky, swirling clouds of snow and an ominous black locomotive between, thrilled Long Islanders for six generations. Here, No. 36, thundering into Carle Place during a winter of her waning existence, recalls the magnificent locomotives which will live forever in the soul of Long Island. Unconcerned with imminent war, the aftermath of which was to alter so drastically the pastoral face of the Island, No. 42, *above,* sped her train westward from Mineola on March 2, 1941. H-10s No. 104, *below,* found herself in the middle of her train as she switched near Bethpage's "B" Tower in 1949.

F. G. Zahn

The Nassau That Is No More

When Joseph Burt focused his enormous 1908 Graflex Press camera on the Long Island Rail Road near his home in Mineola, the results were invariably striking. He long considered this picture to be an unqualified failure, due to the fact that he had inadvertently tripped the curtain shutter too soon. Few photographs, however, better illustrate the rapid change experienced by Nassau County since the late summer of 1931. The phenomenal two-point perspective, in which rich fields of famed Long Island potatoes were bisected by the high iron of the railroad, has been obliterated by thousands of hastily constructed cubicles on postage-stamp-sized plots. The charming farm buildings are gone and crab grass is the only harvest the mutilated fields now yield. Although hemmed in, devoid of the rich scenery and robbed of the beautiful steam locomotives which once traversed it, the LIRR is one of the few major physical ties to Nassau's halcyon yesterdays that still remains.

Steam at Work

Often, during the transition from steam to diesel, a G-5s was called out to rescue a stranded diesel. A crossing guard, *left*, watched as the crippled diesel and its train from Ronkonkoma was brought into Hicksville on a crisp morning in 1954. No. 49, *above*, proved her mettle by whipping thirteen heavy steel cars east of Hicksville in 1931. The long potato extras, often totaling over a hundred reefers, were frequently called "Big Berthas." As late as October, 1952, the railroad could still muster seventy cars, *below*, for a train during the potato harvest east of Riverhead.

Standards on the Main Line

Less than a year before their fires were dropped forever, No. 35 and helper 21, *left,* double-headed through Floral Park in what may well have been the last such spectacular scene to grace Long Island rails. In the mid-1940's train No. 27 (the 8:35 A.M. from Montauk), behind K-4s No. 7938, approached the Ellison Avenue overpass at Westbury, *lower left,* where twenty years earlier Henry Guertin had met his amazing brush with death. Eastbound extra L-44, the local freight, pulled into Hicksville on a snowy December day in 1949, *right.* Hicksville was an important water stop, and 2-8-0's such as No. 112, *below,* often had their thirst quenched there. The station was demolished in 1962 when the grade-crossing elimination project raised both the main line and Port Jefferson branch tracks. An impressive modern depot has replaced the little brick structure. The LIRR owned nineteen H-10's (Nos. 101–119), all built in the 1913–1916 era for the PRR. The Long Island purchased them secondhand between 1928 and 1935. One of a trio of Pennsy 2-8-0 classes (including H-8s and H-9s) to possess an enormous boiler similar to the E-6s, the H-10s was the peak of Consolidation development for the PRR. Although originally hand-fired, all nineteen units received automatic stokers after World War II. Operating under 205 pounds of pressure, with a tractive force of 53,197 pounds, they weighed 124 tons. Always rugged and powerful freight movers, when the necessity arose the H-10s's could also haul passenger trains at 50 mph. These H-10s's performed well until they were retired after nearly forty years of active use.

Two photos, F. G. Zahn

The Port Jefferson Freight

For many years No. 113, a Brooks H-10s built in 1916, held down the freight run from Holban Yard, Hollis, to Hicksville and north and east along the Port Jefferson Branch. In 1953 Norman Kohl photographed the daily routine of this local freight as it chuffed through the hills, pausing here and there and switching many sidings. On the eastbound journey before noon, the engineer snagged his orders on the fly, *far left,* as he left the main line at Divide Tower, Hicksville, and headed toward Syosset. At Smithtown, *left,* engineer Larry Foran filled the cross-head-guide oil cups while the tender took on water. The arguments of the smoke haters were clearly justified when an H-10s got underway. Although very photogenic, the burping 113 could be a filthy machine when she set her stack to the task, as pictured here on the return trip through Smithtown, *right.* One of the most picturesque sights on the railroad was a steam train crossing the long bridge near Kings Park, where Town Line Road and Bread and Cheese Hollow Road meet, *above.*

Colonist Richard Smith founded Smith's Town early in the seventeenth century by claiming all the land he could ride around in one day while mounted on a bull, taking with him a loaf of bread and some cheese for nourishment. The Indians honored his claim, hence the existence of Smithtown, the odd names of the roads under the trestle, and the huge statue of a bull at a highway junction near the railroad.

How to Rerail a K-4s

Although the sandy soil of Long Island has always been prone to washouts, it really wreaks havoc upon the railroad after a hurricane. The first train to be cleared from Port Jefferson after the big storm of September 14, 1944, was No. 647, behind K-4s No. 5406. She left Port Jefferson on time, at 10:05 P.M., but due to numerous pauses to clear the track of debris and a 15 mph slow order west of the summit of Cold Spring Hill, she was an hour and nineteen minutes late in arriving at "S" Cabin (now Amott), the start of double track. At this spot the excavation left by the removal of fill for the Jamaica cross-ing elimination of 1912 cut close to the embankment of the railroad. Because of a washout, the 5406, her tender, and the front of the first coach slid into the excavation. Photographer Don A. Boslet, of nearby Syosset, photographed the rerailing operation the next day. The pilot of the 4-6-2 had burrowed deep into the loose sand, *above left*. A crane removed the tender, *below,* while a worker prepared to cut holes in the cab roof and 4-6-0 No. 145, a work engine, stood by. The cranes lifted the 5406 and replaced her on the rails while an H-10s waited behind, *above right* and *right*. After these pictures were taken, No. 145 towed the sandy 5406 to Jamaica.

Two photos, F. G. Zahn

The Mountain Division

The grades and reverse curves of a portion of the Port Jefferson branch between Syosset and Huntington is the nearest thing to mountain railroading on Long Island. K-4s No. 3655, *below,* looked for all the world as if she were climbing a branch in the Alleghenies. Actually, it was cold Spring Hill in May, 1951, five months before the K-4s left the Island forever. A 2-8-0 passed the field west of the Oakwood Road crossing in Huntington on a crisp winter day in 1954, *above.* The eleven miles of track between Port Jefferson and Wading River were abandoned in 1938. The last train, powered by No. 29, *right,* was photographed one mile west of the end of the branch on October 9th. On the return trip, the G-5s brought out whatever equipment was left and a few months later the track was torn up, after forty-four years of service.

Opposite, F. Rodney Dirkes

J. Burt

They Never Learn

Ever since the infancy of the automobile age on Long Island as elsewhere, reckless motorists have insisted on challenging the railroad for possession of grade crossings. The railroad usually wins—even in the rare instances when a train is derailed. In 1930 a Sterling truck was hit at the New South Road crossing, east of Hicksville, *above*. While the local gentry gathered to survey the damage, a G-5s, pulling the Sunrise Special, streaked by whistling, as if to salute the handiwork of her sister. The driver of the solid-tire vehicle was fortunate: he merely spent a few days in the hospital. But apparently hundreds of grade-crossing deaths teach no one a lesson. In 1964 a sports car, traveling at 90 mph, hit a parlor car doing 60 over the Lumber Lane crossing in Bridgehampton. The three youthful riders and their vehicle were mangled beyond recognition; the parlor car's damage consisted of a bent step and a broken journal.

Front and Rear Mishaps

The cause of the mishap that demolished cabin car (Pennsy for "caboose") No. 19, *above,* is somewhat of a mystery. It occurred on the main line near Pinelawn on August 23, 1943, and wartime security kept spectators away. A bulldozer mounted on a trailer was too high for the clearance limitations of the Tunnel Road underpass near Medford on the night of December 28, 1946. The truck driver, either unaware that he had knocked the bridge nearly two feet out of alignment or just indifferent to the situation, walked away without notifying the railroad. When K-4s No. 3731 roared over the bridge sometime later, she was derailed, along with her tender and a New Haven Railroad express car.

In the Middle of the Island

In the early fifties a 2-8-0, her glass headlight askew, *left*, rolled westward through the Ronkonkoma station with eight empties in tow. The eastbound Greenport freight, *above*, traversed many lonely miles of scrub-pine barrens near Brentwood, which had not been fully developed when this photo was made about 1940. Like a ghostly apparition, a G-5s blasted out of a heavy snow storm and into the Central Islip station in the mid-thirties, *right*. The swirling snow mixed with clouds of smoke portrays better than words Long Island winters when steam was king. Many of the old-timers yearn to ride this train back down the high iron of their receding past, to rendezvous with the glories of steam railroading on Long Island.

G. Hoagland Foster, IV   G. G. Ayling

Harry J. Trede

The Pennsylvania Railroad Management

For twenty-five years, climaxed by the disastrous trio of wrecks in 1950, it was customary to blame all the troubles of the Long Island Rail Road on its owner, the Pennsylvania Railroad. Some of the criticism was justified. Many of the PRR officials sent to Jamaica were unfamiliar with the unique problems of the road and were tactless in their handling of the proud Long Island natives. F. R. Gerard, the first Pennsy manager of the LIRR, was a case in point. (Later, when he was president of the Lehigh Valley, he shot himself after a public scandal.) On his first inspection tour out east, Gerard demanded that the agent at Amagansett dismiss the porter whom he had hired to take care of the station and the grounds surrounding it, whose beautiful condition well merited the local pride in which they were held. When the agent refused, Gerard fired both of them. The agent calmly informed the general manager that he would find the station boarded up and the tracks barricaded if the threat were carried out. When the agent went on to say that he owned the land traversed by the railroad and that the contract guaranteed him a lifetime job, the embarrassed Gerard was forced to recant. For years the railroad had stationed a switch engine at Riverhead which was on call to move refrigerator cars from the yard to the potato houses on the North Fork. Pennsy officials, ignoring the pleas of LIRR men, ordered the locomotive back to Jamaica, and informed the farmers that they could wait for the regular freight to bring their cars. The farmers changed to trucks. The charge that the Long Island pays too much rent for Penn Station is no longer valid. The LIRR receives all the rent from the concessions located in its area and pays for the use of only two of the East River tunnels, although it utilizes all four during rush hours. Such accusations as the PRR selling coal for engine fuel to the Long Island and then charging them for the cinders that were used for ballast, cannot be proved, but the story still persists. The absentee management, while not responsible for late trains and wrecks, as the newspapers sometimes charged, nevertheless was demoralizing for talented native Long Islanders who were well aware that they could "never reach the top." Later on, the Pennsylvania promoted some good PRR men to high positions on the LIRR, among them David E. Smucker, Eugene L. Hofmann, Thomas M. Goodfellow, Walter F. McNamara, and the late Henry A. Weiss. However, some Pennsy officials, seemingly exiled to Long Island, made decisions with their feet in Jamaica and their eyes on Philadelphia. Both the Pennsylvania and the Long Island would have profited greatly if more local talent had been promoted to some of the higher positions on the railroad.

The Waning Years of Steam

The diesel, which was still a rarity when No. 112 brought her caboose through Floral Park, *left,* in the winter of 1947, virtually ruled the railroad a mere five years later, when 107, at *right,* carried several hundred fans down the Creedmoor branch. It was the only passenger operation on that weed-grown spur since the specials had brought the visitors and the "Creedmoor Creeper" full of patients to the state hospital in the 1920's.

Jeffrey Winslow

265

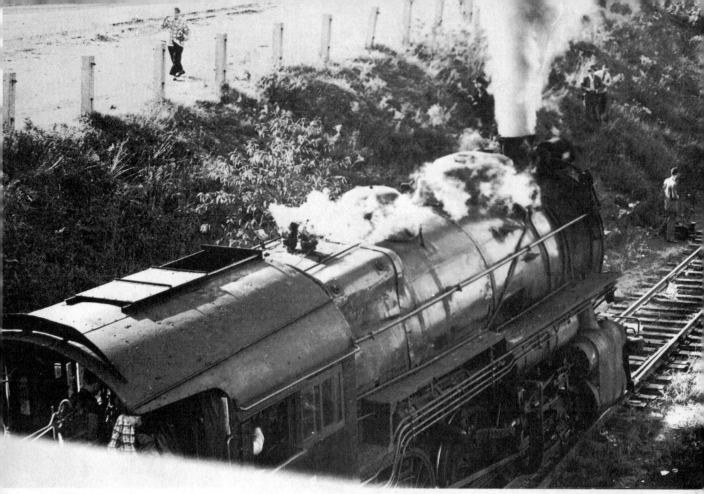

Vincent F. Seyfried

Arthur Huneke

Fading Memories

As the time of total dieselization drew near, several successful railfan excursions were operated by the LIRR. On October 26, 1952, Consolidation No. 107 paused at Fresh Pond during a fan trip, *above.* Handsome 4-6-0 No. 39, *right,* was closely observed by her admirers as she was turned at Greenport during the memorable special run of June 5, 1955. Because of its technical deficiencies, this photograph taken at Morris Park on Memorial Day, 1949, *left,* is more of a stimulus to memory than an accurate portrayal. The photographer and one of the authors, a mere lad of nine at the time, who was with him, recall no more of the scene than the Brownie box camera was able to record: the turntable, the oblique form of the coal tipple, the locomotive, the steam. This observer, recalling that day long ago, sees the blurred image of a K-4s, No. 3738. Dominant features, such as the massive cylinders, solid pilot, and "face-lifted" smokebox front, are vaguely remembered. Most of the other details have been blurred with the years. Yet the emotional impact of this picture is far greater than any made with more sophisticated equipment. Unlike a sharp photograph focused on every detail, this one revives a memory, without destroying it.

Edward Regan

Robert B. Dunnet

A Railroad Loses Its Soul

No. 50, the last of the G-5s's, and the newest steam loco-motive to operate on the railroad, is shown *above*, running under power for the last time. Filthy, with paint peeling, and neglected in all but the most essential maintenance, she spent her last Sunday at Oyster Bay. On the adjoining track smugly sits her successor, a brand-new "growler." The following morning No. 50 ran a com-muter train to Long Island City, then deadheaded back to the ashpit at Morris Park, dumped her fire and was left to cool down—forever. With the exception of a fan trip hauled by sister No. 35 the next Sunday, October 16, 1955, it was all over. Some Long Island steamers were sent to

Pennsylvania for scrapping, but most of them met the torch at Holban Yard. H-10s No. 102 and G-5s's 36 and 27, *upper right,* all appear in dynamic action elsewhere in this volume.

Two G-5s's were preserved for display on Long Island. No. 35, *right,* has been in Nassau County's Salisbury Park since 1956. No. 39, on display at the Carriage Mu-seum in Stony Brook, carries the number plate from No. 38. When the 39 was retired her plate was presented to Roy Campanella, whose Brooklyn Dodgers' baseball uni-form had the same number. After 120 years the steam engines had thundered their last across Long Island, to disappear down the elusive rails of cherished yesterdays.

F. J. Weber, Authors' Collection

New York Daily News photo

270

Efficiency in Gray Paint

As the twentieth century neared the halfway mark, the Long Island Rail Road was plunged into the darkest period of its history. Even the mighty Pennsylvania, which had poured $105,000,000 into the Long Island with no return, could not save it from the combination of natural and human calamities which now befell it. In March, 1949, the hapless LIRR went into bankruptcy and the PRR announced that it was no longer responsible for debts incurred by its subsidiary. The following year three wrecks killed 115 passengers and injured hundreds more. Indeed, the LIRR had descended to the depths of despair; but only ten years later, the railroad had recovered its old vitality and faced a hopeful future.

1950—Year of Disaster

An incredible twenty-four-year safety record, in which the LIRR carried well over one billion passengers without a fatality, was broken in 1950. *Upper left,* on February 19 the lead coach of an electric train was split in half, when it crashed head-on into another train on the gauntlet track, a temporary expedient during the grade crossing elimination, killing thirty-five passengers at Rockville Centre. *Right,* when a brakeman left a switch open at Huntington Station on August 6, a passenger train rammed a sidetracked freight, injuring fifty. This incidentally, was the last major wreck involving two steam locomotives, ending the careers of G-5s No. 29 and H-10 No. 101. The worst disaster occurred at Richmond Hill on Thanksgiving Eve, November 24, when a rear-end collision took eighty lives *lower left.* Typical of the newspaper reaction was the cartoon, *below,* which appeared a day after the Huntington accident. The third bottle, barely visible in the right hand of the inebriated "Long Island R.R." was prophetic—at that time the Richmond Hill wreck was nearly four months in the future.

Three photos, F. J. Weber, Authors' Collection

Collection of W. S. Boerckel, Jr.

Railroad Magazine

The Long Road Back

The Long Island Rail Road, which began its recovery under the Railroad Redevelopment Act, was finally permitted to go ahead with plans which should have been executed long before. One of these was the abandonment of the Rockaway Beach branch—its long timber trestle over Jamaica Bay, built in 1880 by the NY, Woodhaven & Rockaway RR, had always been a maintenance problem. *Above,* ice floes in winter necessitated expensive pile-driving operations to reinforce the structure. *Left,* the worst damage to the Jamaica Bay trestle was caused by fires, which periodically destroyed large sections of the structure. A few years after a particularly disastrous conflagration in May, 1950, the branch was abandoned south of Hamilton Beach and sold to the City of New York, which rebuilt the trestle of concrete and turned the line into an extra-fare extension of the Independent Subway System. *Upper right,* one of the early diesels was the Baldwin switcher No. 403, shown here at Long Island City in 1946 after it had displaced a steam engine. A Fairbanks Morse 2,400 hp demonstrator, *right,* pulled a train up the Port Jefferson branch while steam still ruled the roster. This particular unit wound up on the New Haven but the LIRR ordered four others. Their delivery màrked the beginning of the end for steam, and resulted in the last four K-4s's being sent back to the PRR when the diesels arrived, in October, 1951.

F. G. Zahn

Five photos, Gene Collora

The Coach Rebuilding Program

Passenger-car rebuilding is done at Morris Park. The photos on this page show the basic steps involved in the complete renovation of a car. If necessary, the car is stripped right down to the frame before it is rebuilt. When finished, it emerges with a new interior, recessed lighting, tile floor, and fresh paint inside and outside. The finishing touch is a new number, with a "4" replacing the original first numeral; in this case, 1870 becomes 4870. *Upper right,* as the new cars arrive, the old ones are scrapped at Holban Yard. *Right,* a fascinating pattern is created by white-hot metal fragments as the wheels of an MU car are turned.

274

Harold Fagerberg

Gene Collora

Ron Ziel

Harry Wagner

Old Problems, New Look

The LIRR passed into bankruptcy because of unfair taxes, inept management, and a denial of any fare increase since 1917, although operating costs had doubled. Trains were often late and the road's fleet of passenger cars, averaging thirty-four years of age, desperately needed refurbishing. Amid a rising storm of complaints from commuters, the railroad had to cope with natural misfortunes as well. Just when the blizzard of December 25–27, 1947, reached the point where snowplows were to be called out, a fuel truck was hit by a train at Floral Park. This tied up the main line for hours, allowing the snow to drift and to shut down completely half the railroad. The lamenting newspapers hardly mentioned the Floral Park incident as they lambasted the railroad for its alleged "unpreparedness." When the public outcry rose in volume, the Pennsy sent David E. Smucker to clean up the mess. He arrived in time to oversee the disasters of 1950. Although a good, competent official, Smucker went back to the PRR in 1951, a sacrifice to the gods of public opinion. When a fare increase was finally granted, further abuse was hurled at the LIRR. In 1954, after three years, six general managers and reams of editorial copy, two important changes occurred. The New York State Legislature authorized the twelve-year, $65,613,000 Railroad Redevelopment Act to rehabilitate the LIRR and bring it out of bankruptcy. That same year, Thomas M. Goodfellow came to the railroad and guided it through the rehabilitation period. *Below,* the LIRR turned to gray paint and "Dashing Dan" to symbolize the "de-Pennsification" of the road. *Right,* even before this administration arrived, new diesels, such as the Fairbanks-Morse 2404 at "B" Tower, and many coaches had been painted gray. The PRR tuscan red and keystone symbols became taboo, thus ending the standard era on the LIRR. Much trackwork was done, such as that in the Brooklyn coach yard, *left.* New competition arose in the form of a six-lane road known as the Long Island Expressway. Perpetually jammed, the "crawlway" has been called Long Island's longest parking lot. *Left,* the four tracks of the LIRR which cross the Expressway in Queens can carry as many passengers as seven super-highways, but rubber-happy government officials seem to have ignored this fact as they pour millions of taxpayer dollars into highway development programs which only serve to bring more traffic into the city, forcing the city to provide more parking space which attracts more traffic. The cycle is endless. If one third of the money squandered on highway facilities was spent on the railroads, the problem would probably be solved.

THE LONG ISLAND RAIL ROAD

D. Hamill

Four photos, Ron Ziel

The Last Relics

The flood of modernization which has swept away virtually all the remnants of the LIRR's enchanting past left precious few articles of antiquity in its wake. The most interesting relic to survive is the last wood car of LIRR origin still in existence. Now the property of the seven-mile Moscow, Camden & San Augustine Railroad in Texas, the combine, built at Morris Park in 1898, wends its creaky way through scrub pines reminiscent of its former Long Island habitat, *above.* LIRR lettering is still visible on the cast-truck frames as well as on the car body, *below.* Curious about the problems encountered by such masters as Fullerton when he photographed the LIRR with his cumbersome equipment, one of the authors borrowed the 5- by 7-inch 1908 Graflex Press camera used by J. Burt of Mineola to take most of the fine examples of his work which appear in this volume. Eastman Kodak still manufactures glass plate negatives, so they were used to photograph the Alco-Century diesels delivered in 1963–64. No. 201, *upper right,* about to pass the semaphore on the road near East Moriches, was exposed on this type of plate. One of the few original stations which still survives, *right,* built at St. James in 1873, is another example; the last operational outhouse on the LIRR is visible at the far left. The depot and outhouse were slated for demolition in the spring of 1965. The people of St. James, ever alert to guard their historical treasures, raised such an outcry that the LIRR recanted and completely renovated both buildings.

Creative Vandalism

The Long Island Rail Road has long been a victim of vandalism, most of it the senseless destructiveness of adolescents. In the years before shatterproof glass hundreds of passengers were cut as a result of rocks hurled through train windows. Newly painted stations, of which the LIRR is justifiably proud, are often covered with the scribblings and obscenities of a generation which has known too much freedom too soon. Subtleties such as the Goldwater-Miller streamer on the rear of the *Setauket* at Montauk station, *above,* may be clever campaigning, and the block-lettered "Lionel" on the Nicoll Road Bridge east of Stony Brook, *below,* may seem humorous, but vandalism in any form cannot be condoned. (Both photos on 5- by 7-inch glass plates.)

Four photos, Ron Ziel

Diminishing Splendor

By 1963 service on the main line east of Riverhead had declined to one train daily plus a thrice-weekly freight. *Above,* No. 2004 brought the westbound afternoon train under Bridge Lane between Peconic and Cutchogue in July of that year. It is difficult to imagine this weed-grown stretch of rotten ties as once having been the original high iron to Boston. Despite the silence of the railroad on the matter, the easternmost twenty miles of the main line will probably have to be abandoned unless the proposed Rhode Island bridge radically alters the destiny of that area. Even during its rehabilitation program, rising costs forced the Long Island to close many of its station ticket offices and seek tax relief for the maintenance of the buildings. Though New York City and Nassau County granted these concessions in the interests of its traveling citizens, Suffolk County refused. The road, unable to pay $300,000 to refurbish the buildings in Suffolk, tore down many of them, replacing them with ugly little metal sheds, most of which faced north. Passengers waiting in the "tin coffins" such as the one *below,* erected at Bayport, even before the abandoned depot building was removed, were exposed to the coldest blasts of winter. In most cases, the railroad was justified in demolishing the stations but some, like Amagansett, should have been saved.

Gene Collora

F. G. Zahn

The Many Facets of Operations

Many aspects of running a railroad rarely come to public attention. For instance, for every man in train service, there are seven employees working in administrative, clerical and maintenance jobs. *Upper left,* on the night of September 30, 1962, the "big hook" removed the bridge over Hog Island Creek to let a dredge through. *Left,* in June, 1963, the first welded rail was laid on the main line, west of Forest Hills. Advancing toward the general foreman at left is W. S. Boerckel, Jr., a man who is apt to be seen anywhere on the railroad, supervising such projects. *Above,* a train passed the Nativity scene at Hall Tower in 1963, when Long Island was enjoying a rare white

Christmas. Jamaica station, the general offices of the LIRR, looms behind the diesel. Earlier that year, a huge figure of "Dashing Dan" had been mounted on the side of Hall Tower. It was animated by a motor which moved the legs, in an effort to show "Dan" running for a train. One day the contraption went haywire, sending one of the legs crashing through the large tower window. After chasing his train for the rest of the day on one leg, "Dashing Dan" was removed and never replaced. *Below,* Long Island still has a few old-fashioned snowstorms, as the trackmen working here to thaw switches on January 13, 1964 would be willing to testify.

Ron Ziel

Two photos, Ron Ziel

Gene Collora

Diesel Turnover

Unlike steam locomotives, which had a useful life of at least thirty years, "growlers" rarely last half that long. By the end of 1963 all three classes of Fairbanks-Morse diesels, constructed in 1950–51 and totaling twenty-one units, were ready for retirement. *Left,* the diesel line-up at Morris Park was slightly more interesting than usual, as five classes of growlers posed their snouts in January, 1964. Left to right: No. 1554, Alco, 1955; No. 1505, F-M, 1951; No. 468, Alco, 1950; No. 1551, Alco, 1955; No. 203, Alco, 1964; No. 2402, F-M, 1951. *Below,* during the last days of its usefulness to the LIRR, the 1503 crossed Lumber Lane in Bridgehampton, with the Montauk freight in tow. *Lower left,* the platform sheds at Jamaica sparkle at night under the bright fluorescent lights installed in 1958.

Alfred R. Jaeger

Latter-Day "Scoot"

The Budd Rail Diesel Car, a successful solution for light traffic branch lines on many railroads, originally found a lukewarm reception on the LIRR. Two of them were purchased in 1955, however, and assigned to the Babylon-Patchogue "Scoot." After running the first two RDC's for ten years the LIRR appeared interested in purchasing more of them. This picture, *left,* was taken at Amagansett on a 1961 fan trip.

North Shore Diesels

In July, 1961 Alco diesel No. 459, *lower left,* trundled a lone flatcar as its revenue haul through pastoral forest land near Setauket. The LIRR purchased several Alco units secondhand from the Delaware & Hudson. Two of them paused at Smithtown in 1963, *right.* The lead unit had been repainted and assigned LI No. 1519, but D&H No. 4036, which was on lease, had an electrical fire at Speonk soon after this photo was taken and was sent back to the D&H. *Below,* a lonely afternoon local was headed west toward Syosset in the spring of 1959.

Ron Ziel

Robert Dunnet

Ron Ziel

Alfred R. Jaeger

A Proud Record

By the mid-sixties the railroad had come a long way back. Long Islanders hardly recalled the dismal statistics of 1954: the ridiculous frittering away of valuable real estate holdings for prices at mere fractions of market value, operations running in the red by as much as $6,000,000 annually, inferior equipment, lack of public relations, safety failures, and an attempt to abandon the entire Montauk branch east of Patchogue. The railroad had made tremendous strides to "brighten" commuting: "Dashing Dan" was developed! "Dan," however, was just part of a corporate image program which included lending umbrellas, dispensing cocktail recipes, sponsoring special concerts, station-decorating contests at Christmas, and voting for the colors of commuters' local stations. Commuters had the chance to be "engineer for a day" and ride the head end to work; copies of "Dashing Dan's Diary" were given out; retiring commuters were saluted with certificates of merit (one commuter was heard to say: "They were for courage above and beyond..."), and riders were organized into the Legion of Influential Rail Riders (LIRR), with distinctive caps, membership cards, and a chance to win free commutation tickets. When ground was broken for the new Douglaston station in July, 1962, commuters were invited to attend the ceremonies. Those who appeared were awarded membership cards in the "Three-D Society"—the Douglaston Dirt Diggers. Many of these efforts led to the LIRR's receiving the Twentieth Anniversary Award of *Public Relations News* on September 16, 1958. The management, however, ignored the pleas of railroad men and historians to save a few operational steam locomotives which might have netted the LIRR considerable revenue as well as favorable publicity.

In recent years thirty-one new diesels and 252 new coaches have been put into service and almost 550 coaches have been completely rebuilt. Welded rail was installed and the railroad maintained an enviable on-time record of nearly 97 per cent. The jokes of 1954 were no longer the vogue. Example: Two commuters are speaking— "Did you know that the Almighty built the LIRR?" "Really?" "Sure, the Bible says that He created all things that creepeth and crawleth." The most common story told about the Long Island was of a suicide who died of starvation on the tracks while waiting for a train to run over him.

It is sad that the efficient and conscientious administration which brought the road back to respectability at the same time showed so little feeling for its history. One sign of this was the choice of gray paint and of "Dashing Dan" (p. 277) as the corporate emblem. While "Dashing Dan" running for his train may be a reasonable

Two photos, Robert M. Emery

image of Mr. Suburbia—a grouchy, pot-bellied clock-watcher who probably suffers from ulcers —it is simply not the one for a once-proud railroad which, though it had suffered reverses, was now bent on recovery. Nor does the "Weekend Chief," with his loincloth and arrows, blend in with the Hamptons, the Cannon Ball's parlor-car consist, or the thirteen Indian tribes whose moccasined feet long ago threaded the Sunrise Trail. A more appropriate emblem for "The Main Line to the Mainland," might be one depicting the Montauk Lighthouse (recommended by *Railroad Magazine* editor Freeman Hubbard) or a contemporary typographical design similar to the one used in the early fifties.

Steel Wheels and Rubber Tires

One of the few places where the LIRR still picked up mail on the fly in the 1960's was at Shinnecock Hills. The desolate station, unused by the railroad since 1932, serves as a post office during the summer, *left*. Another little-known operation was that of the "Quogue switcher," *upper left*. Weighted down with sand and a rail, this old truck switched hoppers at a construction company near Quogue. With a large bumper mounted on the front end, the powerful vehicle was capable of pushing six loaded cars. The main line has changed since the days when K-4s's such as No. 3805 pulled ten-car trains through

Cutchogue, *above*. With only one daily train to Greenport, the LIRR has turned to busses to augment its reduced rail service out east. One route runs from Greenport along State Road 25 to South Huntington and terminates at Huntington Station. The second principal route is from Montauk to Amityville depot. *Below,* a westbound bus makes time on the "Road 'n' Rail Route" west of Middle Island, as it travels the Jericho Turnpike, the main line of the sixties. The once-spectacular through route to Boston has suffered a slow and inglorious decline.

The South Fork in the Sixties

Each summer Montauk yard is a busy place as many East Enders and vacationers take the fashionable parlor car service to the farthest point of the LIRR. Although the tracks held few cars the last weekend in September, 1964, when the scene at *right* was recorded on a dry plate, Saturday afternoons in mid-summer may find more than thirty parlor cars laid over. On view here is an eleven-car train made up and ready to leave for Jamaica, as well as an interesting variety of passenger equipment in use at the time. With so many eastern railroads cutting back their passenger service, the Long Island was able to purchase their equipment at bargain prices: the parlor car fleet was leased and eventually bought from the Pennsylvania, while coaches were obtained from the Lehigh Valley, Lackawanna, Reading, Bangor & Aroostook, New York Central, Delaware & Hudson, Maine Central and Boston & Maine railroads. Many of them are visible here, including three MU trailers in the middle of the train. Converted to steam cars in the twenties, the MU's were known as "ping pongs" because they seemed to bounce between the heavier nonelectric cars. *Below,* one improvement of diesel power over steam was the lack of dirty smoke, demonstrated here by a new Alco leaving East Hampton station. *Lower right,* a detail of the same depot as it appeared in 1964.

Three photos, Ron Ziel

CARRIAGES MUST NOT STAND AT THIS PLATFORM EXCEPT WHILE ACTUALLY DISCHARGING OR LOADING PASSENGERS.

Ron Ziel

Gene Collora

Beyond the Soaring Sixties

A stipulation of the $65 million Railroad Rehabilitation Act was that the Pennsylvania Railroad agree to suspend all payments and interest on the debt owed it by the LIRR—a debt which had attained a total of $120,000,000 by 1965. For this reason, the PRR was understandably opposed to extending the plan beyond 1966. The Pennsy wanted a permanent solution to the problem, one which would assure eventual repayment of the debt. The PRR was quite willing to sell the LIRR, a property worth nearly a half billion dollars at 1965 replacement value, but there were no buyers. A flurry of schemes had been proposed, including turning the western branches into rapid transit lines or replacing the standard track with a monorail system. The latter, a frightening prospect to *aficionados* of the road, was as farfetched as the Boynton Bicycle monorail had been seventy years earlier. Another plan, which has often been revived to the horror of the proud LIRR men, called for the conversion of the entire road into a rapid transit line—an extension of the New York subways. That could mean state administration, abandonment of the main line east of Ronkonkoma and the Montauk branch east of Speonk, complete electrification of the railroad, and suspension of the freight service which supplies one sixth of LIRR revenues. In 1942 an elaborate state blueprint was drawn up to electrify the entire railroad in a series of "five year plans" ending in 1965, but fortunately such an impractical scheme was never put into effect. One solution might be to modify the rehabilitation program so as to allow the Pennsy a reasonable return on its investment. Meanwhile, the LIRR had a final fling at the 1964–65 New York World's Fair with its pleasant little pavilion, *upper left*, and it fairly plastered the Island with billboards such as the one at *left* featuring Guy Lombardo. The only railroad actually to exhibit was the L&N, with its much used "General," a Civil War locomotive built in 1856. This was sad indeed as the Association of American Railroads and its membership had given one of the most impressive showings at the 1939 Fair. One of the last five steam locomotives to operate on Long Island, No. 12 of the Brooklyn East District Terminal, photographed in 1962, *above*, was recently purchased by the authors who hope to return her to service. LIRR President Thomas M. Goodfellow had tangible plans to spend $129,000,000 to assure the healthy operation of the road through 1985. When queried concerning the high cost, he answered: "It's considerably less than what is going into the already obsolete Long Island Expressway." The authors concur, and add their opposition to any proposed North Shore Expressway which would destroy the pastoral beauty of the villages along Long Island Sound. Many politicians, whose lack of transportation knowledge showed in their fantastic political schemes to "save" LIRR service, offered advice concerning the dilemma. The only sensible political contribution came from New York Governor Nelson A. Rockefeller in 1965. Since it appeared impossible to operate the LIRR privately on a profitable basis, Rockefeller proposed that the state purchase the railroad and turn it over to a private operating authority. By June the state and the PRR had agreed on a sale price of $65,000,000. The Pennsy also received the Bay Ridge branch, and new contracts were negotiated whereby the LIRR would pay increased rent for use of the East River tunnels and Penn Station. The Metropolitan Commuter Transportation Authority, created to administer the LIRR, contracted with the Goodfellow management to continue operations. The Authority was to take over the administration of the railroad with the expiration of the Rehabilitation Act in August 1966. A $200 million bond issue would finance the purchase of nearly 500 new coaches, extend electrification on four branches, and provide for long-term improvements. The last vestiges of the old LIRR would pass with this program, as the railroad left sixty-six years as an independent line followed by sixty-six years of Pennsy management to become the first government-owned class-one railroad in the United States.

Deluxe Varnish Eastward

In railroad parlance, the term "varnish" once referred to first class passenger trains in days when the natural wood interiors of the cars were kept highly polished. The Long Island Rail Road, known as a commuter conveyor, has amazed even its most ardent devotees with the plush quality of its varnish runs to the eastern forks. No small railroad can match the beauty, luxury, and romance of the Long Island's "Straw Hat Limiteds." In fact, the little commuter road can scoff at some of the transcontinentals in this field. Although the LIRR has always catered to affluent riders, there are three definite periods of luxury train operation in its history. When Austin Corbin was promoting the Fort Pond Bay project in the 1890's, he ran sumptuous parlor cars at record speeds to Montauk. Again, when the railroad was pacing

the emergence of modern Long Island in the 1920's, a number of named trains featuring Pullman equipment were on the timetable. And finally, the LIRR of the 1960's has earned national acclaim for the dynamic promotion of its revitalized parlor car service to the East End. In addition to the regularly scheduled varnish, the LIRR has often operated special passenger trains. In the 1890's Austin Corbin ran fast extras in connection with the Fort Pond Bay project, while Frederick W. Dunton hired trains to carry prospective customers to his south side enterprises. During World War I the "Canning Train" and troop trains were a common sight. Extras were operated in connection with the Montauk boom of the 1920's. World War II saw more troop trains, and the *Freedom Train* (p. 233) followed a few years later. More recently railfan trips, both steam and diesel, have been operated with great success, as well as summertime "daisypicker" excursions. And, as it has since its earliest days, the LIRR continues to bring trainloads of horse-racing enthusiasts to the various race tracks on the Island.

That the LIRR is merely an improved form of rapid transit, an erroneous view which has prevailed throughout its history, was repudiated by a *Brooklyn Eagle* reporter as early as August 25, 1901:

Turn of the Century Varnish

One of the finest action railroad photographs ever made, *left,* dates from the infancy of that art. It shows the Shelter Island Flyer westbound (probably on a Monday morning) through Deer Park in 1904. The Baldwin 4-4-0, whose sixty-seven-inch drivers are propelling the two parlor cars, a combine, and seven coaches at sixty miles per hour, was built in 1893. A shiny extra, *below,* was possibly the first run of the Cannon Ball, at Montauk in 1899.

Two photos, Fullerton, St. James General Store

Collection of Harold K. Vollrath

FAST RIDE TO MONTAUK IN A
LONG ISLAND ENGINE

Eagle Reporter Travels Over the Island on
Cannon Ball Train No. 109.

HOW IT FEELS ON A CAMEL BACK

A Layman's View of a Big Locomotive and
Sixty Miles an Hour.

The man who bumps down to Manhattan Beach from
the Brooklyn Bridge behind a diminutive wash boiler of
an engine, with a deep, hoarse whistle out of all propor-
tion to its size, may be pardoned if he thinks that Long
Island has little to boast of in the way of locomotives. In
fact, it has long been a general, even a popular belief,
among strangers and scoffers, that travel on Long Island
was simply synonymous with the slowness of the Aesop's
tortoise, the jolting of an army wagon and such modern
improvements as were possessed by stage coaches on the
old Boston Post Road. Perhaps in the past some of these
impressions were justified. Certainly they cannot be justified now, and this is nothing less than a description of a
fast run to Amagansett in the cab of a big Long Island
engine.

There is no doubting that it was big. Anybody can
settle that point for himself by journeying over to Long
Island City about three o'clock of an afternoon and watching train No. 109 pull out of the yard. And fast? Yes, there
can be no doubt about that, either, as an Eagle man who
made the run can disinterestedly testify. It has long been
the custom for daily papers to periodically send somebody out with the fast mail, going west, or the limited
flyer going east, and then to print vivid word pictures of
the experience gained, but Long Island has never been
regarded as a feasible field for such material. This story
therefore is designed to abolish prejudice and to add another locomotive yarn to the million, more or less, which
have already been written.

It will not be a scientific story, with observations and
things, because the Eagle man, who took the trip, doesn't
know about such intricate matters. It will be just a layman's view. Train No. 109 has long been one of the best
which the Long Island Railroad makes up in summer. It
runs from Long Island City to Westhampton on the south
shore without a stop and from there it is away to Montauk. When the Eagle man arrived at the depot on Borden

Avenue last Friday afternoon, train No. 109 was without
its engine. Locomotive No. 2 had yet to come down from
its comfortable quarters in the round house, but as soon
as it appeared, with a dignified rumble, the conductor
volunteered to play the part of a reception committee and
introduce the reporter to the engineer.

It had always been a mystery to him how an engineer
dared to be carelessly familiar with so formidable a mon-
ster as a locomotive. The feeling had its origin in the days
when the reporter was told "Nassy engine; burn baby,"
and ever since a sentiment of wholesome respect has been
entertained for all kinds of locomotives except those on
the Kings County Elevated. Now, it is customary, when
introductions are made, for the parties to the transactions
to shake hands and say to each other, "Delighted, I'm
sure," or "Very happy to meet you." That is etiquette,
but it isn't practicable within three feet of a driving wheel
which measures 6 feet 4 inches and five feet from a gigan-
tic cylinder that is perpetually saying:

"Hiss-ss-ss-ss—Swiss-ss-ss-ss—Hiss-ss-ss—Swiss-ss-ss
—B-r-r-r-r-r-r-r," and the same all over again with most
annoying racket.

The conductor of train No. 109 leaned over and yelled
something in the ear of the engineer of No. 2. The reporter
was right alongside and he distinctly saw the conductor's
talking apparatus move up and down, but other than that,
there was no evidence that any one present had spoken.
Pat Murphy, engineer of No. 2, looked in the direction of
the reporter and smiled. The master of the huge machine
—the man who could make that cylinder cock or whatever it was stop roaring—was dressed in a suit of overalls
and in his hand he carried an oil can. With the oil can he
motioned in the direction of the engine and then without
more ado he climbed nimbly and familiarly up the side
of No. 2 and disappeared on the engineer's side of the cab.

Now, it must be understood that No. 2 is a "camel back."
In other words, it has two cabs; one, way up forward and
high in the air, where the engineer sits and scans the
track ahead of him, and the other further astern, where
the fireman stands and feeds coal continually to the
gaping maw of a furnace. Everybody has seen camel
back locomotives and if there is a way to build engines
which will make them as a class more impressive, that
way has yet to be discovered. With boilers elevated far
above the road bed, twice as many cabs as most well

behaved locomotives are allowed to possess at once and extraordinary powers of internal rumbling and growling, any member of the big camel back type may be calculated to inspire a feeling of awe on close acquaintance.

The cylinder, hissing and roaring, expanded suddenly on the principal of geometrical progression; the headlight, when the reporter stepped on the platform supporting the cowcatcher, seemed miles above him, while the iron handle, which it was necessary to grasp before reaching the running board, suggested the summit of Mount McKinley in its lofty altitude. Patient coaxing, however, finally induced the locomotive to reduce its proportions so that the reporter could reach his destination. Once inside the cab, it was hot but secure. Not very many folks, perhaps, are accustomed to riding down town to business daily next to the boiler of a camel back locomotive, so it won't be space wasted in describing how it feels to be on intimate terms with one. In the first place, it is extremely tropical; that is, of course, when the train is not in motion. The windows are open though and it is possible to remove the heat from everything but your trousers' legs by leaning far out. Then, in the process, you look down and see the rods of those six feet four inch driving wheels far beneath and simultaneously realize that there is a suggestion of high life in an engineer's existence. To the reporter, Pat Murphy was out of sight. In camel back locomotives the boiler, very formidable and dignified in its aspect, runs right through the main cab without a stop and from where the reporter sat and wilted there was no way of reaching the engineer except by a somewhat precarious climb over it. This the reporter had no intention of attempting. Pat Murphy's close fitting peak cap could be seen by means of a tiptoe stretch, but at this point all communication ceased. Bob Barry, the fireman, was standing in front of the furnace door, back behind the second cab and No. 2, a piece of machinery weighing a neat 130 tons, was throbbing with pent-up force.

"Take this; it'll keep your hands clean."

Barry, the fireman, had probably spoken in a tone of voice which would have been loud for a concert hall, but it sounded in the cab like a whisper. "This" was a large consignment of cotton waste, a commodity which is used for a multiplicity of purposes around a railroad yard. Clutching it and removing cuffs and straw hat, the reporter felt that he was more of the real thing and less of an imitation. Then, at this juncture, there was an unmistakable evidence that those 6 feet 4 inch driving wheels were about to turn.

The throbbing increased, the roaring grew louder, the bell began ringing, somebody on the station platform whispered something to someone else—he probably yelled, but it sounded like a stage hiss—the stubby smoke stack cleared its throat and around went the wheels on their first revolution. Immediately a welcome breath of fresh air came in the front and side windows of the cab and a breeze which defies the hottest day began to blow. The reporter once more got on good terms with his neighbor, the boiler, and a padded seat provided a comfortable resting place. Steaming past an engine doing duty on the Flushing and Whitestone division, No. 2 towered as high above the cab as an ocean liner does above the pilot boat which goes out to meet it. Bumping over switches, past a crowd of the late Mayor Gleason's fellow townsmen by the lowered crossing gate, train No. 109 left the depot yard behind it and started auspiciously on its run to Montauk, 115 miles distant.

Ordinary trains out of Long Island City skirt the creek to a point past Penny Bridge and thence through stretches of semisettled country, pass through Glendale to a point on Atlantic Avenue just east of the Morris Park repair shops. For trains such as No. 109, however, a more

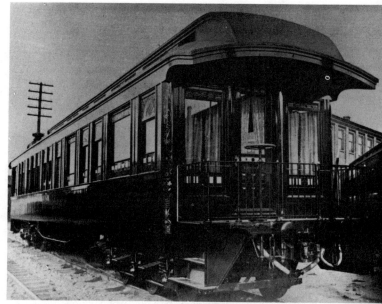

Collection of Jeffrey Winslow

The Eagle Camelback

Opposite is No. 2, the engine on which the *Brooklyn Eagle* reporter rode to Amagansett in 1901, as she appeared when new. Typical of the splendid passenger equipment of that time is the business car *Manhattan*, which often brought up the rear of the Cannon Ball.

exclusive route is provided; a line of track straight as a die, which leaves the North Shore division in the neighborhood of Woodside and extends along the embankment most of the way, through Maple Grove to Dunton. It was over the latter that engine No. 2 escaped from "the maddened crowd" at Long Island City and made its way onward with ever-increasing speed. The reporter put his arm along the window sill, leaned half way out with an attempt at professional ease and watched the block signals as they came in sight up the road.

The newspaper man was not the only one who was watching the block signals. Engineer Murphy governed his movements, and the movements of No. 2 entirely by what the narrow semaphores atop the signal poles told him. A semaphore dropped obliquely; he shot past. A semaphore at right angles with the post, and the grinding of the brakes took the place of every other sound in the anatomy of the locomotive. Then when the signal dropped and the track was clear, what a seeming sigh of relief escaped from the great engine, chafing under sudden restraint and anxious to be off! Phew-ew-ew-w-w, long drawn out and pleasant to hear. From Woodside No. 2, with its train of six dull red coaches, struck across country and made Jamaica on time to a dot. No. 109's run really begins at the junction there, for after leaving the platform at Jamaica it makes Westhampton without a stop.

Brooklyn passengers have to look alive in changing cars for the Cannon Ball, as the train is popularly called. There is no unnecessary delay, and in less than five minutes after it draws into the Jamaica station, No. 109 is pulling out and heading for Hicksville. Sometimes the train takes the south shore route, but on the afternoon that the Eagle man made the trip in the cab of camel back No. 2, it took the straightest road it could find—right down the center of the island to Manor and thence southward to the Montauk division. The track is level and the country, with the exception of an easy grade here and there, as flat as a pine board.

Semaphores were down and nothing interfered with No. 2 in its progress as it whizzed past station after station. Junctions such as those at Mineola and Hicksville necessitated brief precautionary slow downs, but between the two stations named the train fairly flew. The reporter, still grasping his cotton waste, leaned out of the cab window and gazed downward toward the apparently whirling track. The massive driving rods which looked so unwieldy when the engine was in comparative repose at Long Island City, now were spinning like a paper pin wheel on a stick. It is not too late even now to marvel at the power of steam when the point of view is the cab of a speeding locomotive. Hand in hand with admiration and fascination comes an unavoidable sense of apprehension. The old and frayed combination of timid words, "Suppose something should happen?" bobs up before the mental vision before there is time to check it. That is why, perhaps, that the reporter remembered, after a period of forgetfulness covering at least twelve years, that once an engine he had read of blew up without the slightest warning and killed both the fireman and the engineer. The engine was not a camel back, so in all probability No. 2 was exempt. With this reassuring thought, the reporter clasped his cotton waste close to his bosom and let it go at that.

The center of Long Island after Hicksville is left astern is a revelation to any one who has never traversed it. The pretty villages of the south side and picturesque hills and valleys of the north are wholly lacking, and in their stead appears an endless array of pine forests, barrens that have been fire swept, acres of stunted shrubs and huckleberry bushes and here and there a house on the way to rack and ruin. In such a district there are few impediments to fast running, and once clear of all bothersome junctions and crossings, No. 2 simply ate distance. Fifty, fifty-five, and at times sixty miles an hour was its customary speed—seventy miles in a little over one hour. As Engineer Murphy afterward said, there was occasion to be cautious, for another express train was ten minutes ahead of No. 2 on the same line. For that reason, the locomotive was not pushed, but it will stand a lot of pushing when emergencies appear.

"It's all right; needn't move."

It was the fireman's voice. Once more he had yelled and once more the reporter heard some whispered words. The fireman had come up from the rear cab along the after runway to pour oil in the main driving box, the tube leading to which was close by the reporter's seat. Black oil and lard oil were what he used and his trips were frequent.

"Been a wreck out here somewhere today," he shouted, as the express roared past Ronkonkoma Station. "There's the wrecking train on the siding."

The wrecking train was waiting for the Cannon Ball to pass and once more the reporter had a fleeting vision of the engine which blew up thirteen years ago. In a minute Ronkonkoma Station was lost to view in the back distance and another—and much more serious—matter attracted the newspaper man's attention. It was his hat; not the small cap that had been provided for the journey, but the civilized, wear-to-parties hat, which had been carefully stowed away when the engine started. It had just occurred to the reporter to remove the hat from its place behind the cab door and see if it was pretty well, thank you. Examination showed that the article had been jammed up against the side of the cab, tightly gripped there and that it then wore a fine growth of soot whiskers. In his agitation the reporter unsettled the iron support of the fireman's seat and hat, seat, cotton waste, and bogus railroad man went down on the floor of the cab together. The boiler was the only witness of the proceeding and this is the first public confession.

It was with different feelings from those entertained at Long Island City that camel back No. 2 was contemplated in the growing darkness at Amagansett. The feeling of strangeness had gone and the feeling of respect had grown. The engine looked just as big, as a whole, but the individual parts had shrunken and the reporter felt that he could emulate a cat, if occasion demanded, in reaching the fireman's side over the running board. The cylinder cocks were silent and the bell was stilled on its little air ringer, when Pat Murphy, engineer, turned from his omnipresent oil can and spoke.

"How'd you like it?" he asked.

This time it was easy to hear him.

Wartime Special

The "Canning Train" *below, left* was photographed at Patchogue on May 25, 1917. Car No. 708, a baggage and Adams Express Company car, carried exhibits on how to preserve fruits and vegetables. The signs, "Can or Collapse" and "Preserve or Perish" reflected the strong home-front sentiments of the day. These particular slogans were authored by the irrepressible Hal B. Fullerton, who carried out many of the LIRR's wartime projects.

Oil Lamps and Wooden Coaches

Above, a train, probably the Cannon Ball, consisting of two sections behind one locomotive, nears Yaphank, c. 1912. This was split at Manorville, with the head section (locomotive, express car, coach, and parlor car) traveling down the branch to the Hamptons, while a second engine took the combine and two rear coaches to Greenport. The Block Island Express, *below,* was westbound near Blue Point in 1908.

E. L. Conklin

The Great Pickle Works Wreck

For several generations the gaudiest social events in eastern Suffolk were those which revolved around occasional mishaps on the Long Island Rail Road. Consequently repositories of LIRR antiquity reveal a great many pictures of catastrophic occurrences. In view of the railroad's heavy traffic, however, the number of wrecks was actually very minor, though because of their rarity, they attracted much interest. Certainly the most celebrated of all pile-ups out east was the pickle factory wreck in August, 1926. Occurring on Friday the 13th, the Calverton Wreck is remembered with the 1938 Hurricane and the Cape Horn Train as giving rise to some of the most colorful stories to come out of twentieth-century Suffolk. How the Shelter Island Express split a switch and careened into the Golden Pickle Works at seventy miles per hour, and the ensuing rescue operations carried on during a rousing thunder storm, is still a lively topic of conversation among the old-timers. A D-16sb, No. 214, leading the renowned camelback, No. 2, rolled over on her side. Both enginemen were killed when several tons of coal from the tender pinned them against the red-hot backhead. The camelback and train of six cars carrying 387 passengers roared into the siding with such force that the locomotive, *above left,* spun completely around and tore a wall out of the building. One witness told the authors that the train "looked like a big black caterpillar as it bounced along the ties. Then the lead engine rolled over and the train went into the pickle house." The four passengers who perished were among 32 in the Pullman car *Easter Lily, below left* (behind combine), which had thrust itself deep into the pickle plant. One woman died in a hospital after being trapped in the wreckage for six hours. Her two children and the prominent stock broker, Hamilton Fish, had expired earlier— the latter under hundreds of pounds of salt from the building's attic. The camelback's fireman, although in shock, was able to extinguish the fires in both locomotives, thus preventing further disaster. Men of the 62nd Coast Artillery Regiment, on maneuvers at nearby Camp Upton, provided immediate aid in the form of floodlights and rescue workers. Doctors working to aid victims in the deep recesses of the building, however, had only flashlights and the intermittent lightning to see by. The struggle was carried on in a withering downpour, as the dirt, which had been churned up by the engines, quickly turned to mud. Five days had passed and over fifty thousand people had viewed the scene before cranes removed No. 2. A comparison between No. 214 and her sister 213 dramatizes the extent of the damage (note demolished pickle house in left background). *Below,* the two engines stood in Calverton station before their final trip to the scrapper's torch in Jamaica. The *Easter Lily* was blocked up, *below,* while a huge locomotive crane prepared to remove engine No. 2, the famed speed queen which would never again wheel a varnish over steel rails to the sunrise.

Collection of Carol Powell

H. S. Wells

E. L. Conklin

E. L. Conklin

The Sunrise Special

Of all the fine trains operated by the Long Island Rail Road, none has ever matched the splendor and beauty of the Sunrise Special. Until 1926, when the Pullman Company took over operation of the parlor car service, the railroad had operated a modest fleet of extra-fare cars. In 1927 Pullman brought in buffet parlor, buffet club, and buffet lounge cars. The following year saw the introduction of observation lounge cars such as the one at *left*, photographed at Jamaica on May 25, 1928. Train No. 18, the Sunrise Special, became a first class limited in every sense when it began carrying a through parlor car from Washington, D.C. As for speed, the Sunrise made it from Penn Station to Montauk in two hours and fifty-five minutes, compared to three hours, fifteen minutes for the Cannon Ball of the 1960's. The Sunrise usually consisted of a club car, several parlor cars, the Washington parlor car, a dining car and the observation lounge, pulled by the spotless new G-5, *above*, especially assigned to train No. 18. The Sunrise Special's tender sported a beautiful red and gold keystone symbol on its shiny black flanks. *Upper left*, G-5s No. 1589, leased from the PRR, pulled the tender of LIRR No. 21 as she brought train No. 18 through Mineola on June 16, 1928. *Right*, a rear view of the Special as she sped eastward in September of the same year. At this time a through Pullman sleeping car was run from Pittsburgh to Montauk, but it was not part of the consist of train No. 18.

J. Burt

The Fish Trains

In the early thirties, when Montauk was the fisherman's paradise of the Eastern seaboard, the LIRR ran "Fishermen's Specials," but as these trains usually left New York before dawn, there are no known photographs available of them. The Sunday morning New London boat excursion train, however, carried many late-rising fishermen to an afternoon with their sport, so it qualified as a *bona fide* Fish Train. Here K-4s No. 3750, *above,* whistled for the Willis Avenue crossing as she momentarily disturbed the early stillness of Mineola in the summer of 1946. Two hours later she would have delivered her twelve coaches to Montauk. Although many LIRR trains had acquired their names years before, it was not until 1927 that these names were officially recognized in the road's timetables. Two less celebrated trains of the time were the Peconic Bay Express and the Shinnecock Express. The former, *above right,* pulling two Pullman cars and three coaches, topped sixty miles per hour, as an E-3 Atlantic, No. 4176, sped it through Mineola in June, 1928. The latter *right,* with James Eichhorn at the throttle of K-4s No. 5406 and consisting of five Pullmans, a diner, and three coaches, rolled through Mineola on July 21, 1934. For a long time, LIRR passenger engines sported handsome graphite smokeboxes with black doors to offset the red and gold number plates.

G. G. Ayling

The Cannon Ball in Steam Days

Virtually every grade crossing accident out east during the twenties and thirties was credited by imaginative local news reporters to the Cannon Ball Express. It was not intended as a slur, for this crack train of the LIRR has earned a reputation for speed, on-time performance, and winning right-of-way disputes. Through the teens and early twenties double-headed camelbacks wheeled the crack flyer, *below,* to Manorville, where the Greenport section was cut off. This operation was performed in a unique, daring, and illegal (by I.C.C. standards) manner. As the train neared Manorville, the Greenport section was cut off at speed and allowed to coast into the station, where it made a "flying coupling" with a waiting engine. Then the locomotive would bring the Montauk section down the branch to the Montauk division. The only known photo of a train on the Manorville branch shows camelback 4-4-2 No. 1 bringing the Cannon Ball into Eastport in 1924, *upper right.* The Eastport curve of the Montauk division is in the left foreground. Since the abandonment of the Manorville branch in 1949, the Cannon Ball has taken the main line, the Central branch, and the Montauk division. G-5s No. 49, *left,* leads a K-4s with the Cannon Ball through Central Islip during the troubled Depression years.

J. Burt

"Oh, listen to the jingle, the rumble, and the roar..." The smoky splendor which inspired one of the most beloved of all American folksongs—"The Wabash Cannon Ball"—may have faded into oblivion, but another Cannon Ball has created a phenomenon which is now without parallel in this country. On July 9, 1899, when the Montauk division had been completed for four years, the LIRR inaugurated a luxury flyer which came to be known as the Cannon Ball Express. This train was the only tangible survivor of the project to build a deepwater port at Montauk. Though the plan never developed, the Cannon Ball, its name shortened, continued to operate for vacationers and wealthy summer residents who, as automobile traffic began to choke the highways, found the palatial surroundings of the parlor cars most relaxing. Nothing symbolizes the magnificent conquest by the Long Island Rail Road over the trials of the early 1950's better than this famous parlor car train. Although the Cannon Ball puffed through six decades on a railroad of frustrated destinies, it took the present Manager of Special Services, Walter F. McNamara, a reconstructed Pennsylvania Railroad official with a fighting spirit, to revitalize the old train. In doing so he created that much vaunted creature of modern society—a status symbol. As the only all-parlor-car train remaining in the United States, the Cannon Ball has been hailed as the way

to travel to the ultra-fashionable South Fork. Reviewing the social register of the Hamptons, this is no trifle. The following quotation is from the *L. I. Guide* of August 28, 1964: "A man drives out to the Hamptons...in his Jaguar. When he gets there he meets a friend who proudly proclaims that he came out on the Cannon Ball. That's just about as impressive as coming out in your Jaguar." In addition to the chair cars, there is a diner and an open-end observation car. The two observation-lounge cars, *Setauket* and *Jamaica,* are the only equipment of this type to remain in regular service on any first class train in the United States. One observation car is used on the Cannon Ball, while the other usually follows on the East Ender, a Friday-only train. In the dreary diesel era, when all the romance of the Long Island Rail Road appeared to have passed, it is refreshing to see a forward-looking management revive a fine service and turn it into a profitable operation. Not content with having expanded the parlor car fleet from the postwar low of two cars to nearly forty by 1965, Walt McNamara continues to plot additional ways of showing the American railroads how passenger service should be operated. In an age of jet flight, when few people among the fashionable class care to admit that they travel by rail, it is grand to hear diplomats, Broadway stars, and Wall Street brokers proudly announce that they rode to one of America's swankier resort areas aboard McNamara's Cannon Ball. "...She's mighty tall and handsome and she's known quite well by all,/You can find no equal to McNamara's Cannon Ball."

*Friday Only

Glass plate by Ron Ziel

The End of the Sunrise Trail

The afternoon of August 23, 1964, found a gathering of new Alco diesels in a thick Atlantic fog. Nos. 209 and 205, *above*, switched the *Setauket*, while No. 211 left with the parlor cars and coaches of the Ebb Tide, and No. 200 coupled onto another string of cars. Most of the chair cars were named for Long Island towns, but the railroad's only dining car, *left*, was called the *Tuscarora Club*. Walter F. McNamara sat with the late Henry A. Weiss, vice president of passenger operations, while W. F. Wilson, superintendent of special services, stood at the back. "Dashing Dan," *upper left*, was presented in Indian garb on the sides of each car. Compared to the stately red and gold herald which adorned the Sunrise Special, the "Weekend Chief" was an aesthetic calamity. The Cannon Ball, *right*, was a rewarding sight as it passed Napeague Beach, east of Amagansett. Sometimes its consist ran as high as seventeen cars.

No More Mail via Long Island Rail

At 10:18 P.M. on Friday, June 18, 1965, train No. 37 from Speonk brought the last Railway Post Office car into Jamaica. The LIRR, after having carried the U.S. mail for thirteen decades, had lost another battle to the highways. Now all mail service to Long Island villages goes by truck. The letter on which the postmark, *above*, was stamped was posted on that last trip by the authors. In the first year after the suspension of the LIRR mail service there was an atrocious decline in the speed and quality of mail delivery, particularly among the East End villages.

Edith M. Ziel

Appendix

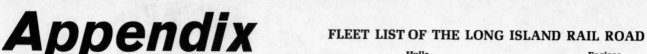

FLEET LIST OF THE LONG ISLAND RAIL ROAD

	Registry Number	Where Built	When Built	Notes	Hull Type	Length	Breadth	Depth	Gross Tons	Net Tons	Engine Type	Notes	IHP
STEAMBOATS:													
New Haven	18189	New York, N.Y.	1835	10	Stm. P. W.	178	22.8	9	342	—	B	C	—
Cleopatra		New York, N.Y.	1836	3	Stm. P. W.	193	23	8.11	402	—	B	A	—
Worcester		New York, N.Y.	1841	10	Stm. P. W.	219	28.6	10	605	—	B		—
George T. Oliphant	10488	Staten Island, N.Y.	1863		Stm. P. W.	—	—	—	146.81	122	—		—
Magenta	17324	East Albany, N.Y.	1863		Stm. P. W.	197	30	9	636	510	—		617
Frances	9313	Wilmington, Del.	1864		Stm. P. Ir.	225	32	10	850	717.82	B		—
W. W. Coit	26725	Mystic Bridge, Conn.	1864	7	—	172	26	9	484.72	—	—		—
Greenport (a Star of the East; b Sagadahoc)	1413T	New York, N.Y.	1866	6	—	244.2	35.2	12.8	1,365	1,267	—		—
Harlem	95131	Brooklyn, N.Y.	1872		Stm. P. W.	165	28	8	465	—	—		—
Jane Moseley (b Minerva)	75537	Brooklyn, N.Y.	1873	9	Stm. P. W.	200	32	11.7	800.62	563	—		250
Nantasket	130127	Chelsea, Mass.	1878	13	—	173.5	29.1	9	498.22	259.51	B	E	500
Manhanset	91176	Mystic Bridge, Conn.	1879		Stm. Sc. Ir.	104.4	19.5	7.7	197	175	C		300
Meteor (b Brazoria)	91527	Philadelphia, Pa.	1883	11	Stm. Sc. Ir.	162	23	8.7	423	338	C		NHP 32
Cape Charles	126278	Wilmington, Del.	1885	8	Stm. P. Ir.	252.5	36	13	940.83	648.68	B		NHP 115
Shelter Island	116107	Wilmington, Del.	1886	8	Stm. P. Ir.	175	31	11	648.02	484.49	B		—
Montauk I (b King Edward; c Forest City; d Montauk)	92294	Wilmington, Del.	1891	8	Stm. P. Ir.	175	31	9.6	570.94	449.47	B		—
Wyandotte (b City of Fort Myers; c Dolphin)	81406	Wyandotte, Mich.	1892	5	Stm. Sc. St.	155.6	33	9	320	160	T.E.	G	900
Long Island (b Pemaquid)	141270	Philadelphia, Pa.	1893		Stm. Sc.	132.5	28	9.8	409	225	—		700
Orient (a Hingham)	-96338	Chelsea, Mass.	1896		Stm. P. W.	142.6	25	9.2	378.58	238.51	I		600
Shinnecock (b Empire State; c Town of Hull)	116712	Wilmington, Del.	1896	8	Stm. P. St.	234	35	14.3	1,250	706	C.	L	1,600
Nassau (a Old Glory)	155325	Noank, Conn.	1898	12	Stm. Sc. W.	133	26.9	9.4	400	235	2 T.E.	B	NHP 52/IHP 1,000
Quaker City (b Sieur de Monts; c USQMD Major L'Enfant; d General Mathews)	20633	Philadelphia, Pa.	1901		Stm. Sc. St.	155.5	32	7.4	469	318	T.E.		1,000
Sagamore (a City of Trenton)	127534	Philadelphia, Pa.	1901		Stm. Sc. St.	155.5	32	7.4	458	311	2 T.E.		1,000
Montauk II (a Queen Caroline; c Transford; d Ramona; e Richmond)	20637	Baltimore, Md.	1902	2	Stm. Sc. St.	193	30.1	11.2	893	487	—		1,000
Patchogue (b Fire Island)	210297	New York, N.Y.	1912	19	Stm. Sc. W.	99.8	23.3	4.3	135	106	2 T.E.	I	—
CHARTERED:													
Narragansett	—	—	1836	22	Stm. P. W.	212.6	27	10.4	835	576	B	J	—
City of Lawrence	5273	Wilmington, Del.	1867	8	Stm. P. Ir.	243	40	11.9	1,678	1,351	—		1,000
Conoho	125882	Philadelphia, Pa.	1881	11	Stm. Sc. Ir.	161.6	23.5	8	366	297	C		260
Northport (a George W. Dohnert)	85880	Wilmington, Del.	1885		Stm. Sc. W.	83	26	7	89	44	—		150
Nantucket	130354	Camden, N.J.	1886		Stm. P.	190	33	9	629	468	—		575 (745/1904)
FLUSHING & NORTH SIDE:													
Island City (b Palisade)	19918	New York, N.Y.	1850		Stm. S.E. W.	146	24	7	196	—	B		—
Enoch Dean		Keyport, N.J.	1852	17	Stm. S.E. W.	135.8	21.6	7.3	194	—	—		—
Mattano	17003	Keyport, N.J.	1859	17	Stm. S.E. W	143	22	6	288	230	B	E	—
FERRIES:													
Louise	*	Greenpoint, N.Y.	1853	20	S.W.D.E.F. W.	125	28	10	341	—	I	J	—
Montague	16984	New York, N.Y.	1859	6	S.W.D.E.F. W.	142	32	11	449	—	—		—
Queens County	20527	New York, N.Y.	1859		S.W.D.E.F. W.	148	31	11	512	396	B		—
Suffolk County	22792	New York, N.Y.	1860		S.W.D.E.F. W.	148	31.7	11.7	512.49	396.5	B	C	—
Kings County	14102	New York, N.Y.	1860		S.W.D.E.F. W.	148	31	11	512	396	B	C	—
Ravenswood	21855	New York, N.Y.	1866		S.W.D.E.F. W.	137.2	29.8	10.7	430.63	314.25			NHP 125
Hudson City	11927	Brooklyn, N.Y.	1867		S.W.D.E.F. W.	203	35.7	12.9	1,008.95	800.5	B	F	NHP 525
Long Island City	15632	Green Point, N.Y.	1869	16	S.W.D.E.F. W.	149.6	33	11.8	562.1	450.43	B		—
Southampton (b Southland)	115028	Wilmington, Del.	1869	8	S.W.D.E.F. Ir.	170.8	33.5	10	673	483	I	G	700
Garden City	85425	Chester, Pa.	1872	4	S.W.D.E.F. Ir.	171.2	33.8	10.4	825.55	575.67	B		900
Pennsylvania (b Old Point Comfort)	20469	Wilmington, Del.	1874	8	S.W.D.E.F. Ir.	136.7	29.4	8.9	430	298	B		350
Flushing (b Tarrytown)	120282	Wilmington, Del.	1877	8	S.W.D.E.F. Ir.	163	32.5	9.5	521	383	I		NHP 400/IHP 300
Rockaway	110389	Wilmington, Del.	1879	8	S.W.D.E.F. Ir.	150	32	10.5	520.83	361.73	B		NHP 400/IHP 500
Long Beach	140399	Wilmington, Del.	1880	8	S.W.D.E.F. Ir.	150.5	32	10.5	519.51	360.41	B		NHP 400/IHP 300
Manhattan Beach (b Harding Highway)	91074	Newburgh, N.Y.	1884	14	S.W.D.E.F. Ir.	152	32.5	12.2	630	436	I	G	600
Sag Harbor	116007	Newburgh, N.Y.	1884	14	S.W.D.E.F. Ir.	152	32.5	12.2	630	436	I		600
Babylon (b Tenafly)	203468	Wilmington, Del.	1906	8	D.E. Sc. F. St.	188.5	45.1	16.5	1,310	890	2 C	G	1,600
Hempstead (b Hackensack; c Islander)	203563	Wilmington, Del.	1906	8	D.E. Sc. F. St.	188	45	16.1	1,310	890	2 C	G	1,600
CHARTERED:													
America	107140	Chester, Pa.	1894	11	S.W.D.E.F. Ir.	156	36.6	13.3	818.21	667.98	B		NHP 600/IHP 500
Henry L. Joyce (a Vermont)	161750	Chester, Pa.	1895	11	S.W.D.E.F. Ir.	156	36.6	13.3	810.29	660.06	B		NHP 2000/IHP 50
TUGS:													
Gladiator	86020	Boston, Mass.	1888	2	—	110.6	22	11.5	167	83	—		55 NHP
Wrestler	30869	Boston, Mass.	1889	1	—	115	25.5	13.2	198	99	C		500
Montauk		Wilmington, Del.	1895		W.Sc.	96.6	22	10	121	51	C		500
Syosset	116895	Philadelphia, Pa.	1899	11	St. Sc.	102.6	23	10.5	176	120	C		NHP 71/700
Patchogue	204384	Camden, N.J.	1907		St. Sc.	90.5	25.4	11.6	190	129	C		800
Cutchogue	217845	Wilmington, Del.	1918		W.Sc.	98.5	25.1	15.1	184	105	C		600
Quogue	219419	Wilmington, Del.	1919		W.Sc.	92.5	25.1	15.7	184	105	C		600
Talisman	22000	Camden, N.J.	1920	18	W.Sc.	94.2	24.5	13	188	127	C		NHP 61/450
Meitowax	226279	Staten Island, N.Y.	1926	15	St. Sc.	96	26	13.3	199	135	Dies. El.	H	680
Long Island	229322	Wilmington, Del.	1930		St. Sc.	104.6	24	13.6	186	129	Dies. El.		550
Garden City	240341	Wilmington, Del.	1941		St. Sc.	101.2	25.2	13	218	148	Uniflow		800
Long Island	140784	Brooklyn, N.Y.	1885	21	Lgt. W.	102	29	8.8	163.73	106.17	S	E	—

*Never issued a number

Cylinders Dimensions Bore & Stroke	Boilers Boiler No.	Boiler Work Pressure	Boiler Type
48x120	—	—	—
44x132	—	—	—
48x132	—	—	—
—	—	—	—
—	—	—	—
50x132	—	—	—
—	—	—	—
—	—	—	—
—	—	—	—
48x132	—	—	—
46x96	2	—	—
22x20	—	—	—
28x36	—	—	—
54x131	—	—	S.C.
—	—	—	—
38x108	2	60	S-E-S
6,24,38x24	2	170	W.T.
20+40x28	—	—	—
40x72	1	—	E
8+56x102	4	130	S-E-S
15½+26x15	1	20	W.T.
0,15+25x18	2	165	L
0,15,25x18	2	—	L
—	—	—	—
9¾,15½x9	1	—	W.T.
56x138	—	—	—
65x132	—	—	—
20+36x28	—	—	—
—	—	—	—
—	—	—	—
—	—	—	—
32x84	—	—	E
—	—	—	—
—	—	—	—
34x108	1	—	R. T.
34x108	1	—	R. T.
—	—	—	—
46x132	—	—	—
—	—	—	—
48x120	1	52	R.T.
48x120	1	—	R.T.
38x108	1	—	L
44x108	—	—	—
44x108	1	50	G.B.
44x108	1	35	G.B.
44x108	1	150	R.T.
44x108	2	150	W.T.
18+38x28	2	200	W.T.
18+38x28	2	200	W.T.
42x120	1	40	R.T.
42x120	1	40	R.T.
20+36x26	—	—	—
17+36x26	2	150	W.T.
17+36x26	2	150	W.T.
20+40x28	2	150	W.T.
18+38x28	2	150	W.T.
17+36x26	2	150	W.T.
17+36x26	2	150	W.T.
18+36x26	1	200	W.T.
—	—	—	—
22+22x24	1	260	W.T.
16 H.P. 28 L.P. x24	—	—	—

Notes—Shipbuilders

1 American Car & Foundry
2 Baltimore Steamboat & Dry Dock Co.
3 Bishop & Simonson
4 Delaware River Iron Shipbuilding & Engine Works (Roach's Shipyards)
5 Detroit Dry Dock Co. (Detroit Shipbuilding Co.– American Shipbuilding Co.)
6 John Englis
7 George Greenman & Co.
8 Harlan & Hollingsworth
9 Lawrence & Foulkes
10 Lawrence & Sneeden
11 Neafie & Levy
12 R. Palmer & Sons Steamboat Co.
13 Pearce & Montgomery
14 Ward Stanton & Co.
15 Staten Island Shipbuilding Co.
16 Henry Steers & Co.
17 Benjamin C. Terry
18 Valley Iron Works
19 Jacobs
20 Eckford Webb
21 Trundy & Murphy
22 Wm. H. Brown

Notes—Engine Builders

A West Point Foundry
B Hyde Windlass Co.
C Allaire Iron Works
D John Roach's (Morgan Iron Works)
E Fletcher-Harrison (Eng. No. 5)
F New Jersey Railroad Co. (Meadows Shops)
G Converted for burning fuel oil while owned by the LIRR
H Ingersoll-Rand Co. (6 cyl. 4 cycle, single action vertical type, with 13" bore and 19" stroke, solid fuel injection, water cooled)
I Seabury
J Novelty Iron Works
K Harlan & Hollingsworth
L Neafie & Levy

Notes—Abbreviations (in order of appearance)

Stm.P.W.	Steamer, Paddle, Wood
Stm.P.Ir.	Steamer, Paddle, Iron
Stm.P.St.	Steamer, Paddle, Steel
Stm.Sc.W.	Steamer, Screw, Wood
Stm.Sc.Ir.	Steamer, Screw, Iron
Stm.Sc.St.	Steamer, Screw, Steel
S.W.D.E.F.W.	Side Wheel Double-End Ferry, Wood
S.W.D.E.F.Ir.	Side Wheel Double-End Ferry, Iron
D.E.Sc.F.St.	Double-End Screw Ferry, Steel
Stm.S.E.W.	Steamer, Single-End, Wood
W.Sc.	Wood, Screw
St.Sc.	Steel, Screw
IHP	Indicated Horse Power
NHP	Nominal Horse Power
B.	Vertical Beam
I.	Inclined
C.	Compound
T.E.	Triple Expansion
Dies.El.	Diesel Electric
R.T.	Return Tube
G.B.	Gun Boat
W.T.	Water Tube
L.	Locomotive
S-E-S	Single-Ended-Scotch
Lgt. W.	Lighter, Wood
S	Propeller engine

Steamship Historical Society of America

The Beginning and the End

One of the earlier boats used on the Greenport–New London route, the *Magenta*, was photographed in action, *above*, in the late 1800's. *Below*, in the last year of LIRR tugboat operations, the *Garden City* nudged two carfloats up the East River toward the Brooklyn Bridge.

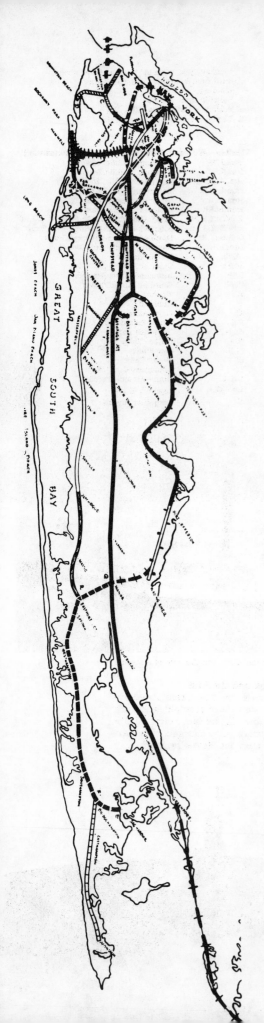

LONG ISLAND RAIL ROAD SYSTEM
DEVELOPMENT MAP

Symbol	Charter Name*	Building Date	Abandonment Data
	Brooklyn & Jamaica RR	1836	
	Long Island RR	1836–1844	
	Long Island RR	1870	E-F, 1939
			Q-R, 1949
	Long Island RR	1861	
	Long Island RR	1868	
	Long Island RR	1865–1868	
	Long Island RR	1910	U-V, 1953
	Hicksville & Cold Spring Branch RR	1854	
	South Side RR of LI	1867–1868	
	North Shore RR	1866	
	Far Rockaway Branch RR†	1869	
	Flushing & North Side RR	1869	
	Hunters Point & South Side RR†	1870	
	Smithtown & Port Jefferson RR	1873	
	New York & Rockaway RR	1872	K-L, } 1934 M-N, }
	Rockaway Railway†	1886	Y-Z, 1953
	Whitestone & Westchester RR	1886	I-J, 1932
	Central Railroad of LI	1873	A-B, 1879
	Central Railroad Extension	1873	
	Glendale & East River RR	1877	S-T, 1938
	New York, Bay Ridge & Jamaica RR	1876	
	New York & Manhattan Beach RR	1877	C-D, c. 1940
	New York, Woodhaven & Rockaway RR†	1880–1886	1953
	New York & Long Beach RR	1880	
	Brooklyn & Montauk RR	1881	
	Long Island City & Manhattan Beach RR	1883	
	Oyster Bay Extension RR	1889	
	New York Bay Extension RR	1893	
	LIRR North Shore Branch	1895	1939
	Montauk Extension RR	1895	
	Great Neck & Port Washington RR	1898	

Indicates lines proposed but never built.

Rail Bridge to Rhode Island, proposed, 1965.

*After many of these companies were chartered and the track laid, they were immediately leased to the LIRR.
†Subsidiary of South Side RR of Long Island prior to merger with LIRR.

STATION NAME CHANGES
(Mostly in 1880's and 1890's)

FROM	TO
Fresh Pond	Bushwick Junction
Bushwick Junction	Fresh Pond
Good Ground	Hampton Bays
Locust Avenue	Locust Manor
Clarenceville	Richmond Hill
Hunter's Point	Long Island City
Pearsalle's Corner	Pearsalls
Pearsalls	Lynbrook
Baldwinsville	Baldwins
Baldwins	Millburn
Millburn	Baldwins
Baldwins	Baldwin
Ridgewood	Wantagh
South Oyster Bay	Massapequa
Belmont	Belmont Junction
Wellwood	Breslau
Breslau	Lindenhurst
Forge	Mastic
Moriches Station	Eastport
Moriches	Center Moriches
Center Moriches	Centre Moriches
Centre Moriches	Center Moriches
Fanny Bartlett	Bartlett
Bushwick Avenue	Bushwick
Ocean Point	Cedarhurst
Woodsburgh	Woodmere
Fenhurst	Hewletts
Hewletts	Hewlett
Norwood	Malverne
South Lynbrook	Center Avenue
Barnum Island	Jekyl Island
Baiting Hollow	Calverton
Jerusalem	Central Park
Central Park	Bethpage
Brushville	Queens
Queens	Queens Village
Kew	Kew Gardens
Hinsdale	East Hinsdale
East Hinsdale	Floral Park
Hyde Park	New Hyde Park
Hempstead Station	Hempstead Branch
Hempstead Branch	Mineola Junction
Mineola Junction	Mineola
Melville	Pinelawn
Babylon Station	West Deer Park
West Deer Park	Wyandance
Wyandance	West Deer Park
West Deer Park	Wyandanch
Old Holbrook	Holbrook
Waverly	Holtsville
Bellport Station	Bartlett
Millville	Yaphank
St. George's Manor	Manor
Manor	Manorville
Franklinville	Laurel
Hermitage	Peconic
Newtown	Elmhurst
West Flushing	Corona
Brookdale	Great Neck
Glendale	Parkside
Springfield	Springfield Gardens
Willis	East Williston
Nassau	Glen Cove
Woodbury	Cold Spring
Cold Spring	Cold Spring Harbor
Centerport	Greenlawn
East Northport	Northport
St. Johnland	Kings Park
Ramblersville	Howard Beach
Cypress Hills	Railroad Avenue
Railroad Avenue	Autumn Avenue
Union Course	Unionville
Unionville	Union Course
Woodville	Woodhaven
Woodhaven Junction	Woodhaven
Fords Corners	Rugby
Kings County Cent. Jct.	Flatlands
Flatlands	Vanderveer Park
Panataquit	Bayshore
Bayshore	Bay Shore
Golf Station	Golf Grounds
Easthampton	East Hampton
Bridge Hampton	Bridgehampton
West Hampton	Westhampton
Suffolk Station	North Islip
Rockaway Junction	Hillside
Lake Road Station	Lakeland
Lakeland	Lake Ronkonkoma
Lake Ronkonkoma	Ronkonkoma
Hollands	Holland
Sea Side	Seaside
Seaside	Babylon
Hammels	Hammel
Wardenclyffe	Shoreham

Alfred R. Jaeger

In the Twilight Years
Only nineteen steam locomotives remained on the roster of the LIRR when No. 24 reposed at Port Jefferson in February, 1952. A Fairbanks-Morse diesel was occupying the adjoining track.

Milestones in LIRR History
The Long Island has many distinguishing features: for instance, it is the only class-one railroad to derive more of its revenue (75 per cent) from passengers than from freight; and it has never owned a General Motors diesel locomotive. It has more significant "firsts" to its credit than any other railroad; here is an impressive list of its pioneering ventures:

1836—Developed the now standard rail spike.

1836—Installed the first locomotive steam whistle.

1868—Launched the first iron-hulled ferryboat (the *Southampton*) at the Port of New York.

1885—Invented the "piggy-back" concept, which may help to save the United States rail industry. Unfortunately, it is no longer of any practical use to the short-haul LIRR.

1905—Purchased the first all-steel passenger car.

1905—Was the first to utilize extensive main line electrification.

1926—Placed the first United States diesel locomotive in road service.

1927—Was the first to retire all wood passenger cars.

1930—Installed the first completely remote-controlled electrical substations.

1931—Was the first to use electronic rail detector cars (see page 206).

1951—Devised the first completely modern automatic speed control system.

1958—Installed the first fully automatic IBM inventory control.

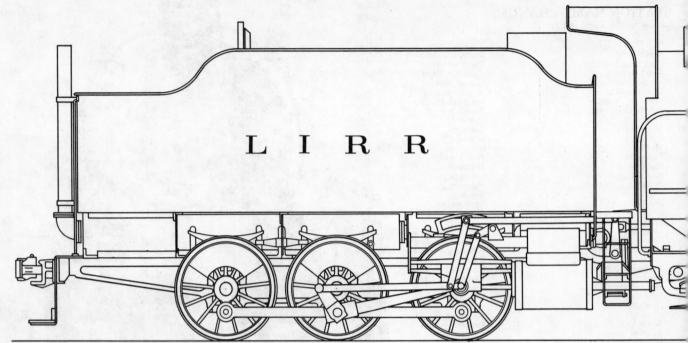

L I R R

ROSTER OF ALL STEAM, ELECTRIC, AND DIESEL LOCOMOTIVES KNOWN TO HAVE OPERATED ON THE LIRR, ITS AFFILIATES AND PREDECESSORS, 1835–1965.

This roster was compiled from many sources, but the efforts of the following individuals were chiefly responsible for it: Vincent F. Seyfried, William J. Rugen, Harold Fagerberg, Robert M. Emery. Certain odd classes of locomotives appear in photographs, but there is no further record of their existence. One class, numbered in the 500's in the 1902–04 period (pp. 122-123) was due for retirement after the imminent electrification. It is presumed that they were of an older series, temporarily renumbered. A few locomotives numbered in the 370's appear circa 1900. They were probably from roads recently absorbed by the L. I. Virtually all of these odd types as well as the older pre-1890 engines were scrapped by 1906, after the first electrification and the arrival of nearly seventy new steam locomotives in the years 1901–06.

Abbreviations (in order of appearance): LCC, Locks and Canals Co., Lowell, Mass.; PLC, Poughkeepsie Locomotive Co.; BVH, Baldwin, Vail & Hufty; RK&G, Rogers, Ketchum and Grosvenor; H&D, Hinkley and Drury; DC&C, Danforth, Cooke and Co.; WFS, Withdrawn From Service (scrapping) date.

EARLIEST LIRR STEAM LOCOMOTIVES, 1835–1875

Name	Builder	Date	Drivers	Notes	WFS
Ariel	Baldwin	1835	54″	1, 2	1855
Post Boy	Baldwin	1836	54″	2, 3	c. 1881
Hicksville	LCC	1836	60″	2	1848
John A. King	PLC	1838	60″	2, 4	1869
Chichester	BVH	1840	48″	5	1853
Crabb	BVH	1840	42″	5	*
Brooklyn	*	*	42″		c. 1859
Brooks	RK&G	1844	60″	6	c. 1860
Fiske	RK&G	1844	60″	7	1869
James H. Weeks	BVH	1844	60″	8	1862
Len Crossman	Baldwin	*	*		1865
Elihu Townsend	Norris	1844	60″	9	*
Derby	H&D	1844	69″		1859
Boston	H&D	1845	72″		c. 1861
Little	Norris	1845	69″	10	*
Ruggles	Norris	1845	69″		1860
New York	RK&G	1845	72″		c. 1863
Moses Maynard	RK&G	1851	66″	11	c. 1880

Name	Builder	Date	Drivers	Notes	WFS
Long Island	RK&G	1852	60″		1867
Peconic	Norris	1853	60″		1869
Wyandank	Baldwin	1853	40″	12	1862
Montauk	Swinburne	1854	60″		1874
Orient	RK&G	1854	66″		*
Atlantic	RK&G	1855	66″	13	*
Nebraska	*	1856	*	14	*
Pacific	Rogers	1857	66″	15	*
Phoenix	Rogers	1860	60″	16	*
Nassau	Norris	1860	60″		*
James Sedgely	Northern RR	1862	*	15	*
Hempstead	Taunton	1862	*	17	*
Quincy	H&D	1862	*	18	*
Glen Cove	Norris	*	*	19, 20	*
Richard Schell	*	*	*	21	*
George F. Carman	Rogers	*	*	15	*
Queens County	DC&C	*	*		*
Suffolk County	DC&C	*	*		*
Corona	DC&C	1864	*	22	*
General Grant	Rogers	1865	*		*
General Sherman	Rogers	1865	*		*
Aaron J. Vanderpool	Ellis	1866	*		*
Horace Greeley	Ellis	1866	*		*
James M. Waterbury	Ellis	1866	*		*
Thurlow Weed	Schenectady	1867	*		*
Charles R. Lincoln	Schenectady	1867	*	23	*
Riverhead	Schenectady	1867	*	24	*
Huntington	DC&C	1867	60″	25	1878
Woodbury	McQueen	1867	*		*
Northport	McQueen	1867	*		*
Alden B. Stockwell	Schenectady	1871	*		*
Charles A. Dana	Schenectady	1871	*		*
Peter Cooper	Manchester	1871	*	26	1881
Robert C. Brown	*	1873	*	27	*
Benjamin W. Hitchcock	Schenectady	1874	*	28	1896
St. Johnland	Schenectady	1875	*		*
Lakeland	Schenectady	1875	*	29	*

NOTES. 1. 19th engine built by Baldwin. 2. Brooklyn & Jamaica R.R. 3. Duplicate of *Ariel*, sold 1852. 4. Only engine built by this company. 5. Purchased 1842 from Annapolis & Elk Ridge R.R. 6. Rebuilt 1853. 7. Retired after hauling ballast trains, const. of Sag Harbor branch. 8. Traded for *Len Crossman* 1862. 9. Rebuilt 1865. 10. Renamed *Fanny*, c. 1860. 11. Rebuilt *James Gordon Bennet* (later No. 25). 12. 0-6-0 rebuilt to 4-4-0, 1856; sold to U.S. Govt. in Civil War. 13. Renamed *Horatio Seymour*, 1868. 14. First LIRR coal-burner, 1857. 15. Sold, 1869. 16. Sold, 1873. 17. Dummy, for Hempstead branch. 18. Similar to *Hempstead*, rebuilt as *Fred* with 40″ drivers; sold to Canarsie R.R., 1876. 19. Scarce roster information, 1863-69. 20. Probably old *Nassau*. 21. Renamed *Orient* or *Elihu Townsend*. 22. Bought from N.Y. & Flushing R.R., 1871. 23. Tank engine, renamed *Long Island City*. 24. Similar to *Lincoln*. 25. Bought from Brooklyn Central & Jamaica R.R.; later No. 40. 26. Very beautiful but poorly built. 27. Renamed *Deer Park*. 28. Renamed *Port Jefferson* (later No. 49). 29. No. 51.

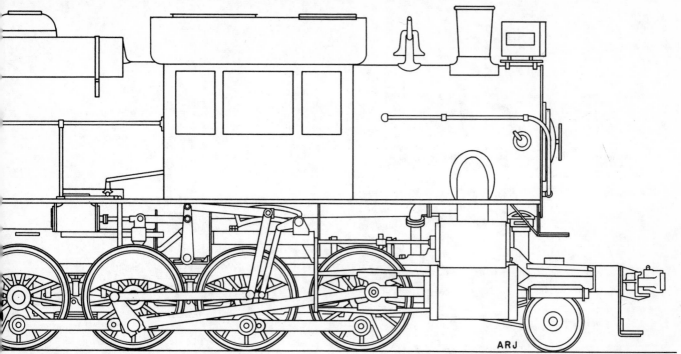

Drawing by Alfred R. Jaeger

South Side R.R. of Long Island Locomotives, 1865–1876 (WFS dates unknown)

Name	Builder	Date	Notes	LIRR No.
Nos. 1-3	Hinckley	1865	1	*
Charles Fox	Mason	1867	2	16
Daniel T. Willets	Mason	1868		18
Alex McCue	Mason	1868		23
John Tappan	Mason	1868		20
J. B. Johnston	Grant	1868		41
R. O. Colt	Mason	1868		21
Pewit	DC&C	1860	3	*
Fire Fly	DC&C	*		19
A. J. Bergen	DC&C	1870		17
Francis B. Baldwin	Grant	c. 1870		*
A. McLean		c. 1870	4	*
Massapequa	Grant	1870		*
Norwood		1872		*
South Side		1872	5	26
Islip	Brooks	1873	14	
Patchogue	Brooks	1873		15
Montauk	Schenectady	1873	6	32
Springfield	Manchester	1875		27

NOTES. 1. No further information. 2. Renamed *Merrick*. 3. Built for CNJ R.R., purchased by S.S.R.R., 1869. 4. Probably rented. 5. Probably built by Rogers. 6. Renamed *Creedmoor*.

New York & Flushing R.R. Locomotives

Name	Builder	Date	Notes	LIRR No.
Flushing	Rogers	1853	1	*
New York	*	1853	1	*
Manhasset	DC&C	1864	2	46
Uncle Tom	B&P RR	1851	3	*

NOTES. 1. Engine weight 18 tons; drivers 60″. 2. Sold to LIRR, 1871, renamed *Corona*. 3. Boston & Providence RR sold *Dedham* to Fitchburg & Worcester, which renamed it *Uncle Tom*. Arrived on NY&F in 1866 as 4-4-2 (!) tank engine.

Flushing & North Side R.R. Locomotives (all had 60″ drivers)

Name	Builder	Date	Notes	LIRR Name, No.
College Point	Rogers	1868		Newtown No. 4
Whitestone	Rogers	1868	1	5
Flushing	Rogers	1869		2
Woodside	Rogers	1869		3
Bayside	*	1869	2	New York No. 1

NOTES. 1. Rebuilt tank engine, 1885; renumbered 296 in 1888; retired c. 1905. 2. Rebuilt tank engine, c. 1885 (probably type which appears on p. 40). LIRR Nos. 5, 2 and 3 retained F&NS names.

Double-Expansion Camelback

An early experiment with the 2-8-6-0 camelback, *above*, nearly got off the drawing boards before somebody asked: "What happens when the tender runs low on coal and water?" The plan had been to rebuild the class of H-51s camelbacks with piston valves and additional steam pipes; the chassis of retired B-53 0-6-0's were to be used to support the tenders.

Central R.R. of Long Island Locomotives

Name	Builder	Date	LIRR Name, No.	No. After 1898
Newtown	Rhode Island	1871	Bayside No. 6	*
Winfield	Rhode Island	1871	Winfield No. 7	7
Farmingdale	Rhode Island	1872	Farmingdale No. 8	9
Babylon	Rhode Island	1872	Hinsdale No. 10	*
Garden City	Rhode Island	1872	Garden City No. 11	11
New York	Rhode Island	1872	Hyde Park	*
Hempstead	Brooks	1873	Babylon No. 12	3
Hyde Park	Brooks	1873	Hempstead No. 13	4
Fire Island	Brooks	1874	*	*

In 1876, all of the above roads were merged into the LIRR.

LIRR STEAM LOCOMOTIVES, 1876–1955

Name	No.	Builder	Date	4-4-0's
Arrow	72	Baldwin	1879	See page 22.
Comet	73	Baldwin	1879	No further information
Meteor	74	Baldwin	1879	available.

New York & Rockaway Beach R.R. (LIRR in 1898) 60″ Drivers

LIRR Nos.	Builder	Date	N.Y. & R.B. Nos.	WFS
301	Rogers	1879	6	1904-06
302-303	Hinckley	1879	2-3	1904-06
304-305	Rogers	1879	4-5	1904-06
306-308	Rogers	1879	8, 7, 1	1904-06
309-312	Baldwin	1893	9-12	1904-06

All of these engines were 4-4-0's.

Suburban Passenger Tank (0-4-4T)

Nos.	Builder	Date	Drivers	Pre-1898 Nos.
201-206	Baldwin	1878	40″	105-110
207-216	Baldwin	1892	51″	150-159*
217-220	Rhode Island	1893	44″	160-163*
221-222	Rhode Island	1894	44″	164-165
223	Rhode Island	1893	44″	166
224-226	Rhode Island	1894	44″	167-169

*Vauclain Compounds.

315

Suburban Passenger Tank (2-4-6T)* New York & Manhattan Beach R.R.

Nos.	Builder	Date	Drivers	N.Y. & M.B. Nos.
227-231	Rogers	1883	48″	61-65

*At least one NY & MB 2-4-6T numbered in 300's; see page 79. Nos. 201-231 used as main-line rapid transit engines, Brooklyn to Rockaway Junction. All were retired by the electrification of 1905. Road Nos. 201-231 were immediately assigned to new D-16's.

Passenger (4-4-0) D-52

Nos.	Builder	Date	Pre-1898 Nos.	Notes
27-32	Rogers	1882	80-85	Nos. 39-41, still
23-42	Rogers	1883	86-95	active in 1912

Suburban Passenger (4-4-0) Nos. 43-63, Baldwin rebuilt Camelbacks.

Nos.	Class	Builder	Date	Drivers	Original Nos.
43-46	D-53	Rogers	1888	67″	111-114
47-48	D-53b	Rogers	1888	67″	115-116
49	D-53a	Rogers	1888	67″	117
50	D-53a	Rogers	1889	67″	118
51-54	D-53a	Rogers	1889	60″	119-122
55	D-53b	Rogers	1889	67″	123
56	D-53	Rogers	1889	67″	124
57	D-53	Cooke	1890	67″	125
58	D-53b	Cooke	1890	67″	126
59-60	D-53a	Cooke	1890	67″	127-128
61	D-53a	Cooke	1890	60″	129
62	D-53a	Cooke	1891	67″	130
63	D-53	Cooke	1891	67″	131

Converted to Camelbacks, c. 1895 (pp. 104-107). WFS 1915-22.

Passenger (4-4-0)

Nos.	Class	Builder	Date	Drivers	Pre-1898 Nos.
64-67	D-54	Baldwin	1893	67″	1-4
68-73	D-54	Baldwin	1893	67″	27-31, 37
74-76	D-55	Baldwin	1893	67″	38-40
77-78	D-55a	Brooks	1898	67″	6, 8
79-81	D-55a	Brooks	1898	67″	33-34, 42
82-85	D-56s	Baldwin	1903	68″	
86-100	D-56s	Baldwin	1904	68″	WFS c. 1930

Switching (0-6-0) 51″ Drivers

Nos.	Class	Builder	Date	Pre-1898 Nos.
170-171	B-53sb	Baldwin	1913	
172-175	B-53	Baldwin	1906	
176-180	B-51	Schenectady	1889	16-20
181-183	B-51	Schenectady	1891	21-23
184	B-52	Baldwin	1893	24
185-188	B-52	Baldwin	1892	25, 147-149
189	B-52a	Baldwin	1899	
190	B-52a	Baldwin	1901	
191-192	B-53	Baldwin	1902	
193-194	B-53	Baldwin	1903	
195-197	B-53	Baldwin	1905	
198-199	B-53a	Baldwin	1911	

Freight (2-8-0) Camelbacks, 51″ Drivers

Nos.	Class	Builder	Date	WFS
151-153	H-51	Brooks	1898	All gone
154-155	H-51a	Baldwin	1903	c. 1928

Freight (2-8-0) Class H-3 50″ Drivers

Nos.	Builder	Date	Ex-PRR No.	D.O.A.*	WFS
159	PRR**	1893	1724†	11/1905	12/1922
160	PRR	1892	1505	10/1903††	5/1924
161	PRR	1892	1539	10/1903††	12/1922
162	Baldwin	1892	1568	10/1903††	6/1924
163	Baldwin	1892	1586	10/1903††	6/1924
164	PRR	1893	4186	11/1905	5/1924
165	PRR	1892	1492	11/1905	7/1915
166	PRR	1887	1701	11/1905	12/1921
167	PRR	1888	1779	11/1905	7/1915
168	PRR	1887	1780	11/1905	12/1921
169	PRR	1894	4187	11/1905	

*Date Of Arrival (on LIRR). **Pennsylvania R.R. (Altoona or Juniata Shops). †Ex-No. 110. ††First PRR engines on LIRR

Passenger (4-4-2) Class E-1 Camelbacks, 80″ Drivers

Nos.	Builder	Date	Ex-PRR Nos.	D.O.A.	WFS
198-200	PRR	1899	698, 700, 820	12/1903	1911

Built by PRR for W.J. & S.S. R.R. to compete with Reading 4-4-2's.

Passenger (4-4-2) Class E-51sa Camelbacks, 76" Drivers

Nos.	Builder	Date	WFS
1-4	Baldwin	1901	No. 1, 7/1929; No. 2, 8/1926

Dual Service (4-6-0) Camelbacks

Nos.	Class	Builder	Date	Drivers	WFS
5-6	G-54sb	Baldwin	1901	68"	No. 7—
7-9	G-54sa	Baldwin	1902	72"	3/1928.
10-15	G-54sb	Baldwin	1902	68"	All gone
16-19	G-54sa	Baldwin	1903	72"	by 1931.

Passenger (4-4-0) Class D-16b, D-16sb

Nos.	Builder	Date	Drivers	WFS
201-210	PRR	1905	68"	205, 8/1927; 211, 4/28;
211-231	PRR	1906	68"	212, 5/34; 214, 8/26; 225, 230, 8/27

Freight (2-8-0) Class H-6sb 56" Drivers

Nos.	Builder	Date	Ex-PRR No.	WFS
300	Baldwin	1906	987	
301	Baldwin	1905	2920	3/1949
302	Baldwin	1906	3117	12/1947
303	Baldwin	1906	3108	3/1949
304	Baldwin	1905	2904	
305	Baldwin	1906	3109	2/1949
306	Baldwin	1906	1689	12/1948
307	Baldwin	1907	3802	1935*
307	Baldwin	1906	3062	4/1948
308	Baldwin	1905	2754	2/1949
309	Baldwin	1906	3064	4/1949
310	Baldwin	1906	3571	4/1948
311	PRR	1906	3832**	5/1948
312	Baldwin	1906	3576	8/1947
313	Baldwin	1906	2811	12/1947
314	Baldwin	1905	2830	7/1949

All H-6sb's except second No. 307, arrived 1916. *Wrecked on Bay Ridge branch, scrapped. **Ex-Cumberland Valley R.R. No. 101.

Suburban Passenger (2-6-2T) Class S-51

Nos.	Builder	Date	Drivers	Sold*	WFS
20-24	Baldwin	1904	63"	11/1911	7/1945

*Central R.R. of New Jersey; renumbered 220-224.

Shop Engines (Steam, Electric, Diesel)

Power	Wheel Argt.	Class	Builder	Date	WFS
Steam	0-4-0T	"Pop"			c. 1900
Electric (#320)	0-4-0	A-1	Blw.-West.*	1927	12/1958
Steam (#321)	0-4-0T**		Rhode Island	1894	8/1927
Electric (#322)	0-4-0***		LIRR	1912	1927
Electric (#322)	0-4-0	A-1	Blw.-West.*	1927	12/1958
Diesel (#398-399)†		GS-1	General Electric	1958	

*Baldwin-Westinghouse. **Purchased from Chicago Elevated R.R., 1898. ***Homemade cab on MU truck. †150 hp. 0-4-0.

Dual Service (4-6-0) All WFS by 1925

Nos.	Class	Builder	Date	Drivers	Pre-1898 Nos.
101-105	G-51	Rogers	1886	54"	101-2, 98-99, 100
106-107	G-51	Rogers	1884	54"	96-97
108-112	G-51a	Cooke	1891	60"	132-136
113-117	G-52	Baldwin	1892	60"	137-141
118-122	G-52a	Baldwin	1892	60"	142-146

Freight (4-6-0) Camelbacks, 60½" Drivers

Nos.	Class	Builder	Date	WFS
123-127	G-53	Brooks	1899	#124, 1/1930; #126, 4/1929

Freight (4-6-0) 60½" Drivers

Nos.	Class	Builder	Date	WFS
128-132	G-53a	Brooks	1907 }	c. 1930
133-136	G-53b	Brooks	1911 }	
137-140	G-53sc	Schenectady	1913	c. 1935

Dual Service (4-6-0) Class G-53sd

Nos.	Builder	Date	Drivers	WFS
141, 143	Brooks	1917	60½"	2/1949
142	Brooks	1917	60½"	5/1948
144-146	Brooks	1917	60½"	7/1949

An E-6s and a G-5s met east of Mineola in 1945.

O. Winston Link

Winter at "S" Cabin

In February, 1921, Ralph Kaiser, the operator at "S" Cabin, Syosset, photographed this D-56s battling up Cold Spring Hill after a heavy snowfall.

ROSTER OF DIESEL LOCOMOTIVES

Road numbers usually determined by horsepower rating (i.e., No. 2403 had 2400 hp). Exceptions: Nos. 1501-1509, 1551-1560 were 1600 hp. 2000 hp. Alcos were numbered in 200's for simplicity.

Nos.	Class	HP	Builder	Date	WFS
400	GS-4	400	G.E.	1950	11/1963*
401	AA-2	600	Schen.-G.E.	1925	6/1951
402	AA-3	600	Schen.-G.E.	1928	6/1951
403**	AA-4	600	Blw.-West.	1927	1951
403	B-S6	660	Baldwin	1945	9/1963
404-408	A-S6	660	ALCO	1946	
409-412	B-S6a	660	Baldwin	1948	3-7/1964
413-421	A-S6	660	ALCO	1949	

*Sold to C.R.R. of N.J. this date. **'A' and 'B' units.

Units Purchased During and After Dieselization

Nos.	Class	HP	Builder	Date	Notes
446-449	A-S10	1000	ALCO	1949	
450	B-S10ac	1000	Baldwin	1948	WFS 3/1964
451-460	A-S10c	1000	ALCO	1949	
461-465	A-GP10sc	1000	ALCO	1948-49	
466-469	A-GP10sc	1000	ALCO	1950	
1501-1502	FGP-16	1600	F-M*	1951	
1503**	FGP-16	1600	F-M	1949	WFS 1964
1504-1509	FGP-16	1600	F-M	1951	
1551-1560		1600	ALCO	1955	
2001-2008	FP-20	2000	F-M	1950	WFS 1-4/1964
2401-2404	FP-24	2400	F-M	1951	WFS 2-4/1964
200-221	AGP-20***	2000	ALCO	12/1963-7/1964	

*F-M, Fairbanks-Morse. Other abbreviations: Schen.-G.E., Schenectady-General Electric; Blw.-West., Baldwin-Westinghouse; ALCO, American Locomotive Co.) **F-M demonstrator, purchased by LIRR, 1951. ***"ALCO Centurys"; may be only class of road diesels on LIRR by 1970, totaling 30-40 units.

Diesels Purchased from Delaware & Hudson R.R.

Nos.	HP	Builder	Date	D.O.A.	D&H Nos.
439	1000	ALCO	1948	6/1964	3025
440	1000	ALCO	1948	1/1964	3020
441, 442	1000	ALCO	1948-49	6/1964	3017, 3030
443	1000	ALCO	1947	1/1964	3013
444-445	1000	ALCO	1944	8/1963	3001, 3003
1519-1520	1500	ALCO	1949	8/1962	4019, 4020

RDC (Rail Diesel Car)

LIRR purchased two Budd RDC's in 1955. Plans for purchase of at least 20 more from Boston & Maine R.R. in 1965, for use on Oyster Bay branch and some Huntington and Northport trains, as well as main line east of Ronkonkoma were cancelled.

GAS TURBINE POWER

In 1966 the Metropolitan Commuter Transportation Authority, in one of its first acts affecting the operations of the LIRR, ordered extensive track work on the main line between Bethpage and Ronkonkoma, for the purpose of testing gas-turbine trains at speeds up to 150 mph. The outcome of these tests would determine whether or not electrification would be necessary on the East End branches.

Switching (0-8-0) 56" Drivers

Nos.	Class	Builder	Date	WFS
251-254	C-51s	Schenectady	1916	1949
255	C-51sa	Pittsburgh	1918	2/1949
256	C-51sa	Pittsburgh	1918	9/1948
257	C-51sa	Pittsburgh	1918	5/1952
258	C-51sa	Pittsburgh	1918	8/1950
259	C-51sa	Schenectady	1922	4/1951
260-264	C-51sa	Schenectady	1922	1949
265	C-51sa	Richmond	1924	9/1948
266-268	C-51sa	Richmond	1924	1949
269	C-51sa	Richmond	1924	5/1951

Freight (2-8-0) Class H-10s 62" Drivers †

Nos.	Builder	Date	Ex-PRR No.	WFS
101	Baldwin	1913	7146	8/1950
102	PRR	1913	7174	12/1948
103	Baldwin	1913	7205	6/1951
104	Lima	1915	7732	12/1954
105	Pittsburgh	1913	7558	11/1951
106	Baldwin	1913	7140	12/1954
107	Baldwin	1915	7616	12/1954
108	Baldwin	1915	7152	10/1955
109	Brooks	1916	7952	5/1951
110	Brooks	1916	8610	6/1950
111	Brooks	1916	8239	10/1955
112	Brooks	1916	8246	12/1954
113	Brooks	1916	9732	10/1955
114	Lima	1915	8222	12/1954
115*	Lima	1916	8814	11/1951
116	Baldwin	1915	9888	6/1951
117**	Lima	1915	7931	12/1954
118	Baldwin	1913	8527	5/1951
119	Baldwin	1913	8566	5/1951

†Arrived on LIRR, 1928-1930. *Ex-Vandalia No. 419. **Ex-Little Miami No. 8931.

Passenger (4-6-0) Class G-5s 68" Drivers

Nos.	Builder	Date	WFS
20-25	PRR	1924	No. 36, 4/1950; Nos. 23, 44, 6/1950; Nos. 29,
26-28	PRR	1925	45, 46, 8/1950; No. 43, 11/1950; No. 20, 1/1951;
29-39	PRR	1928	No. 30, 6/1951; No. 47, 8/1951; Nos. 25, 26, 27,
40-50	PRR	1929	31, 33, 34, 37, 41, 42, 48, 49, 11/1951; No. 40, 6/1952; Nos. 22, 28, 7/1955; Nos. 21, 24, 32, 35, 38, 39, 50, 10/1955.

ROSTER OF ELECTRIC LOCOMOTIVES

No.	Class	Builder	Date	WFS
323	AA-1	Juniata	1905	1937

Ex-PRR No. 8; first PRR electric locomotive.

Nos.	Class	Builder	Date	WFS
324-337	B-3	Juniata	1926	1953-1956 (No. 337, 1950)
338-360	DD-1	Juniata	1910-1911	1948-1952

23 DD-1's purchased secondhand from PRR, 1927-1942.

No. 3522 was one of seventy Pennsylvania class H-9s Consolidations leased to the LIRR. *F. J. Weber, Authors' Collection*

PENNSYLVANIA RAILROAD STEAM LOCOMOTIVES LEASED TO LIRR, 1916-1955

This roster is presumed accurate, however, some locomotives were on the LIRR for only a few weeks and may have been missed by observers. Others spent more of their service time on the L.I. than they did on the PRR (i.e., No. 5406). Some locomotives were leased, returned and leased again (No. 1737 was on the LIRR in 1937 and again in 1947).

Switching 0-4-0: Class **A-6**; No. 3906. Class **A-6b**; No. 3905.

Switching 0-6-0: Class **B-6sa**; No. 1418. Class **B-6sb**; No. 2015. Class **B-8**; Nos. 27, 229, 539, 664, 665, 919, 1056, 1105, 1108, 1109, 1152, 1249, 1415, 1504, 2362, 2502, 2504, 2784, 3134, 3243. Class **B-4**; No. 0288.

Passenger 4-4-0: Class **D-16b**; Nos. 485, 3171, 3192, 5226, 5320.

Passenger 4-4-2: Class **E-3sd**; Nos. 186, 917, 955, 1044, 1413, 2985, 2999, 3005, 3148, 3149, 3152, 3154, 3158, 4106, 4170, 4176. Class **E-6s**; Nos. 51, 169, 198, 230, 402, 435, 460, 530, 563, 645, 737, 779, 1179, 1238, 1287, 1321, 1333, 1347, 1351, 1470, 1564, 1600, 1611, 1680, 1694, 5209. Class **E-7s**; Nos. 7213, 7315, 7379, 7407, 7482, 7484, 7497, 7601, 7622, 7685, 7766, 8033, 8075, 8482, 8492, 8496, 8498, 8499, 8534, 8587, 8631, 8633, 9713, 9714, 9716, 9719, 9720, 9723, 9818, 9819, 9820.

Passenger 4-6-0: Class **G-5s**; Nos. 1589, 1961, 5703, 5704, 5706, 5707, 5714, 5717, 5724, 5741.

Freight 2-8-0: Class **H-3b**; Nos. 0781, 0783. Class **H-6**; Nos. 1665, 1868. Class **H-6a**; No. 2387. Class **H-6sb**; Nos. 158, 701, 1038, 1114, 3042, 3047, 3077, 3835, 5043, 8557, 9771. Class **H-8sa**; No. 7507. Class **H-8sb**; Nos. 125, 345, 693, 1340. Class **H-9s**; Nos. 155, 237, 357, 363, 392, 429, 486, 540, 543, 580, 614, 692, 746, 813, 910, 1084, 1111, 1144, 1370, 1382, 1421, 1484, 1493, 1495, 1500, 1504, 1508, 1532, 1558, 1559, 1561, 1795, 1797, 1803, 1806, 2090, 2386, 2486, 2824, 2826, 2927, 3217, 3419, 3468, 3470, 3475, 3478, 3493, 3513, 3521, 3522, 3523, 3526, 3527, 3530, 3534, 3539, 3540, 3601, 3602, 3615, 3620, 3685, 4147, 4153, 4180, 5139, 5172, 5264, 5624.

Passenger 4-6-2: Class **K-2s**; Nos. 732, 1245, 1458, 3325, 3366, 3378, 3570. Class **K-2sa**; Nos. 1387, 3228. Class **K-3s**; Nos. 7149, 7793, 8091, 8232, 8659. Class **K-4s**; Nos. 269, 383, 389, 518, 719, 830, 920, 958, 1139, 1384, 1395, 1554, 1730, 1737, 1984, 1985, 3655, 3728, 3731, 3734, 3738, 3740, 3741, 3744, 3750, 3751, 3752, 3753, 3754, 3757, 3771, 3805, 3838, 3841, 3843, 3854, 3873, 3880, 3887, 5072, 5238, 5296, 5336, 5348, 5349, 5365, 5375, 5385, 5387, 5389, 5393, 5394, 5395, 5396, 5406, 5407, 5409, 5410, 5411, 5414, 5428, 5432, 5434, 5438, 5455, 7267, 7270, 7275, 7938, 8225, 8378.

Freight 2-8-2: Class **L-1s**; Nos. 714, 1286, 1385, 1478, 1542, 1625, 3078, 3408, 3518, 3580.

A PRR K-4s was Babylon-bound on the Central branch in 1949. *Collection of W. S. Boerckel, Jr.*

One of the few LIRR stock certificates in existence, this one was signed by
President Austin Corbin and Treasurer E. B. Hinsdale. *Collection of James A. Schultz*

Recommended Reading

The Long Island Rail Road: A Comprehensive History, Vincent F. Seyfried (published by the author), Vol. I, 1961; Vol. II, 1963; more to follow. *Pennsy Power*, Alvin F. Staufer (published by the author), 1962. *Apex of the Atlantics*, Frederick Westing, Kalmbach Publishing Company, 1963. The story of the development and operations of the E-6s locomotive. *Walt Whitman's New York*, edited by Henry M. Christman, The Macmillan Co., 1964. *Early History of the LIRR, 1834–1900*, Mildred Smith, Salisbury Printers, 1958. *LIRR Information Bulletin*, LIRR, 1920–1931 (most complete set on file at the Queens Borough Public Library), *Long Island Forum* (a monthly historical magazine, published in Suffolk County).

Authors' Notes: Glossy prints of most of the photographs in this volume are available to collectors for framing, personal use and, in specific instances, for reproduction. Contact the authors for details. A seven-inch EP high fidelity recording of the sounds of steam locomotives which operated on the LIRR is available from the authors for $1 each postpaid. Manufactured by Ralbar Productions, this is the only recording of LIRR steam sounds ever produced, made from the only such tapes known to exist.